Method in the Madness: Research stories you won't read in textbooks

EDITED BY
KEITH TOWNSEND
AND
JOHN BURGESS

Chandos Publishing
Oxford · Cambridge · New Delhi

Chandos Publishing
TBAC Business Centre
Avenue 4
Station Lane
Witney
Oxford OX28 4BN
UK
Tel: +44 (0) 1993 848726
E-mail: info@chandospublishing.com
www.chandospublishing.com

Chandos Publishing is an imprint of Woodhead Publishing Limited

Woodhead Publishing Limited
Abington Hall
Granta Park
Great Abington
Cambridge CB21 6AH
UK
www.woodheadpublishing.com

First published in 2009

ISBN:
978 1 84334 493 3

© The contributors, 2009

British Library Cataloguing-in-Publication Data.
A catalogue record for this book is available from the British Library.

Typeset in the UK by Concerto.
Printed in the UK and USA.

Printed in the UK by 4edge Limited - www.4edge.co.uk

Contents

List of contributors

Vikki Abusidualghoul completed a BA in music and related arts at the University of Chichester in 1992, and worked as a music teacher, youth worker and orchestral conductor for three years. She then turned to linguistics and taught English as a foreign language in schools in Poland, Greece and Britain until 2001, when she undertook an MEd at the University of Exeter. Since then she has taught English for academic purposes at London Metropolitan University and currently at the University of Leicester. Her interests include cross-curricular issues in curriculum design; teacher development; autonomous learner aids; support networks in educational establishments; social constructivism in second-language learning and teaching; state school policy implementation; and chaos theory in relation to educational organisation systems. E-mail: vjl8@le.ac.uk.

Rowena Barrett is a professor of small business and HRM at De Montfort University, Leicester, UK. She moved to the UK in September 2006 from Monash University in Australia, where she had worked for many years. Rowena's research focuses on small business and particularly work, employment and management issues, looking at them qualitatively and incorporating employer and employee perspectives. At De Montfort University she is director of the Small Business and Entrepreneurship Research Group, which brings together academics involved in small business, entrepreneurship and enterprise research and teaching. Despite what many may think, she does have experience in establishing and running a small firm. This experience, and that of growing up in a dysfunctional family farming business, ensures she will be sticking to her 'day job'. E-mail: rbarrett@dmu.ac.uk.

Ken Bridge is an adjunct staff member at Adelaide University's Centre for Labour Research, and has a long career in teacher education, community action and labour studies. With postgraduate qualifications in sociology and occupational health, he has spent the last decade researching health and workplace issues, with a focus on health professionals, workplace training and the impact of work on family life. Since 2007 he has been assisting with the Work, Home and Community Project at the Centre for Work + Life, conducting interviews and analysing the resulting material; his insights are enhanced by feedback from his extended family, which includes eight children and nine grandchildren. E-mail: Kennedy.bridge@unisa.edu.au.

Kaye Broadbent is a senior lecturer in the Department of Employment Relations at Griffith University. She received her PhD in 1999, examining the construction of part-time work in Japan. From 2004 to 2006 she was an Australia Research Council research post-doctoral fellow, conducting research on women-only unions in Japan and Korea. Her research interests focus on women and work, and women and union organising in a comparative context. She has published widely in these areas, including *Women's Employment in Japan: The Experience of Part-time Workers* (Routledge Curzon, 2003) and a co-edited volume, *Women and Labour Organizing in Asia: Diversity, Autonomy and Activism* (Routledge, 2008). E-mail: k.broadbent@griffith.edu.au.

John Burgess is a professor in the School of Business & Management, University of Newcastle, Australia. He coordinates the Work, Employment Relations and Organisations Research Group within the Centre for Institutional and Organisational Research. His research interests are employment relations developments, the labour market, gender and work, and labour regulation. Edited books (with Julia Connell) include *Globalisation and Work in Asia* (Chandos, 2007), *Developments in the Call Centre Industry* (Routledge, 2006) and *International Developments in Temporary Agency Work* (Routledge, 2004). Other recent co-authored books include *Industrial Relations in Australia* (Pearson Education, 2006) and *New Employment Actors: The Case of Australia* (Peter Lang, 2008). E-mail: john.burgess@ newcastle.edu.au.

Jane Clarke currently works as an educator at the ACTU Organising Centre, having begun working in the union movement at the ASU; her positions include educator, women's officer and organiser. She worked in an industrial capacity at the SA Working Women's Centre in the 1990s. Jane has also worked on a number of research projects with Barbara Pocock, including 'Women Count'; 'Women and Work'; and 'Work and Children and Consumption'. E-mail: JClarke@saunions.org.au.

Tony Dundon is college lecturer in the J.E. Cairnes School of Business and Economics at the National University of Ireland, Galway. He has published widely on systems of employee and employment relations in small firms. He is co-author of *Employment Relations in Non-Union Firms* (Routledge, 2004) and *Understanding Employment Relations* (McGraw-Hill, 2007). He is also editor of the *Human Resource Management Journal*. E-mail: tony.dundon@nuigalway.ie.

Bradon Ellem teaches a range of employment relations units in work and organisational studies at the University of Sydney. He is a co-editor of the *Journal of Industrial Relations*, an associate editor of *Labour History* and co-convenor of the Union Strategy Research Group in the Faculty of Economics and Business. His PhD thesis examined the history of unionism in the Australian clothing industry; in subsequent years he wrote on peak unions, the Cold War and local industrial relations. His research now concentrates on geographies of work, union strategy and particular aspects of government industrial relations policy. He is writing a history of industrial relations in the Australian iron-ore industry. E-mail: b.ellem@econ.usyd.edu.au.

Alan Felstead is research professor at Cardiff School of Social Sciences, Cardiff University. He holds degrees from the Universities of Cambridge, Warwick and London, and has held posts at Nuffield College, Oxford, and the University of Leicester, where he was professor of employment studies. His research focuses on training, skills and learning; non-standard forms of employment; and the spaces and places of work. He has completed over 30 funded research projects (including seven funded by the UK Economic and Social Research Council), produced six books and written over 150 journal articles, book chapters and research reports. He is regularly invited to give expert advice on these matters to policy-makers in government departments, public sector agencies, international bodies and private sector organisations. E-mail: alanfelstead@cf.ac.uk.

Alison Fuller held research and academic posts at the Universities of Lancaster and Leicester prior to joining the School of Education at the

University of Southampton in 2004. Alison is now professor of education and work and head of the Post Compulsory Education and Training Research Centre at Southampton. Her main research and publishing interests are in the fields of education – work transitions; vocational education, training and apprenticeship; workplace learning; and patterns of adult participation in education. She is co-director of the ESRC-funded research project 'Learning as Work: Teaching and Learning in the Contemporary Work Organisation' (see http://learningaswork.cf.ac.uk), with Alan Felstead, University of Cardiff, and Lorna Unwin, Institute of Education. E-mail: a.fuller@soton.ac.uk.

John Goodwin is a reader in sociology and head of the Centre for Labour Market Studies, University of Leicester. He holds a BSc in sociology and social psychology from Loughborough University, and a PhD from the University of Leicester. His research interests include young workers and the transition from education to work; biographical methods; and the history of sociology. He is currently working on articles exploring issues such as youth transitions as 'shock experiences', and 'fantasy and reality' in the transition to retirement. He is also undertaking research for a biography of the Leicester sociologist Ilya Neustadt. E-mail: jdg3@le.ac.uk.

Donald Hislop is a senior lecturer in organisational behaviour and HRM at Loughborough University Business School. Donald has research interests in the areas of knowledge management and mobile working. He has published articles in a wide range of business and IT journals, including *Management Learning, New Technology Work and Employment, Journal of Management Studies, International Journal of Human-Computer Studies* and *Journal of Information Technology*. He also recently edited *Mobility and Technology in the Workplace* (Routledge, 2008), and has published a textbook on knowledge management, *Knowledge Management in Organizations: A Critical Introduction* (Oxford University Press, 2009). E-mail: d.hislop@lboro.ac.uk.

Nalita James is a lecturer in employment studies in the Centre for Labour Market Studies at the University of Leicester. She obtained a DEd, specialising in academics' workplace learning and communities of practice, from the University of Leicester. Her methodological research interests include the use of the internet in qualitative research, and she has recently published in this area in the *International Journal of Research and Method in Education* and the *British Educational Research Journal*. She is currently co-authoring a book with Hugh Busher, *Online Interviews: Epistemological, Methodological and Ethical Considerations in Qualitative Research* (Sage, 2009). She is also researching and writing about the impact of creativity on young adults' learning transitions, and creative professionals' workplace learning. E-mail: nalita.james@leicester.ac.uk.

Nick Jewson is a senior research fellow in the Cardiff School of Social Sciences, Cardiff University. His research interests include the spatial organisation of work and employment, processes of workplace learning and the dynamics of productive systems. E-mail: nickjewson@cf.ac.uk.

Konstantinos Kakavelakis is currently employed as a research associate in the Cardiff School of Social Sciences, Cardiff University. He holds a BA in methodology, history and theory of science, and an MBA and diploma in social science research methods. In 2006 Kostas completed his PhD in organisational analysis at Cardiff Business School. His research interests include workplace learning, knowledge management and organisational change. E-mail: konstantinoskakavelakis@cf.ac.uk.

Paula McDonald is a senior lecturer in the School of Management at the Queensland University of Technology. Paula completed her PhD in 2004, examining the factors influencing women's labour-force participation. Her current research interests include gender and youth employment issues, work-life integration policy and practice, and negotiation in work and family arrangements. Paula has published over 25 journal articles and book chapters and has been awarded two ARC Linkage grants. In 2007 Paula was awarded the ANZAM and Tilde University Press Early Career Research Award. She works closely with several organisations in Queensland which provide advice and advocacy to vulnerable workers. E-mail: p.mcdonald@qut.edu.au.

Barbara Pini is a professor of sociology in the John Curtin Institute of Public Policy at Curtin University of Technology, Perth. She has published widely in the area of gender and rurality in a range of journals, including *Journal of Rural Studies, Sociologia Ruralis, Gender, Work and Organization, Work, Employment and Society* and *Sociology*. She has recently published her first book, *Masculinities and Management in Agricultural Organizations Worldwide* (Ashgate, 2008). E-mail: b.pini@curtin.edu.au.

Barbara Pocock, inaugural director of the Centre for Work + Life, has been researching work, employment and industrial relations for 25 years. She has worked in many jobs – as a researcher and academic, advising politicians, on farms, in unions, for governments and as a mother. Her main areas of study have been work, employment relations, unions, inequality and vocational education. She was initially trained as an economist and has a PhD in gender studies. She is actively engaged in public discussion about work issues and has extensive media engagement. She has published many book chapters, reports and articles in academic journals, led the Association of Industrial Relation Academics of Australia and New Zealand, is a board member of the Australia Institute and the South Australian Festival of Ideas and gives around 40 invited public addresses a year in Australia and internationally (including in China, Canada, the USA and New Zealand in 2006–2008). Her books include *Kids Count: Better Early Childhood Education and Care in Australia* (edited, Sydney University Press, 2007); *The Labour Market Ate My Babies: Work, Children and a Sustainable Future* (Federation Press, 2006): *The Work/Life Collision* (Federation Press, 2003); *Strife: Sex and Politics in Labour Unions* (edited, Allen & Unwin, 1997); and *Demanding Skill: Women and Technical Education in Australia* (Allen & Unwin, 1988). In 2007 Barbara won the 'society' category of *The Bulletin*'s 'Smart 100 Australians'. She has been a Dunstan fellow (2006), a Queen Elizabeth II fellow (2003–2007), a visiting fellow at the International Institute for Labour Studies, International Labour Organization, Geneva (May 2005) and a visiting fellow at Ruskin College, Oxford (May–June 2005). E-mail: barbara.pocock@unisa.edu.au.

Robin Price has held a lecturing post at Queensland University of Technology since 2004, but is currently seconded to a post-doctoral fellowship position. She has an arts degree from the University of Queensland, a graduate diploma in adult and vocational education, and a BCom and a PhD in industrial relations from Griffith University. Robin's research interests are in service sector employment generally, and retail industry labour usage and practices specifically. Her post-doctoral research is investigating secondary school students' experience of paid work. E-mail: r.price@qut.edu.au.

Al Rainnie is professor and director of research at the Centre for Labour Market Studies at Leicester University, UK. Before joining the CLMS in February 2007, he worked at Monash University in Australia. Born in

Leeds in 1955, Al has also worked for the Low Pay Unit in the north of England and the University of Hertfordshire. He has researched and written widely in the fields of globalisation, work, employment, regional development and trade-union organisation. He has carried out research with and for trade unions in the UK, Poland, Latin America and Australia. He has published books on work and industrial relations in small firms, regional and employment restructuring in Central Europe, public sector restructuring and community unionism. Current research interests include work, space and place, social movement unionism, and trade unionism and community engagement. E-mail: al.rainnie@le.ac.uk.

Paul Ryan received his PhD from the Judge Institute of Management Studies, Cambridge University. He previously lectured at the Smurfit Business School, University College Dublin, and is now based at the J.E. Cairnes School of Business and Economics, National University of Ireland, Galway, where he lectures in strategic management and international business. He is also a project leader at the university's Centre for Innovation and Structural Change (CISC) in the area of industrial clusters, strategic networks and collaborative innovation. He is of the phenomenology tradition and engages in multifaceted research utilising a qualitative research approach. E-mail: paul.a.ryan@ nuigalway.ie.

Shaun Ryan is a lecturer in employment studies and management at the University of Newcastle, Australia. His PhD in work and organisational studies, at the University of Sydney, examined employment relations and organisational culture in the New South Wales commercial cleaning industry. He is currently working on a longitudinal study of change and employment relations after the corporatisation of a major NSW water utility, as well as continuing his ongoing research into work organisation and unionisation in the Australasian cleaning industry. E-mail: Shaun.ryan@newcastle.edu.au.

Jennifer Sappey, BA (CSU), Dip Teaching (CSU), MBus (IR) (QUT), PhD (Griffith), is a lecturer in sociology in the Department of Social Sciences and Liberal Studies at Charles Sturt University, Bathurst. Her research interests lie in industrial sociology and the changing nature of work, with recent research focused on higher education and the commercial health and fitness industry. In 2007, with Professor Greg Bamber (Griffith University), Jennifer engaged in a public debate through the press, conferences and journal publication on the unintended consequences of the national ethics regime for social science research. She is currently a CSU Flexible Learning Institute fellow, redesigning academic work for the online teaching environment. E-mail: jsappey@csu.edu.au.

Phil Taylor is a professor of human resource management at the University of Strathclyde, Scotland. He is the co-editor of *Work, Employment and Society* and has published extensively across a range of areas, including call centres and trade-union organising.

Keith Townsend has worked in many forms of employment – as a manager of a medium-sized business, swimming coach, gym instructor, aerobics instructor, off-licence bottle-shop attendant and petrol station attendant – all of which place him in an excellent position to be an employment relations academic. Prior to his current work as a research fellow in the Centre for Research on Work, Organisation and Wellbeing (WOW) at Griffith University, he was employed in the Department of Industrial Relations (Griffith) and the School of Management at Queensland University of Technology. His research interests are focused in the areas of employee misbehaviour and high-performance human resource management systems. However, his limited attention span has meant that he has also investigated a range of other areas, including popular culture, working time and work-life balance, mobile phones and work, and workplace closedowns. E-mail: k.townsend@griffith.edu.au.

Lorna Unwin is professor of vocational education at the Institute of Education, University of London. Her research focuses on the creation and use of vocational knowledge and skills in and outside work, and transitions from education to work. E-mail: l.unwin@ioe.ac.uk.

Katharine Venter holds a BSc and PhD from the University of Leicester, and is a lecturer in the Centre for Labour Market Studies at the same university. She lectures on the centre's international distance-learning programmes and has conducted research on the experience of learning and distance learning in different cultural contexts. Other research interests are learning, skills and development in Chinese organisations, women and management, work-life balance and family-friendly employment. Katharine is currently researching into carers' experiences of employment. E-mail: k.venter@leicester.ac.uk.

Jennifer Waterhouse is a senior lecturer in the School of Management, Faculty of Business, Queensland University of Technology. She has a

BCom from Griffith University, with majors in industrial relations and accounting. Her PhD from Queensland University of Technology presented findings from a longitudinal study of organisational culture change within the public sector. She has extensively researched corporate culture, organisational change and human resource management practices within the public sector, and has published in the areas of corporate culture, organisational change, public sector reform and employment relations. E-mail: j.waterhouse@qut.edu.au.

Melissa White is a lecturer in the Centre for Labour Market Studies at the University of Leicester. She completed her PhD in the Collaborative Program in Comparative, International and Development Education at the Ontario Institute for Studies in Education, University of Toronto. Her research interests include the political economy of adult education and training, regional and community development, leadership, public policy and post-industrialism. E-mail: melissa.white@le.ac.uk.

Philippa Williams is a research fellow at the Centre for Work + Life in the Hawke Research Institute for Sustainable Societies, University of South Australia. Her educational background includes a BSc (psychology) from Charles Sturt University, a master's degree in public health from the University of New South Wales and a PhD in public health at the University of Adelaide. Combining a background in psychology and social science with research degrees in public health, Philippa has developed a track record in the social determinants of health for diverse populations. She is currently exploring the interactive effects of work, home and community on the well-being of men, women and children in suburban Australia. E-mail: pip.williams@unisa.edu.au.

Acknowledgements

We would like to thank the contributors, the referees and Chandos (in particular Glyn Jones) for their support and perseverance. There have been many people who have contributed to some way to the chapters, and the book in general: Linda Colley, who first helped initiate the excitement over the smokers, and countless colleagues and friends who have been involved in (or endured) conversations about research and methods. We also owe a big thanks to Sidsel Grimstad, who provided editorial and coordination support for the book and kept it all together. Finally, we would like to thank the Faculty of Business and Law, University of Newcastle, and the Centre for Research on Work, Organisation and Wellbeing at Griffith University for financial support with this project.

List of acronyms

ABS	Australian Bureau of Statistics
ACCI	Australian Chamber of Commerce and Industry
ACD	automated call distribution
ACTU	Australian Council of Trade Unions
AFR	*Australian Financial Review*
AIR	Australian Industrial Registry
ALP	Australian Labor Party
ASCO	Australian Standards Classification of Occupations
AT&GWU	Amalgamated Transport and General Workers Union (Ireland)
BHP	Broken Hill Propriety (Australia)
CEO	chief executive officer
COSBOA	Council of Small Business Organisations of Australia
CSR	customer service representative
DG	director-general
DTI	Department of Trade and Industry (UK)
HREC	human research ethics committee
HRM	human resource management
IT	information technology
JIR	*Journal of Industrial Relations*
JNC	joint negotiating committee
NSW	New South Wales (Australia)

PDA	personal digital assistant
QIRC	Queensland Industrial Relations Commission
SCC	sectional consultative committee
TG	task group
TQM	total quality management
UFD	unfair dismissal
WA	Western Australia
WLB	work-life balance
WRA	Workplace Relations Act 1996 (Australia)

Foreword

That the outcome of our research endeavours in the final analysis is the printed word is a truism. The published journal article, book chapter or monograph, even the conference paper, is the permanent record of the academic labour process. But even though these carefully crafted artefacts might successfully explicate the research philosophies and approaches underpinning them and the specific methods and techniques involved in operationalising the study, and however much these might then convince the reader of their validity, something of value often gets lost. Just as the recently constructed building does not bear witness to the problems its builders had when laying its foundations, so the final published academic work often fails to reveal the difficulties its authors encountered during the research process.

Accumulating the empirical evidence upon which our arguments are based is rarely unproblematic. Instead, as this collection vividly illustrates, the research process is all too often bedevilled by problems of access, the intelligibility of the hard-won evidence and the downright unwillingness of participants to respond as we would wish them to. It does not matter whether the cause is the difficulty in winning the trust and confidence of key informants or the more prosaic circumstance of equipment failure, the outcome can be the same – we end up with no usable data.

This collection of experiences from the research front line, edited by two respected Australian academics working in the fields of employment relations and the sociology of work, succeeds in depicting both the habitual and the unexpected difficulties encountered when engaging in fieldwork. These rarely make into print. An overarching theme embracing the book's diverse contributions might be Goethe's epithet, 'All theory, dear friend, is grey, but the golden tree of life springs ever green.' In other words, no matter how valuable the texts on methods that inform our research approaches and assist in the selection and application of our techniques, there comes a point at which prescription will fail us. It is not possible to swim without getting a bit wet.

Many of the chapters are concerned with mining the depths of organisational life, and thus implicitly, if not explicitly, they acknowledge the rich ethnographic tradition within the sociology of work and employment. Arguably the key contribution was Huw Beynon's (1973) *Working for Ford*, which ushered in a fertile period of ethnographic study and publication (e.g. Nichols and Beynon, 1997; Pollert, 1981; Cavendish, 1982; Haraszti, 1978; Kamata, 1982). What the authors of these and other works had in common was the desire to uncover the hidden realities of the workplace, to reveal the lived experiences of workers and understand the dynamics of employment relations. These academic accounts were paralleled by oral histories and the memorable worker testimonies of Studs Terkel (1972) and Ronald Fraser (1969).

This compulsion to tell things as they were was never simply about presenting compelling narrative accounts, but was designed to impart a greater understanding of the social relations of capitalist production at work. In sharing these objectives the editors and contributors to this book are seeking to reconnect with earlier traditions which placed worker voices and agency at centre stage. This worker-centric focus, we should remember, had tended to become marginalised by the dominant academic discourse of the late 1980s onwards in its managerial and post-modernist variants. Indeed, it is ironic that the adoption of the so-called Foucauldian perspective, in its insistence on the return of the subject (a captured subject), further contributed to the move away from undertaking ethnographic research which had the explicit purpose of analysing the dynamics of workplace social relations. When disarticulated from context, workers' voices were often wholly discursive and devoid of broader explanatory purchase.

In exploring the meaning of work and worker experience, this book should be seen as reflective of and contributing to a revival of such concerns. We could cite many instances of this mini-renaissance. Of course, there is the epic work of Pierre Bourdieu and his colleagues (1999), *The Weight of the World*, which recorded and analysed a mass of individual narratives from community, housing estate and, strikingly, the workplace. There are memorable passages documenting the relationships between permanent and temporary workers at Peugeot and the dismantling of the 'old system of social relations that governed shop life', the engineered decline of work collectives (ibid.: 267–81). Bourdieu's purpose was to convey the profound sense of material and spiritual impoverishment caused by neo-liberal economics and the 'abdication of the state'. We note also the work of John Bowe and his colleagues (2000), which sought to offer the 'unscripted voice' of workers across industries and occupations, preventing the mediation and distortion of workers' accounts.

In sum, this book succeeds in telling how it is in two related senses. Firstly, it provides some tremendous insights into the reality of working life and the meaning of work in a range of contemporary workplaces. Secondly, the authors present the most honest 'warts-and-all' descriptions of the means by which these authentic accounts have been excavated. The reader will be struck by their willingness to immerse themselves in their various research milieux and their profound empathy with their research subjects. The editors should be congratulated for having gathered together such a varied collection that succeeds simultaneously in reconnecting with the traditions of workplace ethnography and confirming for newer and older researchers alike the value of these approaches.

Phil Taylor

Serendipity and flexibility in social science research: meeting the unexpected

Keith Townsend and John Burgess

Introduction

This book contains a collection of essays that highlight the challenges, frustrations, the unexpected and the rewards attached to the research process. For the student or academic researcher there are countless books and journal articles that explain the different research methods and examine the stages of data collection, from ethics clearance through to data storage and data analysis. The choices are vast and the starting position, the view of the world, the nature of truth and the role of the researcher in the process are fundamental in determining the research process. Indeed, the last century has seen a wonderful array of research methods that have illuminated various aspects of the world of work. Some of many examples include Frederick Winslow Taylor's (1911) time-and-motion studies of the early twentieth century; Elton Mayo and his team in the infamous workplace experiments in the Hawthorne Studies (Mayo, 1933, 1949); industrial sociologists of the post-war era investigating shop-floor activities through covert ethnographies (Roy, 1952, 1954; Beynon, 1973; Burawoy, 1979); and modern-day nationwide time-series surveys (such as WERS in the UK – Kersley et al., 2005; and AWIRS in Australia – Morehead et al., 1997).

Over the past decade there has been an explosion of books and journal articles on research methods, reflecting in part the systematisation of the research process (especially related to ethics requirements for methodological reviews) and the expanding frontiers of methods. The terrain of research methods is as vast as are the choices confronting researchers (Creswell and Piano Clark, 2007: 29). In particular, for those undertaking quantitative research the number and range of tests have become more extensive and sophisticated, and for those undertaking qualitative research the scope of the field has been extended to include feminism, queer studies and post-modernism. The interpretive paradigms (including Marxism) reject the assumptions of the independent researcher and objective knowledge (Denzin and Lincoln, 2005: 24; Ezzy, 2002: 17). Feminists stress the importance of shared experience, and highlight the exclusion of women's voice in both theory and methods (ibid.: 20, 45). In both qualitative and quantitative studies the sophistication of data collection and analysis has been facilitated by hardware and software developments. While it is true to say that there remain strong elements of logical positivism and replication of the research methods of the natural sciences (especially in behavioural studies of organisations – leadership, commitment, perception, trust), it is also apparent that this model has been rejected by feminist researchers, ethnographers and post-modernists. This makes for interesting choices about how to conduct research, in particular positioning the researcher in the research process – as a participant with a pre-set framework of analysis, or as on objective scientist who systematically analyses data.

This book is different. It should not be seen as a textbook. It is not a 'checklist' of things to do prior to starting data collection. Nor is it a book about how to do research, although there are a few reflections on what to avoid and how to cope with difficult situations that occur in the research process. Rather it is a set of personal narratives where researchers reflect on their own experiences in doing research and offer observations about the process and the research experience. The stories themselves are entertaining and instructive. Rhodes and Brown (2005: 167–9) remind us that the story is itself a valid form of research and provides valuable data for research. Equally, narratives and reflections about doing research offer insights for other researchers. Here we present the experiences of researchers who broadly have been examining work and workplaces. This extends to those who are out of work (see the vignette by John Goodwin) and to the families and dependants of workers (see the chapter by Barbara Pocock and her colleagues). This field of research spans several disciplines (industrial relations, human resource management, labour economics and industrial sociology) and many different methodologies, from surveys through to interviews, case studies, ethnography and feminist analysis.

As a generalisation, this area of research has largely been dominated by case studies, ethnographies and small surveys. Again as a generalisation, it appears that there is a trend in the leading journals towards logical positivism and quantitative analysis. The researchers here are predominantly ethnographers, but there are reflections on surveys and feminist research. Indeed, the chapter by Felstead et al. highlights the complementary results that can be generated through utilising both surveys and interviews. Here the researchers highlight that social science research is conducted in everyday settings, with associated challenges and complexities that you meet in everyday life (Flick, 2005: 5), such as being able to organise a meeting between four or five very busy people, organising a place for a meeting, dealing with people you have never met before and dealing with problems such as equipment failure and non-cooperation. The researchers here report on their investigations of workers and workplaces throughout Australia, North America, Asia and Europe. Through reflecting on their experiences the researchers are able to identify a number of themes about the research process that are instructive and are not covered in the standard textbooks on research methods. This book is not only about doing research, but living and experiencing the research. Textbooks can provide extensive lists and advice about how to conduct research, but they never really prepare the researcher for the actual encounters in the field when you are conducting interviews, distributing surveys or observing work processes. There are a multitude of issues and obstacles to confront and prepare for. The texts have their place in terms of articulating and preparing for the research process, but living the process is entirely different. Ethics clearances can provide systematic rules and review procedures to screen and verify research processes, but in themselves they cannot guarantee ethical research (Ezzy, 2002: 51). As the chapters demonstrate, the lived experience oscillates from the exhilarating to the depressing, from the inspiring to the frustrating and from the unexpected to the mundane. We suggest that there are a number of abiding themes that emerge from the volume.

Emerging themes

The first theme is the important role of serendipity in research: being in the right place at the right time, and/or talking to the right person. Conversely, you could be in the wrong place at the wrong time and your research programme could evaporate. Often it is the unforeseen event or a chance meeting that is important in allowing a research programme to develop and proceed. Chance events or unplanned situations are often crucial in the research process. These events cannot be planned for, but when they happen they must be built upon in the research process. Here we can identify the importance of chance meetings and chance events. The chapter by Ellem discusses his role as an 'accidental' ethnographer: he became involved in a research project at a deeper level and over a longer period of time than he had planned or expected. In one sense the research took over his life for a few years; however, he would also suggest the research enriched far more than his professional life. In many of the other chapters there is discussion about how research took unexpected turns or was shaped by unexpected events. The chapter by Barrett discusses an experience of being transformed from observer to participant in research through the single event of a letter to the editor of a national newspaper.

The second theme is the importance of gaining access to your research subjects. Dealing with organisations, workplaces, managers, employees and the families of workers is invariably associated with obstacles to access. These range from the formal, such as ethics approval and written consent, to negotiating with gatekeepers regarding the protocols for access. Even in research projects where access is guaranteed in writing and underwritten by organisational funding, there can still be considerable problems associated with access (see the chapter by McDonald et al.). Then there are the informal barriers, such as arranging suitable times and meeting places, gaining the cooperation of local managers and overcoming hostility and suspicion. This problem is noted in many of the chapters: if you wish to interview employees but your research is organised through managers, there is a natural suspicion that you are an agent of management (see the chapter by Ryan and Dundon). Having formal access to organisations is not the same as having access to key informants for the research project. Many of the chapters report on the difficulties of access. These can range from language and cultural barriers to the problems created by staff turnover and having to renegotiate access to informants through new gatekeepers. Others report on innovative routes to access (see the chapter by Price and Townsend on smokers as key informants).

The third theme is that key attributes of the researcher are humour, identification and empathy. Gaining access to informants requires trust in the researcher's ability, the confidentiality of the process and the relationship between researcher, organisation and informants. The researcher needs to be able to empathise with subjects and get them to participate in the research. This will involve developing relationships, demonstrating an understanding of the context of the research and developing an empathy with the participants. When you research on work and workplaces, conflict, rivalry, mistrust, politics and suspicion inevitably confront the researcher. Developing trust in the research relationship is crucial. Humour is an important tool, and being able to establish a rapport with the participants is crucial. The chapter by Ryan and Dundon outlines a story about developing rapport with trade-union officials based on drink and sports. Having empathy with the respondents is important. Broadbent and Ryan in their respective chapters were employed in the jobs they were researching, to live the experience and access workers as colleagues. Several of the studies demonstrate how trust can be developed – and dissolved.

The fourth theme is the importance of commitment to and belief in the research. You not only have to convince grant committees and ethics panels, you have to convince participants of the value of the research and why they should commit time and resources. This means being able to articulate your research clearly to all participants, from managing directors to temporary employees. It also involves being able to demonstrate that commitment. Again, there are examples of participant observation where the researcher experienced the conditions of employment and worked side by side with the research subjects (see the chapter by Ryan on cleaning, and the chapter by Broadbent on retail work in Japan). Living the research is an important aspect of these ethnographic studies in retailing and cleaning, and travelling extensively around the mining communities of the Pilbara was important in Ellem's research.

The fifth theme is the importance of reflexivity in research. This is the ability to examine the research process continuously and critically in the context of prior knowledge and the ongoing research (Flick, 2005: 6). Several of the researchers highlight the importance of keeping a research diary that records the research process and personal reflections on the process (O'Reilly, 2005: 3). This is crucial in ethnographic research, but has validity in all research processes. The chapter by Pini highlights the importance of reflexivity in the research process, and the key role performed by her research notes in understanding what was happening in her difficult research project.

The sixth theme is the importance of flexibility in research. There is inevitably a gulf between research plans and research processes. There will be failures to gain or sustain access, there will be problems of record-keeping and recall (especially if the research also involved alcohol consumption) and there will be opportunities that arise that should be developed (for example, talking to smokers outside the workplace environment). Introducing a survey into the research protocol was important in being able to access individual respondents for subsequent interviews in the study by Felstead and colleagues. The researcher has to be prepared to modify and adapt the methods to the emerging circumstances (Denzin and Lincoln, 2005: 5). This means not only being prepared for the serendipity that is associated with research, but being able to modify the research according to changing circumstances. Improvisation is important, and often the sites of research cannot be planned – you have to see what is convenient for your respondents: a car, a bar, a café or in cyberspace. In the experiences of Abusidualghoul and colleagues, in many of the examples discussed flexibility was important in the light of obstacles, equipment and memory failure.

The seventh emerging theme is that of perseverance. There will be obstacles, struggles, knock-backs and accidents along the way in conducting research. Many of these will be unexpected, and at the time may appear to be terminal in terms of the research project (see the chapter by Sappey on the problems of dealing with ethics clearances processes). Many of the studies outlined here were, at various stages, faced with major obstacles. The researchers persevered with the project, although often they had to change direction or approach (the importance of flexibility) and adapt their research protocol to the changing circumstances.

Eighth, the importance of preparation is evident in all the studies. This is not only in academic terms, but also involves having recording equipment that is operational, knowing how to get to an interview site, being familiar with the details of the participating organisation and being prepared for the purposes of establishing empathy with the respondents. The chapter by Ryan and Dundon highlights the importance of being familiar with the details of a participating organisation and trade union, and having knowledge of local culture and customs (drinking Guinness and Irish hurling).

Finally, we would suggest that having a perspective on what you are doing is also important. Your research may be crucial to you (especially if you are doing a PhD or have a grant-funded project), but to those who you are researching it may be novel, amusing or inane. The world of the researcher and the world of the research subjects are completely different. As a young, excited researcher, one of the 'city-boy' editors was told in a 'country' focus group that the participant was 'tired of pointy-headed academics coming up here to stop us from doing our job'. A decade later those words are still a lesson that what may be important to the researcher might be quite an intrusion to the research subjects. The researcher is the outsider, and has to convince subjects to participate in research projects. Here we can cite the example of Ellem, with the researcher based in Sydney and the respondents based in the Pilbara several thousand kilometres away, as a physical manifestation of the gulf that invariably exists between researcher and research subjects. Having a sense of perspective and being able to accept that the researcher is the peculiar beast are important in terms of developing rapport and trust. Having a go and being an object of fun in the chapter by Ryan and Dundon were instrumental in building trust with trade-union officials.

Book organisation

The chapters are organised around a number of broad themes. The sectionalisation is broad and not exclusive – many of the chapters cross the identified boundaries. One issue that comes through the reported experiences of conducting research is that the researchers have to perform multiple tasks: there is rarely a straightforward research experience that goes according to plan and involves a few discrete tasks. This reminds us of Denzin and Lincoln's (2005: 4) description of the qualitative researcher as scientist, naturalist, fieldworker, critic, performer, journalist and quilt-maker. We start with particular research approaches, and move our way through to observations and experiences about various aspects of the research process. The first part of the book (Chapters 2–4) deals with the experience of conducting workplace ethnographies. Here the researchers recount their experiences in living the research. They all recount the experience of sustained and direct contact with the research (O'Reilly, 2005: 3). The second part (Chapters 5 and 6) examines issues surrounding access to organisations, workplaces and research respondents. These chapters cover a range of issues, from ethics through to hostility and suspicion on the part of respondents. The third and largest part (Chapters 7–11) reports on conducting interviews. These chapters highlight important issues linked to preparation and establishing empathy in the interview process. The fourth part (Chapters 12–14) covers the research process, and includes discussions linked to preparation, technology and dealing with fear and intimidation.

Chapter 2 by Kaye Broadbent recalls her experience as an ethnographic researcher in Japan. Her research project examined the experience and conditions of female part-time workers in the retail industry. Like many ethnographic studies (ibid.), this research project is about 'non'-workers to the extent that they are marginalised, rarely incorporated into institutional career paths and very little is known about them. Broadbent engaged in participant observation and experienced the research through being employed as a part-time worker in a major department store. This enabled her not only to experience the conditions of work but also to access women workers, build trust and develop empathy with them. In this chapter there are the familiar issues of access and the trust of subjects. The role of socialising as a research tool in order to access managers and workers away from the work site was important. Events such as a retirement party and an organised company holiday to a ski and spa resort were very important in gaining access, developing empathy and organising group discussions of work and the workplace among workers and managers – an occurrence that could not take place at the work site. This leads to the problems associated with mixing research and alcohol. One issue that comes to the fore in this chapter is doing research in unfamiliar territory. Broadbent was conducting her research in another country, with different cultural mores and a different language. Once again, preparation in conducting the research was important. The various anecdotes outlined in the chapter highlight the importance of serendipity and the need to maintain an accurate record (no mean task for an ethnographer who is also a participant, in a country where the research must be conducted in a second language!).

Chapter 3 by Shaun Ryan reports on his ethnographic research of the commercial cleaning industry in Australia. Ryan obtained work as a commercial cleaner in order to experience the job and access the cleaners. Once again, these are invisible workers who work outside normal hours, are contracted or subcontracted, have casual employment conditions and are often migrants who are recruited through informal family networks. Again the researcher faced a long battle in gaining access, and perseverance and flexibility were important attributes required in order to complete the research. To win trust and acceptance Ryan found that being upfront about his research project and being prepared to do the job were important attributes. His research involved observation and note-taking. As with many of the recorded research encounters, there was suspicion and even hostility. For Ryan, as with many other research experiences related in this book, one of the major obstacles is the perception of workers that researchers may be spies of management. In this case one of the ironies was that some workers did not have any idea of the organisation employing them, since they worked in multiple client workplaces and only had contact with a supervisor. As in other industries and occupations where work is insecure, fragmented and lightly regulated, the research provided important insights into a form of work that is largely undertaken by migrants. In this research there were multiple sites and the place of work was in reality someone else's workplace or office. This contributed to the 'hidden' nature of the work: the cleaners are rarely seen and, as the chapter notes, rarely acknowledged.

Chapter 4 by Bradon Ellem provides an entertaining account of undertaking research in the iron-ore mines in the Pilbara, a remote region of Western Australia. Over more than a decade there has been a series of bitter disputes between the unions and the main mining companies, centred on attempts to deunionise the workplace. Ellem recounts how he became an accidental ethnographer, immersed in the industrial struggle and in the lives of miners and their families living in remote communities. The anecdotes are amusing and there is a clear identification between the researcher, the unionists and the communities in which they live. Again, access and empathy were important, as was establishing credentials with respondents. Being able to socialise, in this case consuming copious amount of alcohol, was a necessary aspect of developing a relationship with the research respondents. The site of research shifted, as the location of the project was vast and dispersed, and this in itself was challenging: the car became an important site for conducting the research. Ellem lived the research in terms of spending long periods of time in the mining communities; but, unlike some of the other participant observers, he was not employed as a miner. There is an important issue about distance and objectivity raised in the chapter: being so closely identified with the mining unionists and their struggle made it difficult to switch from participant to researcher.

In Chapter 5 Paul Ryan and Tony Dundon discuss how they developed rapport with the officials of an on-site trade union at a Waterford Crystal plant in Ireland. Once again, it is a story that highlights the difficulties of access and the importance of building trust with respondents. The research process involved undertaking workplace interviews with trade-union officials. However, the problem they faced was hostility and indifference, since the interviews were organised by management and held in the offices of managers. To move from hostility and non-cooperation, the researchers outline the strategies they adopted and the processes they went through in order to convince the respondents to participate fully in the interview process. By going through a series of amusing transitions that involved changing the location of the interviews (one of the researcher's secret fantasies to emulate Patrick Swayze's nightclub bouncer in the movie *Roadhouse*) and establishing common ground with the respondents, the researchers in the end were able to win trust and respect, and were also shown parts of the factory that they would not have ordinarily seen. Perhaps more importantly, they each received a Waterford Crystal glass gift from the union. In this case study it was important that the researchers persisted and were flexible: the chapter highlights some strategies that can be employed in interview situations where there are problems of hostility, indifference or a lack of trust. Finally, it is important to be prepared and to learn about the organisation, the respondents and the local environment (the close relationship between drink and sport).

Chapter 6 by Barbara Pocock, Jane Clarke, Philippa Williams and Ken Bridge discusses the processes of conducting focus groups. The rationale for focus groups and their limitations are discussed. The researchers have used focus groups as a key research instrument over a number of years. For these authors, focus groups encompass large problems, including ethics, access and sustaining the research, but at the same time they generate rich and detailed information about how particular social issues are experienced and negotiated. While many of us understand the complexity of completing research at the best of times, Pocock et al. were surely looking to make the research process more difficult for themselves by arranging focus groups with children to talk about parents' work. Nevertheless, perseverance delivered wonderfully rich stories that, again, illuminated an area of work that was formerly not understood. As with many of our contributions, this chapter highlights the importance of being prepared, of confronting the problems associated with extensive qualitative research and of negotiating large studies through to their conclusion.

Chapter 7 by Robin Price and Keith Townsend discusses an unusual source of workplace information – smokers located outside the workplace. Australian legislation prohibits smoking in the workplace, so smokers are forced to congregate outside if they wish to have a 'ciggy'. This group of workers are effectively outsiders, and their smoking areas are generally exposed and unpleasant. However, here is an opportunity to meet workers outside the controls and constraints imposed by conducting interviews within the workplace. The smokers' turf is a neutral ground where the smokers feel outside the control of managers and supervisors. Price and Townsend engage with the smokers and build rapport through smoking (or at least being willing to spend time with the 'gutter scum', in Townsend's case). This demonstrates empathy and can build up trust. The smokers can provide information that in turn can be triangulated with other information. Through illustration and stories from three case studies, Price and Townsend demonstrate that, as social outcasts, the smokers can be a valuable source of information, often confirming or contradicting official sources. This chapter highlights the importance of being flexible in conducting research, developing empathy with subjects and taking advantage of serendipitous events – although the researcher does need to take up smoking in order to access this source.

Chapter 8 by Barbara Pini highlights the problems of access and trust. Researching the (non-)participation of women in a large agricultural lobby group generated difficulties of access and completing the project. This chapter highlights the centrality of gender in the research process. A female researcher questioning men in senior positions about the barriers facing women within the organisation was never going to have an easy task. Pini outlines the hostility and resistance of her male research subjects to her and to the research programme. Organising and conducting interviews was a feat in itself. Pini persisted, and discusses the importance of the record beyond the interview. Not only were the interviews informative; equally important was recording the processes and experiences that went with the interviews. These included hostility, non-cooperation, body language and paternalism. A detailed research record of the experience was an invaluable research tool. Once again, the importance of reflexivity in the research process is highlighted. Going beyond the interviews and reflecting on the politics of the research process within the case-study organisation was an important component of the research project.

Chapter 9 by Alan Felstead, Nick Jewson, Alison Fuller, Konstantinos Kakavelakis and Lorna Unwin highlights how quantitative and qualitative research can be used in concert to allow for the completion of a research project. The authors indicate that quantitative and qualitative research approaches are not necessarily alternatives, but can be effectively harnessed so that they complement each other (Cresswell and Piano Clark, 2007: 9); and outline how their project investigating work at a call centre used a survey of call patterns in order to gain access to operatives and develop a rapport with workers at the centre. Once again this chapter highlights the problems of access and trust, and also demonstrates how the researchers were flexible and innovative in the conduct of their research. At the call centre in question it transpired that the managers (who were the gatekeepers for the project) did not know too much about the work performed by operatives. This ignorance was used by the researchers as justification for developing and conducting a survey of the call-centre operatives regarding the content of their calls. In turn this led to discussions with and greater engagement with the operatives, who were then able to provide very detailed and rich qualitative information to the researchers.

Chapter 10 by Paula McDonald, Jenny Waterhouse and Keith Townsend recalls the experiences of three Australian early-career researchers on industry-funded projects. In all projects the industry partners provided a financial, an in-kind and a written commitment to support the work and provide access for the researchers to the organisations. However, despite these undertakings the researchers were faced with various barriers and road-blocks in the conduct of their research, including staff turnover (key personnel leaving the organisation), accessing key informants (too busy), political barriers (the research viewed as being sensitive) and even natural disasters. This chapter highlights the importance of persistence and flexibility in the conduct of research. The researchers had to modify their protocol and stay the course, despite a mounting list of obstacles. Unlike many of the other access situations reported in the book, these examples are interesting in that the organisations sponsored and sanctioned the research project and guaranteed access. However, through time, written and financial commitments have to be tempered against organisational and political change. The chapter also outlines the problem of 'research fatigue': it is difficult to sustain engagement through time. When conducting research that spans time and involves continuous engagements there is always the potential that at some stage access rights will be modified or even terminated.

Chapter 11 by Jennifer Sappey emphasises three issues faced by workplace researchers: access, ethics and time. Researching the fitness industry posed a number of problems, not the least being that it did not exist for purposes of industry and employment classification, nor for the purposes of employment regulations. Where work is irregular, undocumented, unregulated and fragmented there are problems in accessing workers (see the chapter by Shaun Ryan on contract cleaning). Emerging industries (call centres are another spectacular example) pose particular problems for researchers as they often lack the points of access that are found in established industries, such as trade associations or trade unions. The second problem is that of ethics clearance. Sappey endured difficulties in her research, since it overlapped between the pre- and post- periods of national ethical guidelines for university research. The Australian system is complex and convoluted, and is based on the medical research ethics guidelines (even many of the questions are the same). For ethnographic researchers there are problems in terms of both access and validity. To interview employees requires the approval of managers. To observe the organisation and processes of work requires the approval of all those being observed. Formal ethics clearance procedures require very extensive approval processes before the research can commence. Finally, time brings other problems: not only institutional and organisational developments, but changes to the access regime (and changes in ethics protocols). The research process does involve politics and the exercise of power. Research itself can be seen by some groups as a threat to the existing order. Playing by the rules can in itself reinforce the status quo, especially with human ethics procedures. As with the study by McDonald et al., where your research is associated with ongoing access, developments can not only limit this access but even endanger the viability of the research. The story of research in this chapter once again reinforces the importance of persistence and flexibility: be prepared to change your research protocol in order to obtain access and clear ethics requirements, and be prepared to take advantage of serendipitous events.

Chapter 12 by Vikki Abusidualghoul, John Goodwin, Nalita James, Al Rainnie, Katherine Venter and Melissa White gives the insights and vignettes of a team of researchers from the University of Leicester. They highlight some of the challenges and traumas associated with conducting research. Once again there are stories about the alcohol and research relationship, but also the social engagement necessary in order to achieve access. There are stories about fear and danger attached to research encounters when conducting interviews with respondents who are drug affected or researching in areas noted for high levels of violence and drug abuse. There are issues of access raised, the importance of engagement and empathy and the importance of being prepared and flexible in the conduct of research. You have to be prepared if you are researching in another country, and when dealing with equipment failure (no batteries in the tape deck) or inaudible recordings of interviews. Gender is an issue that is again implied: particular encounters are very gendered, as in the study of unemployed men in Ireland. In this chapter there is a discussion of the process and limitations of conducting online research, where the technology can overcome the limitations of space but lead to reduced and unsatisfactory engagement, or the emergence of new and different personas.

Chapter 13 by Donald Hislop on mobile work in trains reports on the experiences of conducting a research project that involved gathering data from commuters who engaged in work while travelling by train. This chapter is about planning and executing research. It highlights the importance of being prepared for fieldwork and being flexible in the conduct of the field research. A well-considered and strongly developed plan is essential, but a researcher cannot control everything. Flexibility to change plans and the capacity to think on the run are essential parts of research methods in the social sciences. Once again there is the issue of the context and the location of research. The train is both a form of transport and an extension of the workplace. Commuting falls between leisure time and work time. However, the space is public and subject to non-controllable issues such as delays, overbooking and noise. Developing and implementing a research programme around working commuters required extensive preparation, and especially innovation in dealing with the problems that arose in a non-controlled and public space.

Chapter 14 by Rowena Barrett discusses the research process and highlights how research can take on a life of its own, with unexpected turns and developments. A letter to the editor of a national newspaper in Australia regarding the impact of unfair dismissal laws set in chain a process whereby a research programme unfolded. Barrett was quickly transformed from observer to researcher in the political debate surrounding the application of unfair dismissal laws to small business. This was not planned: it was responding to the unexpected and accommodating serendipitous events. The chapter highlights the role of vested interests and power in research. There are often power relationships within the research process (for example researchers and gatekeepers), but there are also power relationships when research addresses issues of public policy. Invariably, in research around work and employment there are vested interests and politics, since the state has an array of laws and regulations that relate to employment conditions, work and workplaces. Where researchers challenge public policy, or the beliefs behind public policy, they can expect that vested interests will react and challenge their work and their credibility.

Chapter 15 concludes with some observations regarding obstacles facing researchers in the area of work and workplaces. Challenges identified include the role of gender in the research process; the essentially political nature of research, and how power relationships play an important part in the process; the lack of a visual record in this field of research; and the ongoing challenge that ethics protocols present for workplace ethnographers.

Part I
Living the research

2

There are ways and then there are ways: conducting research in social settings in Japan

Kaye Broadbent

Introduction

From 1988 to 1990 I spent two years conducting interviews and researching in Japan. During these years I narrowed my research focus to women working part-time in supermarkets. When I returned to Japan in August 1991 I had enrolled in a PhD programme, and the following 18 months of fieldwork and research contributed towards this. I decided I wanted to work in a supermarket and interview workers and management. When conducting research in 1988–1990 I had met senior union officials from the three major supermarket chains; as there wasn't much difference between them, my selection of workplace was based on a convenient neighbourhood location.

I negotiated six weeks' full-time work (as a casual) in the supermarket, and started in October 1991. My job continued until early 1993. Despite the pressures of work on the supermarket shop-floor, my co-workers were extremely generous with their time, with many conversations conducted while restocking the shelves. Getting access to management and their interaction with workers was always difficult, but social occasions provided the opportunities needed. The first was a farewell for a long-serving part-time worker, and the second a two-day (compulsory) company ski trip/visit to a hot springs. Note-taking (I didn't use a tape recorder) during social situations may be familiar to many – doing it in a second language presented all sorts of challenges. Interestingly, after a couple of drinks I thought my language skills were better!

So how did it all start?

My contact with union leaders and members began when, as a university student in the early 1980s, I was employed as a casual at the Newcastle (Australia) workers' club. At this time I also unconsciously adopted participant observation as a research technique when I heard many stories of strikes and struggles in large mines and railway workshops, plus the experiences of workers in smaller manufacturers when workers at Broken Hill Propriety (BHP – then one of the town's largest employers) went on strike. Sometimes the wives told their stories, too.

When I went to Japan for my first research trip in 1988 to 'learn' about Japan's union movement, I learnt two valuable lessons – one, a social situation can be just as productive (or more) than the original 'research' situation, and second, small group social gatherings can allow the interviewees to take control of a situation, providing discussions and information hitherto not considered by the researcher.

My first experience of learning from a social setting occurred in late 1989 when I travelled with my then supervisor from Tokyo to Hiroshima to meet a leader of a major Japanese union. This union was one of a very small minority which had succeeded in building a strong, activist union despite management's repeated union-busting attempts. It was a valuable experience and an opportunity to gain significant insight into past struggles between Japanese capital and labour, and the extent to which capital would go to prevent workers forming unions. My supervisor, the union leader and I were all staying overnight in a Japanese-style inn, where we dined together and then spent the next day on a fishing boat. My supervisor was keeping up to date with the union's progress and I was there to hear first hand of a well-documented struggle. The union leader had many stories to tell and was a seasoned drinker. I'd heard it was polite to drink when it was offered. Many hours of politeness later resulted in my being barely able to stand. I subsequently discovered that my supervisor had turned his glass upside down, indicating he wasn't drinking any more – an option he'd neglected to tell me about. At the end of the evening I managed to get to my feet and make it to my room, but was very unwell for the rest of the night, to put it politely. I managed to survive the next day's activities and the fishing trip. When I discovered that the union official was also feeling 'under the weather' I didn't feel quite so foolish, but needless to say I have almost no memory of what was discussed that evening and my notes were very little help at all. This was an important lesson, and based on this experience I moderated my alcohol intake in social settings with a fieldwork aspect. The following discussion focuses on two examples of conducting fieldwork in a social setting where the interviewees for my research (part-time and casual workers) were able to 'take charge' of the situation. As a 'passive' participant observer I gained information and insights which I may not have gained in the workplace setting.

In the beginning...

From 1988 to 1990 I conducted many interviews with union leaders, officials and members in Japan. I also attended many rallies, protests and pickets as a way of 'learning' about Japan's industrial relations context and determining the focus of my research for a PhD, and I gave talks to unions keen to understand industrial relations in Australia. I was very fortunate, and grateful for the generosity of everyone concerned, but a vague feeling of unease remained. I hadn't decided the area of research I was interested in pursuing, nor had I decided on the research methodology I would use. I was interested in the experiences of women workers, but had spent a lot of time with male union leaders and officials from male-dominated unions. I wanted to know 'where are the women workers?', which is not an original question (Kessler-Harris, 1975). Six months into my fellowship, in June 1989, I had the good fortune to meet a very dynamic woman professor from a different university to the one I was attached to. When I talked to her about my vague ideas for a project and told her who I had met and how I was attending a range of union conferences, her response was that I was conducting research like 'a middle-aged man'. She suggested that if I wanted to meet Japanese women workers I should just go and talk to them about their work. I loved the idea in principle, but thought the practicalities would limit the efficacy for data gathering. Apart from the difficulties of cornering someone for a chat when they're busy, and having worked 'on the other side' in a supermarket it is always extremely busy, I wondered how people would respond to a 'foreigner' suddenly asking about their work. I decided that I wanted to focus on women workers, and selected part-time work in supermarkets, an industry and employment status predominantly occupied by women. I spent the remaining 18 months of my fellowship, until March 1990, interviewing supermarket union leaders, officials and part-time workers from Japan's (then) three largest supermarket chains. I had met senior union leaders from these chains in 1988, so when I returned in 1991 I selected the Daiichi company (pseudonym) because it was the largest chain and also it had a store in my local neighbourhood – I could walk to work and not have to be 'stuffed' into overcrowded subway trains! After sitting an aptitude test and an 'interview', I started at Daiichi's Hachiban store in October 1991.

Unsure how long I would be permitted to conduct fieldwork and thinking I might be perceived as an inconvenience, I requested a six-week 'contract'. At my 'interview' I was hired for six weeks' full-time work (as a casual) in the 'hard' section (stationery, toys, novelty, haberdashery, manchester and non-electrical household goods). By year-end, when the store was approaching the busy season, I was approached and asked to stay on until the early new year. I was ecstatic, as six weeks had proved to be too short a time to conduct fieldwork. I needed not only to learn the language of 'retail' but to learn it in Japanese. From the beginning I advised my co-workers that I was conducting fieldwork for further study and was focusing on the nature of part-time work in Japan. My presence became a source of interest, and led to me gaining many more willing interviewees. Many co-workers from other departments were curious as to why a native English speaker would work in a supermarket for about AU$6 per hour when they could earn AU$100 per hour teaching English.

My 'six-week stint' as a full-time casual ended in August 1992, nearly ten months after I'd started, but I continued to work one day a week until early 1993. After having my 'contract' renewed until the new year, the store left it to me to decide how long I wanted to stay – it indicated it was quite happy for me to continue indefinitely. I estimated I needed several more months, and the store was happy to comply. I was useful as an employee, as the Japanese economy was suffering serious labour shortages, and while 'retail' was not considered a 3K job (translated to be dangerous, dirty and hard), it was low paying and thus unappealing to many workers. For the company, any worker was better than none.

My experience as a casual worker differed from my part-time co-workers because I worked from 10am to 4pm, five days a week, which was at least an hour less per day than most part-time workers. I worked no Saturdays and very few Sundays, which again differed from most part-time workers. I reasoned that I needed a few hours each day to write up fieldwork notes, conduct research and begin writing my dissertation. Unlike other casuals or part-time workers, I was able to reduce my workload to one day a week – a decision reached through a combination of exhaustion and needing to speed up the process of completing the fieldwork component of interviews and surveys. Despite the pressures of work on the supermarket shop-floor, my co-workers (mostly women) were extremely generous with their time, with many conversations conducted while restocking the shelves, during lunch hours, after work and on outings arranged on common days off.

Minamoto san's *sōbetsukai* (farewell party)

I had been at Daiichi about three months when Minamoto san (pseudonym) turned 60 years old and had to retire as a part-time worker. Her farewell party presented my first real opportunity to listen in and observe conversations between the 'hard' section manager and a small group of part-time workers. I spent most of my time at Daiichi working in the 'hard' section, with short rotations through all the 'hard' departments except for manchester and household goods. I also had a short rotation in the women's clothing department ('soft' section) to get to know a different group of workers. Regular day-trips with part-time workers and an 'overnight' ski trip meant I got to know a large number of part-time workers in other sections as well. At the time of my fieldwork I was 30 years old, at least eight years (sometimes as much as 12 years) older than many of the young female full-time staff. The combination of my research focus and casual status meant I spent more time in the company of, and socialising with, my part-time co-workers aged 50-plus than I did with young full-time workers.

Minamoto san (part-time) had been with the store 17 years. Even though the company demanded she retire as a part-time worker at 60, it rehired former part-time workers on a casual basis. Minamoto san started again as a casual and also requested to work only four hours a day, instead of eight hours as a part-time worker. Her request was refused, and it seems the section manager, Hashimoto san, refused to give her a satisfactory reason. When I asked our department manager why Minamoto san's request had been refused, he simply mumbled something about company policy and indicated that the conversation was ended. My guess is that it was because the store wanted Minamoto san to continue to work long hours, given that it knew her husband worked full-time and she had no dependants at home (aged parents, children or grandchildren) to present a constraint or justify, in the section manager's eyes, her working shorter hours. Management also knew that it would be difficult to get someone with Minamoto san's length of experience so cheaply. The experience of Minamoto san and other part-time workers led me to formulate the argument that part-time work in

Japan was constructed to benefit employers' demands and not the needs of part-time workers (Broadbent, 2003).

I had worked closely with Minamoto san in the toy section, and her appearance suggested a sour and sullen demeanour. On the contrary, she had a dry sense of humour and was easy to work with, but had been ground down by many years of low-paid work with poor conditions, unrelenting pressure to reach sales targets and the need to manage her emotions with both customers and management. She was a patient teacher whose best efforts (combined with those of others) in teaching me even the basics of the beautiful Japanese style of gift-wrapping were to no avail. About 25 of us attended Minamoto san's *sōbetsukai* at a Japanese-style bar near the store; managers, including the toy department manager and the manager of the 'hard' section, Hashimoto san, were also there. Having managers, but especially the section manager, present seemed to offer unprecedented access opportunities for all the staff, but especially for part-time workers who were considered marginal to the store's operations – although, with casuals, they were numerically the largest section of the workforce. Japan's unions are regularly criticised for their close relationship with management (see Kawanishi, 1986), and recent surveys indicate the reluctance of union leaders to organise non-regular workers, such as part-timers and casuals (Rengō-Osaka, 2001), or to fight management to organise the growing non-regular workforce (Broadbent, 2008); this is also the case in the supermarket sector. At Daiichi a minority of part-time workers have been 'permitted' to join the union (Broadbent, 2003). That only a limited group were permitted to become union members is one reason why the national part-time union membership is estimated at only 3 per cent (Japan Institute of Labor, 2006).

Once the dinner was finished and the speeches concluded, the various groups joined and the next hour-and-a-half became a 'conversation' between part-time workers and the managers. Hashimoto san, the section manager, was asked to justify a number of changes to staffing and working conditions. While I have no evidence of this, my guess is that many more criticisms, comments and suggestions were volunteered here than were ever heard by management through other channels. The benefit of suggestions 'offered' in this way was that Hashimoto san could ignore or accept them as he chose, and the offerer could feel uninhibited because the tacit understanding was that it was a social setting and so the atmosphere was less constrained, and the offerers had been drinking so they were not thought any less of for making critical comments. Yoshizumi san from haberdashery was a key interviewee for me. She conversed with Hashimoto san for about 15–20 minutes, with myself and others also present. I suspect this represented more time spent with him than any part-time worker had done in a long while. The part-time workers at the Hachiban store were a little unusual, as many of them had more than the average work experience of part-time workers, with the majority having worked over ten years at the store. What I also found out later was that in 1980 Yoshizumi san and many of the other part-timers I knew had been instrumental in successfully agitating for part-time workers at Daiichi to be unionised.

Shattā renkyū – to Kusatsu we will go!

In late January 1992 the Hachiban store closed for two days, the longest consecutive period of time that the store was closed. It was a break in lieu of the traditional New Year holiday in Japan (1–3 January), when most businesses close but more and more retail outlets remain open, and it is at this time the store chooses to hold its company 'bonding' session. This trip provided the second opportunity to observe interactions between part-time workers, casuals and managers in a relaxed atmosphere away from the workplace. It was the first time that it occurred to me that my part-time worker friends were asking questions to assist my fieldwork process.

This year, staff from the Hachiban store were to take their *shattā renkyū* at Kusatsu, a ski resort with hot springs, approximately two hours by bus west of Tokyo. The *shattā renkyū* was a company-paid trip to thank staff for their efforts during the year. It was not voluntary, as almost all full-time workers had to attend and were expected to ski; for the first time part-time and casual workers were invited, but their participation was voluntary. The 20 or so part-time workers who attended were excused from skiing and were free to enjoy the hot springs. I opted for the hot springs, because of my research focus, so I spent many hours with my part-time colleagues sightseeing around the area.

The Daiichi group arrived at the resort hotel around mid-morning and, once we got our rooms and room-mates sorted out, about ten part-time workers from various departments/sections and I gathered in one of the part-timer's rooms and started a party. People had brought scotch, *sake* and beer. We used icicles hanging from the spouting outside the window to mix with the scotch, while debating the possible pollution levels and toxicity of using this ice! The background noise to the party was the televised announcement and commentary on the engagement of the Crown Prince and his fiancée Owada Masako. This went for eight hours – about the same time as our party. This was the era of the Princess Di phenomenon, with the emphasis on accessibility of the monarchy to the people. Through the young Japanese couple, Japan's powerful Imperial Household Agency was demonstrating that Japan's monarchy was also accessible.

As the party progressed various people came and went, including a few managers. After things had been in full swing for about three hours, the manager of the household goods department, Koma san, joined us. I hadn't met him before, so it was a good opportunity to hear his views. Mikawa san, a casual in his department who had 15 years' experience, claimed that she had both the length of service and the job knowledge to be a manager – something many part-time workers and casuals asserted, though not quite so publicly. His response was that these were not the most important criteria, commenting that it was the content of the job you performed, your employment status and whether you made 'decisions' that were most important. As many of the part-timers I worked with knew their job and how it compared with those of full-time workers, few were persuaded by company arguments that their jobs differed from those of full-timers. In light of the fact that many of these part-time workers were solely responsible for a small department, his comments underscored the discrimination practised by companies towards part-time workers. The attitude was that part-time workers were incapable of taking on management roles because they were 'part-time', which in Japan still remains code for 'housewife'. Recently Daiichi and the other large supermarkets, spurred by the need to cut costs, have replaced full-time workers by 'promoting' part-time workers to managerial positions.

Mikawa san and the other part-time workers at the party continued to ask questions such as these, questions that I may not have considered, and provided me with evidence to support my argument that the construction of part-time work in Japan is gendered. Over the course of an eight-hour drinking party I was able to get notes on most of the conversation – not all of which was relevant for my fieldwork. I did notice that when managers were present, 'work'-related conversations dominated. The social situation provided part-time workers with the opportunity to pursue issues which weren't addressed in other forums. Many of the part-timers I knew well also asked questions they considered important to my fieldwork.

To summarise the experience

Over the course of my fieldwork I did have conversations with two managers I worked with, but generally I kept my contact with management to a minimum for two reasons: first to maintain my credibility with part-time workers, and second because I was interested in the 'voices' of part-timers. Parties and social occasions (there were a couple of others) provided opportunities to hear managers' responses to the issues affecting part-time workers, and the situation was such that they were confronted by several part-time workers who would not be satisfied with evasive responses. The discomfort of managers confronted in this way was clear, but, unlike the store manager, most responded directly and it seemed to me with candour. After all, the part-timers had more experience working in a supermarket than almost all the managers did, but by virtue of their gender, age and marital status they were confined to low-paying, low-status jobs with almost no prospects for promotion. It also benefited my research because I participated in discussions on issues I may not have considered and gained insights that I wouldn't have had access to in a workplace setting.

While participant observation was only one of the methodologies I utilised, it is time-intensive and not for everyone. It suited the topic of my research and my personality, and I benefited from the experience. I made close friendships with many of my part-time co-workers, learning so much more about Japan, Japanese people and industrial relations in Japan than I could have from only reading, questionnaire surveys or conducting 'one-off' interviews. My research only scratched the surface of the work experiences of part-time workers in supermarkets, but the cooperation of my co-workers and the invitations to participate in their social activities meant the data I gathered were richer as a result.

Acknowledgements

This research was assisted by many people, with acknowledgement due to the staff at Daiichi supermarket's Hachiban store – in particular the part-time women I worked with, who befriended me and contributed to a rewarding research experience.

3

'On the mop-floor': researching employment relations in the hidden world of commercial cleaning

Shaun Ryan

Introduction

This chapter explores some of the challenges and tribulations of studying the hidden and hitherto unresearched world of work in the New South Wales (Australia) cleaning industry. The findings and analysis presented here are informed by my research into employment relations, labour management and the organisation of work in the NSW commercial cleaning industry (Ryan, 2007). This research used primarily a case study of an industry exemplar, and made extensive use of participant observation to obtain evidence on the perceived realities of work and organisation for those on the front line of cleaning work – the cleaners and their supervisors – and to understand how they make sense of their working world. The discussions and findings presented in this chapter support the use of an ethnographic approach to work, and provide some guidance as to how a participant observation study might be carried out and what might be found through the use of this method.

Ethnographic approaches to work

Research into employment relations in Australia has traditionally made use of the case-study method and focused on institutional and collective organisation at a macro level. My examination of the NSW commercial cleaning industry adopted an ethnographic approach to analyse employment relations and work organisation from a micro perspective, with the aim of incorporating cleaners' subjective experiences of the 'mop-floor'. I adopted an ethnographic approach to gain first-hand experience of cleaning and overcome some of the challenges arising from the peculiarities of the cleaning industry. I followed Smith's (2001) call for an 'ethnographic approach to work' in order to illuminate the complexity of work normally considered 'unskilled' and explore in some detail power, conflict and inequity at work. My aim was to demonstrate that, far from being unskilled, 'dirty' and unempowered, cleaners were able to construct a positive identity and maintain control over their work. By adopting participant observation as an ethnographic research technique, I was able to incorporate employee voice into my analysis and come to terms with an industry where the work and those undertaking it are stigmatised as 'dirty' (Ashforth and Kreiner, 1999). By entering the working world of cleaners I was able to experience how they organise their work to cope with unrealistic demands and expectations from their managers and clients.

Adopting an ethnographic approach to the work of cleaning meant that I was able to come to terms with some of the organisational and structural characteristics of the cleaning industry. In an industry dominated by non-English-speaking background, part-time and casual workers, where multiple job-holding is common across different employers but within the same industry, issues of coordination meant that focus groups or formal interviews with cleaning employees were not feasible. In order to access employees and understand the lived experience of cleaners, time would need to be spent on the mop-floor. A defining characteristic of the industry is organisational and spatial fragmentation. Cleaning firms formally organise workers on the site of a third party – the client (Allen and Henry, 1996). These firms coordinate and manage work across numerous work sites and at all hours of the day. The case-study firm that formed the basis of my research (known by the pseudonym 'Complete Clean'), for example, organises 1,600 cleaners and managers across some 1,500 sites in NSW. The need to coordinate work across multiple sites leads to a tension between the formal organisation of work and the imperative to get work done, resulting in informal (or precarious) employment practices and giving rise to an industry culture whereby 'formal and informal practices co-exist within large [cleaning firms] as a means of "getting the work done"' (ibid.: 67). This gives rise to a culture whereby managers and supervisors have enormous amounts of formal power, and calls into question normative models of human resource management. These organisational arrangements tend to lead to informal management and reproduce a regime of precarious employment. That cleaners engage in work activities on a site owned by someone else raises interesting questions about the nature of management and whether or not the cleaning firm or the client is the 'employer'. It was felt that such questions could only be addressed by visiting a range of different sites.

The cleaning industry is unusually competitive, with low barriers to entry. This characteristic has led to the Australian industry being labelled among the most competitive and efficient in the world (see Ryan, 2007), with rates of productivity many times higher than elsewhere as firms struggle to compete, often trading quality for cost. It is often argued that Australian cleaning firms achieve high rates of productivity and remain profitable at the expense of their employees. In order to explore this phenomenon, it was felt that time would need to be spent engaging in cleaning work and talking to cleaners on the mop-floor.

Negotiating and securing access

The first challenge was securing a cleaning firm as a major case study. Gaining access to industry consultants, union officials and cleaning industry association representatives was relatively straightforward. Cleaning firms, on the other hand, were reluctant to give access to a researcher. I put this down to two main reasons. Firstly, many cleaning firms operate in the grey areas or margins of the economy, confirmed by Australian Tax Office investigations into the industry and union prosecution of employers for non-payment of entitlements and unsafe working conditions. Managers spoken to were often aware of the industry reputation for precarious employment and did not want to run the risk of adverse exposure (despite assurances of confidentiality). Secondly, cleaning firms are by nature 'lean' organisations. Managers tend to be generalists and undertake a wide range of functions in the normal course of their duties. They work long hours and are on call 24 hours a day, seven days a week. Many simply did not have the time or energy to entertain a researcher. Difficulties in securing access meant a hard lesson in patience and perseverance. At one stage I considered abandoning using a cleaning firm as a case study in favour of a more 'conventional' employment relations study oriented towards the union representing cleaners and its activities before industrial tribunals.

It took me nearly two years of rejection to secure a firm that would serve as the major case for my thesis. Letters to employers and managers went unanswered and phone calls unreturned. In desperation I sought help from the university. Facility management at the University of Sydney fell under the responsibility of an academic; he was sympathetic to my plight and arranged for access to the university's internal cleaning staff. He also suggested to the external contractor (at that stage the university was cleaned by a large commercial firm and the contract was worth millions of dollars) that it might like to take part in my research. This contractor expressed some initial enthusiasm, but discussions led nowhere (cleaning firms at the university around this time were involved in subcontracting arrangements and were under investigation by the union). In the end, by chance, one of my professors suddenly recalled that he had taught a director of a cleaning firm during this person's postgraduate study, and he would be happy to write a letter on my behalf. This letter eventually led to me gaining access to one of the largest cleaning firms in NSW. In an example of support and generosity I was granted complete and unrestricted access to this firm's records, management and cleaning staff. I would be permitted, subject to agreement of clients, access to any of the firm's sites and contracts. In return, the firm requested a copy of my research findings and an undertaking that I would ensure the confidentiality of their trade name for five years. The managing director was aware of the reputation of the cleaning industry, and saw my research as an opportunity to seek feedback from managers and employees and gain the perspective of someone removed from the industry.

Maintaining regular contact with senior management, along with a visible presence in the office and a willingness to give presentations, ensured their continued interest. A vital aspect of maintaining a working relationship with middle-level operational managers was knowing when to keep my distance. For example, Complete Clean divided NSW into geographic territories. Each month the regional managers met with their customer managers. In an industry where 'you are as good as your last profit and loss sheet', these meetings were characterised by high tension as budgets were discussed and the financial performance of each manager was scrutinised. Shouting, swearing and heated exchanges were not uncommon. While it was understood that I was free to attend these meetings, it became clear that my presence made the participants uncomfortable. Eventually I stopped attending and only showed up to these meetings when invited. In any case, managers were happy to stop in the corridor to chat and discuss the meeting informally afterwards.

Conducting research on the mop-floor

Originally it was my intention to gain employment as a cleaner and undertake a period of participant observation research. After negotiation with the relevant managers, I spent a period of three months working as a cleaner and visited 11 different sites. Sites were chosen in conjunction with management, selected on the basis of potential interest to me, ease of access, willingness of the client, exposure to the maximum number of cleaners and the opportunity to experience a range of cleaning across a number of geographic locations. The work sites I visited reflected the market strength and core business of Complete Clean, and included retail, industrial and commercial and office sites. I also spent time on a pharmaceutical site and at a private hospital. The amount of time spent on a site varied according to the site's size, the number of cleaners and hours of work. For example, on some sites I spent only an evening; on other sites I worked for periods of up to two weeks, spending time with cleaners on morning, day and evening shifts.

Time spent on the sites enabled me to overcome my difficulties in interviewing cleaners. I had made it clear to managers that it was my wish for them to place me on a site and treat me like any other cleaner. When it became clear that cleaning was solitary work, I requested placement alongside other cleaners where practical. Typically, a visit to a site for a period of participant observation involved a session with the manager or supervisor followed by a more extensive period of time with cleaners. On each site I wore a Complete Clean uniform and the site manager or supervisor would introduce me to the cleaners I was to work with. I was introduced as a university student who was interested in the cleaning industry and the experiences of individual cleaners, and was writing a thesis on cleaning. The manager or supervisor usually informed the cleaners that I had permission from Complete Clean Australia to be on the site, that what they said to me would be confidential and they would not be identified in the research. On a number of sites the manager or supervisor tried to play a joke on the cleaners and introduced me variously as the new managing director of Complete Clean, the managing director's son (who was himself a cleaner) or a new regional manager. As introductions were often made in Greek, Portuguese, Spanish or Italian, I was not aware of this until much later.

On most sites I was paired with a cleaner and spent the morning, day or evening shift with them. On larger sites where the majority of workers were employed on a part-time basis, which generally meant doing a three-hour stint on a site, the site manager would rotate me around cleaners every hour. On larger sites where day cleaning was common, I worked alongside cleaners for six to eight hours and was able to spend much time in conversation. As the fieldwork unfolded, I found myself following Spradley's dictum for ethnographic researchers, that 'initially ethnographic data should be gathered by listening and observing, "not to discover answers, but to find which questions to ask"' (Spradley, 1970, cited in Schwartzman, 1993: 56). This approach was most useful given the paucity of research into the cleaning industry, and enabled me to approach the research project with an open mind. Time spent on cleaning sites proved invaluable for later semi-structured interviews with managers. On those sites where the work was mainly part-time (three hours a day), I tended to spend around ten to 20 minutes at the beginning of work talking to the cleaner. We would then work together to make up the lost time and complete the allotted work within the three-hour period.

On these sites I would work as directed alongside other cleaners. Often we established an exchange relationship: in return for spending time talking and answering questions, I would help cleaners complete their tasks. During the three-month participant observation period, I gained a wide range of cleaning experience and learnt to operate a range of machines, from polyvacs and polishers through to outdoor scrubbers. I cleaned toilets, scraped chewing gum off floors in public areas, cleaned graffiti, vacuumed floors, emptied rubbish, polished windows, mopped and dusted and completed a wide variety of cleaning duties. The ethnographic research enhanced my human capital in ways that I could not have imagined at the outset!

In most cases the reception from the cleaners was extremely welcoming and positive. In the cleaning world much of the work is solitary and repetitive in nature, and many cleaners welcomed the company and the diversion. Most expressed amazement that someone was interested in them and their work. More than one thought that I was a little crazy. Here, I should point out that my New Zealand origins were a great help. Cleaners expressed interest in my accent, a number had visited New Zealand and Peter Jackson's enormously popular film *The Lord of the Rings* proved to be an ideal ice-breaker. On only two occasions did I experience hostility from cleaners. On one site a mother and daughter accused me of being a management informant and would not talk to me until I had established my credentials as a student. In this case, the mother had suffered an accident at work and her supervisor was putting pressure on her not to report the accident. She was suspicious of the supervisor and of me. Her daughter, who worked with her in one of the few examples of teamwork within Complete Clean, was a student. After production of my student card, both relaxed and agreed to talk to me. In another case, a supervisor was having an ongoing dispute with his manager. He pointedly told the manager and me that he did not want me present, that he was too busy to 'babysit' someone and he was short-staffed on the site. I told him that I was proficient at cleaning and could do any task he put me to. This supervisor relaxed when he realised that I was not a management informant. He also told me he was grateful that I did not 'dob' him in when he brought his niece and nephew to the site as he was caring for them at the time, in direct violation of Complete Clean's and the client's rules on occupational health and safety. He consequently became one of the most invaluable informants that I met during my participant observation.

In many instances cleaners made it clear that they were pleased to have me on site. I was willing to undertake jobs that cleaners tended to dislike, particularly vacuuming and dusting. I was also prepared to do some of the more unpleasant tasks. This was an important lesson learnt during my study, and opened up relationships and conversations that may not otherwise have occurred. For many cleaners, having an extra person to assist them meant they could get ahead in their work and, in some cases, complete their task on time. Again, the emphasis was on fostering reciprocity. In exchange for their time and talk, I willingly gave them my labour. During time spent at the work sites, I was also incorporated into the cleaners' networks. I learnt the secrets of the sites and the clients. Cleaners willingly shared their meals with me, and I became acquainted with the delights of Spanish, Portuguese and other food.

In another unexpected twist, I became the conduit between Complete Clean and its cleaning workforce. Because of the nature of work organisation, many cleaners have little information about their employer. In many cases the continual turnover of contracts meant that often the only sign of the employer was evident in the uniform the cleaners wore or the company name on their pay slips. Cleaners often grilled me about Complete Clean, asking who its owners were, the size of the organisation (which caused surprise to many) and whether or not it was making a profit.

On the sites, and when I was in the offices of Complete Clean, I collected brief fieldnotes according to accepted ethnographic practices. I carried with me a small notebook. When meeting cleaners I explained to them what I was doing, outlined the confidentiality of the research and asked if they minded my taking brief notes and jottings. I followed a policy of openness, and recorded brief jottings in front of cleaners and their supervisors. This practice appeared to work, and cleaners would often stop and ask me to write something down that they were about to tell me. Depending on the individual, I would modify this practice. I refrained from 'jotting down' those matters which participants regarded as secret, embarrassing, overly revealing or potentially harmful (Emerson et al., 2001: 357). Generally speaking, I tried not to make notes and jottings in the field, since I was aware that the process of note-taking could distract me 'from what was happening in the immediate scene' (ibid.). Where possible, I sought to rely on memory and made jottings to record technical details regarding the arrangement and organisation of work and the operation of equipment. These jottings were written up in full in a journal on the same day and frequently expanded during the train journey home, or at home.

Fieldnotes described the setting, the people I met and observed, their reaction to me and my feelings towards them and the work that I was doing. I recorded in detail the conversations I had, the work I observed and took part in and how work on each site was organised. I also recorded in some detail the reactions of the client's workforce and general public to myself and the cleaners I worked with or was observing. On the completion of the field research, the fieldnotes were indexed, reviewed and sorted into organising themes and categories for analysis and to reveal wider patterns. Where possible, I made use of detailed notes to include the 'voice' of the cleaners and present 'multiple voices' in my analysis. Fieldnotes were an invaluable source when it came to forming questions to put to management in semi-structured interviews.

The aim of my research was to capture a 'warts-and-all' view of working life in the cleaning industry from those on the mop-floor, and this was largely achieved. If anything, most cleaners seemed unperturbed by the presence of a researcher in their midst. For example, on some sites cleaners were comfortable in engaging in cheating of clients and unsafe and unhygienic cleaning practices in front of and alongside me (Ryan, 2007). In other cases I was asked to join cleaners in expropriating clients' resources and time from the employer. At a food-processing factory, for example, one of the cleaners asked me to help her load goods produced by the client into her car! On another site, an industrial factory that was impossible to clean, one of the demoralised cleaners spent most of his day on the phone to his girlfriend. I should stress that these examples in no way confirm the popular misconception that much workplace theft can be attributed to the cleaners. As cleaners pointed out to me, in their experience much theft was carried out by the client's own security employees. During the course of the research, I became the repository for much dissatisfaction and discontent. It was this honesty from the cleaners and my ability to listen that filled my study with a contextual richness. In my experience, an open mind and an awareness of potential opportunities paid rich dividends. Cleaners offering to escort me to the train station, giving me a lift home or sharing seats on trains and buses became valuable opportunities to gather data and share experiences in an atmosphere less pressured and hurried than that encountered on the mop-floor.

Middle management (known as 'customer service' or 'area' managers), who serve as a major conduit between the client, cleaner and the employer, play an important role in the employment experience of cleaners. A small number of these were reluctant to be interviewed. This challenge was overcome by conducting interviews off site and stressing the confidential nature of the interview. Invariably, the reluctant manager or supervisor became most helpful and informative, and initial reluctance was not so much to do with me as with some other factor in their working lives. Other managers were eager to 'spill their guts' and share their experiences. A willingness to help out on sites when a cleaner was sick or injured won trust and respect from managers and cleaners alike. Flexibility and a willingness to undertake interviews in places and times convenient to managers and supervisors were crucial in securing their cooperation. In one case I conducted an interview with a manager in a building basement surrounded by bins of stinking and decomposing garbage. On another site the supervisor demanded that I interview him as he polished corridors in a pharmaceutical laboratory. We walked up and down corridors behind a polisher for an hour or more while I conducted the interview and answered his questions about the firm that employed him. He also insisted that I hold my pen and notebook and take notes of our conversation. Another interview with a manager in a building basement was abruptly terminated when the fire alarm went off and he scrambled to ensure that the cleaners were leaving the building.

On all the sites I visited I was acutely aware that I was an outsider. I spoke with a different accent; I was white and removed from the ethnic, kinship and social networks evident on most cleaning sites. Some cleaners were embarrassed by what they perceived to be their 'poor' English-language skills. Managers having a joke and introducing me as a new senior manager to their cleaners did not initially help my situation as an outsider. I overcame this challenge by learning to say hello and greet people in their native language (I learned greetings in Greek,

Portuguese, Spanish, Italian and Macedonian – the main ethnic groups that I encountered) and by developing a reciprocal relationship where I assisted cleaners in their work in exchange for their time to discuss their work and experiences. Taking an interest in their food, sharing their humility and stigmatisation before clients and the public and turning a blind eye to cleaners expropriating clients' goods and their employers' time helped to open doors. Family networks and multiple job-holding among cleaners meant that my reputation preceded me on some sites. In some cases managers were proud of the sites they managed and the work of their cleaners. Invitations to staff barbecues and social events where managers hoped to show off their accomplishments facilitated ease of entry on to sites.

Life on the mop-floor: ethnographic approaches to understanding work

While there is not sufficient space in this chapter to explore fully the findings from my time on the mop-floor, a few brief examples demonstrate the potential of the participant observation method as opposed to surveys and interviews – features of conventional case studies – and allow us to turn conventional assumptions and analyses on their heads. The task of cleaning is universal and is not bounded by job position, title or status, as exhibited by the client's employees. Cleaners are given the freedom to traverse dominant spaces and have access to areas prohibited to the public or other employees. As a cleaner I entered the space of senior managers, high-technology computer research centres and pharmaceutical laboratories and studios, as well as spaces closed to the public and normally reserved for dignitaries and the 'important'. As a cleaner, had I chosen to do so, I could have accessed documents and files that were forbidden or off-limits to the client's employees. As a cleaner I was able to access the forbidden world of management and privilege, but by collecting their rubbish, cleaning their bathrooms and kitchens and collecting their towels etcetera, the aura of privilege, celebrity and seniority was significantly reduced. Through the spatial practices of cleaning, where space becomes bundles of surfaces, the symbolic power of social space experienced by the client's employees as an expression of managerial control loses aura and meaning.

As discussed above, cleaning is often stigmatised as 'dirty work' and those performing the work as 'dirty'. Time spent on the mop-floor demonstrates the complexity of stigmatisation and how cleaners sought to maintain an identity that rejected the concept of them and their work as dirty. As a researcher I also become entangled in the complexity of maintaining one's dignity and identity. My fieldnotes record an experience on one site (a prestige retail and professional studio). It was evening and there was a sense of excitement among the cleaners, as a red-carpet event had been scheduled by the client. The site was crawling with security guards, television cameras and numerous Australian actors and celebrities. I was rather uncomfortable and embarrassed walking and working among all the glitterati wearing my cleaner's uniform. I noticed that people seemed either not to notice the cleaners or to look right through us, despite the fact that we were mingling among them and cleaning between their feet at tables. Some of the guests barely moved out of our way, and I had the impression that we were supposed to show deference and move out of *their* way. Some threw cigarette butts in our direction. I was aware of the stigmatisation of being a cleaner and the servile nature of our work as we cleaned among patrons that night. I noted that the younger male cleaners rejected their *otherness* through the objectification of the women present. I was invited to stare, ogle and rate the attractiveness of those attending the gala evening.

Time spent working with cleaners highlighted the formal organisation of work, informal relations caused by employment tension that comes with coordinating work across multiple sites and the competitive nature of the cleaning industry. While cleaning contracts prescribe a level of quality or cleanliness that is supposed to be achieved by detailing the specificity and frequency of tasks, the reality was that most cleaners colluded with their managers to deceive clients. The reality of cleaning is that the work cannot be completed in the typical three- to four-hour shift or for the amount the client is willing to pay. This is particularly evident in commercial and office cleaning, where the sharp edge of competition is most prominent. In cleaning, cutting corners and maintaining an impression of cleanliness is a game played by cleaners and their managers in order to cope with unrealistic demands on their time. On the sites where I visited and spent time, I became an active and willing participant in such activities. Typically, we would clean those areas subject to client complaint, like toilets, entrance areas and the offices inhabited by senior managers. Dusting, vacuuming and the spaces inhabited by the client's employees were often 'spot cleaned'. In 'spotting' we would pick up the obvious pieces of paper and litter off the floor in order to give the impression that it had been vacuumed. In many cases, cleaning often only meant emptying the rubbish bin and cleaning the toilets. Such activities ensured that cleaners were able to get around an office floor in their allocated time. Other cleaners coped by coopting and organising the client's employees. On a number of sites where I spent time, cleaners encouraged, through flattery, flirtation or doing 'favours', the client's employees to undertake tasks normally done by cleaners. A willingness on my behalf to engage in these activities meant acceptance by cleaners and their managers into their world.

Conclusions

This chapter has highlighted the potential uses of an ethnographic approach in the study of employment relations and work organisation in the cleaning industry. It has discussed the challenges of securing access to a case-study firm and provided some guidance for establishing and maintaining relations with cleaners and their managers. I do not claim that is a definitive guide to an ethnographic approach to work; rather, I have offered some insights from my own experience of participant observation across multiple sites. Indeed, some purists may claim that my method is nothing more than a 'slash-and-burn' approach to ethnographic research. On the other hand, the study I undertook has given a rich and contextualised understanding of cleaning work. Given the fragmented nature of the cleaning industry, it is uncertain whether or not a more formal (read as 'longer') period in the field would have proven more fruitful. Used in conjunction with traditional case-study methods, an ethnographic approach enables the incorporation of the subjective experience of workers into employment relations research.

Acknowledgements

I would like to acknowledge the guidance of Dr John Shields, who supervised the PhD research on which this chapter was based. The experiences recounted in this chapter are a result of working alongside and interacting with cleaners and their managers. Thanks go to all the cleaners I came into contact with and who taught me the meaning of 'hard work'.

4

Drinking with Dessie: research, mines and life in the Pilbara

Bradon Ellem

Prologue

At three o'clock in the morning the dozen or so blokes still going are, funnily enough, still vertical. We are standing around Dessie's lounge room or, more accurately, leaning against the walls. It could be we all know that if we sit down, we'll never get up again. The union meeting I attended 12 hours ago is long forgotten; the function I addressed eight hours ago seems a lifetime away; the journey from pub to house is not one I could readily retrace. This really is the serious time of the morning: we have gone past talking about the job, gossip, politics, even the bullshitting. Men I have met only two or three times talk to me about their lives, wives, work, family, hopes and, yes, sometimes, the union. When I awake back in my motel much later that morning, not too well, I ask myself what the hell I am doing here... hung-over in the heart of the Pilbara? How did this happen?

Thinking about the Pilbara: industrial relations, history, geography

As teachers and researchers, we often tell would-be research students that they must have a passion for their subject: 'If you don't care about it, no one else will.' But that passion can be unexpected. A project might come from chance, from friends or from nowhere to be, dare I say it, love at first sight. Sometimes an entire research project can be, if not accidental, unforeseen in scope. My study of the iron-ore industry in the Pilbara region of the state of Western Australia (WA) was like that. It was meant to be just one section in a comparative overview of how employer and union strategies intersected in different ways in different places, but it became an all-consuming study in itself. If that was unexpected, so were the paths it took: from mine sites to tribunal hearing rooms; from union meetings to the homes of men once derided as scabs; from Karratha in WA to Cardiff in Wales.

To have some kind of interest in the Pilbara's mines is not that odd for students of Australian industrial relations. After all, for all the talk of the 'new economy', the 'old' resources sector has been booming for years. Although most employees in Australia do work in the services sector and the like, it is in the mines that record levels of investment, export income and company profits are being generated. Furthermore, the Pilbara has long been the site of truly dramatic and far-reaching changes in industrial relations. These changes have exemplified, and sometimes led, wider transformations in Australian work and society: from the union closed shop in the 1970s to some of the defining deunionisation disputes of the 1980s, at Robe River (Smith and Thompson, 1987; Thompson and Smith, 1987; Swain, 1995), and 1990s, at Hamersley Iron (Hearn McKinnon, 2007). When I first went to the Pilbara in June 2001 the only remaining unionised operator was BHP (not yet the merged entity BHP-Billiton), which was taking on the mining unions in what looked like a last stand. In November 1999 the company had 'offered' its workforce individual contracts after stalling in negotiations with the unions and making it plain that it did not wish to deal with them any more. This battle to keep mining unionism alive in the region was still at a high point on that first visit.

I had gone to the Pilbara, as I said, to try to see what was happening 'in different places'. In June 2001 there was a major campaign over union recognition to examine. The importance of 'place' came from my fascination with what the academic discipline of geography could tell me – as someone with a background in history and industrial relations – about work and unionism. I had a head full of ideas that I subsequently wrote about (for example, Ellem, 2004, 2006), ideas about how so many of the 'big-picture' stories of our time were playing out in the Pilbara. After all, what a geographical mix it was: the *multinational* companies selling ores into *global* markets and tangling with and seeking to change *national* and *state* labour laws to manage their *local* labour forces. And all of this – which geographers call a set of 'scaled processes' – was happening in this place with a rich history and immense economic significance. At this stage I had a very clear set of questions that I wanted to ask. I knew, or thought I knew, what my research problems were. The rather vague formulation of 'seeing what was happening in different places' did have specific measures such as union membership, for example, and common questions about the nature of management strategy, union action and senses of 'community'. I also had comparators in mind with other mining regions. However, the project suddenly got a lot bigger on me.

There was much more to my rapidly growing interest than these reasonably well-grounded and organised questions. In part, this was because of the peculiarities of the place. I was thrown into what seemed like the quintessential Australian outback landscape. The Pilbara is a place so physically vast and inhospitable, so stunning to all the senses, that despite my new-found interest in human geography, I found the physical geography overwhelming. I wanted to convey that, but I knew I didn't have the writing skills to do it. So, in trying to describe it in an academic article, all I could do was borrow from one of our great novelists to speak of country that looked 'dreamt, willed, potent' (Winton, 2001: 227), where:

> bluffs and peaks and mesas rise crimson, black, burgundy, terracotta, orange against the cloudless sky... on scree slopes the colour of dry blood, the smooth white trunks of snappy gums suspend crowns of leaves so green it's shocking. (Ibid.: 228)

Yet, in spite of the physical difference to the urban landscape around my workplace back in Sydney, I felt that I understood some of the issues I had to come to grips with. To my surprise, years of reading, writing and talking about industrial relations somehow seemed to lead to this. I felt like I was in a place I wanted to be. I was hooked.

So, that is how it happened.

Accidental ethnography?

I was locked into something bigger than I had anticipated. What was I now trying to describe and explain? The answer to that lay in reflection and reading, not more research as such. Although writing about the actual arguments in our research is beyond the focus of this book, it should be signalled that all my documents, interviews, observation and travel were not going to solve the problems of what it all meant and why I should be doing this research. The key breakthrough was in the work of many of the geographers I had been reading (notably Doreen Massey and Andy Herod). In addition to my starting point, focusing on the place, I became sure that *as well as* the local what I had was a study of globalisation, largely because of some of the players involved in those intersections already mentioned. This put the human geography and the physical geography together and wove both of them (in ways I am still working out) through history and industrial relations in the Pilbara. Yes, the Pilbara was a long way from 'the east' and yes, it was physically isolated, *but* it was also locked right into multinational business and global flows of capital, ores, labour. It was the tension between these different ways of looking at a place (from Massey, 1994: 138–9), in this case the Pilbara, that made it what it was. These thoughts took a lot of time (and a lot of writing) to become clear to me, but that is where I was headed. By the end I wanted – and still do – to put this together not just in the contemporary studies I have been doing but also in a study of the history of industrial relations in the Pilbara iron-ore industry.

There was still the question of method, of exactly how I was actually going to do this research. Here I faced lots of problems. My primary interests were and remain around the future of organised labour, but even among union people I could not be more of an outsider. I was a university researcher from 'the east' (where all the wise men came from, the locals observed) among working people in the 'wild west' of Australia. And, once in the Pilbara, I was as much an outsider as the union officials and activists themselves seemed likely to become at BHP. They already had that unfortunate status in other parts of the region, in what they themselves called 'Rio territory'.

I had done – and would do a lot more – reading and background research but 'access' was going to be a problem. With this kind of contemporary research, I needed to be able to meet people, go to meetings and get my hands on internal documents. The unions were on the outside and so was I. My visits to the Pilbara have been, because of the nature of my job, only short, so I do not really qualify as a 'proper ethnographer', a researcher who just about lives in the situation, but I felt I had to be part of the scenery as much as possible. And so I became a kind of ethnographer, by accident and necessity.

Four aspects of how I went about the study were important: to stay with the story over time; to think about what it means to try to break down the gaps between the researcher and the 'subjects'; to understand these very local processes in a global framework; and to think about the connections between this one study and other arguments about work and unions. All four aims pose real problems, perhaps especially in my field of industrial relations where there is an uneven history of this type of research and writing. (This is based on the discussion of 'extended case studies' and 'global ethnography' in Burawoy, 2000: esp. 26–8.)

I could not have got started at all without personal contacts. One of my friends and colleagues back in Sydney knew one of the organisers, Troy, who had done a stint in the Pilbara for the Australian Council of Trade Unions (ACTU). And of course he knew his successor, Will, in that position. I secured the necessary ethics clearances from my university (a six-month story we don't have space for here) and sent polite letters and e-mails. I also made a call to Troy. Being well aware of the ways in which union people (often rightly) regard academics, I simply asked if he could vouch for me with Will. 'Tell him I'm not a dickhead', I suggested. No replies came to my written requests, but a while later the phone rang, with an unknown caller ID. 'I hear you're not a dickhead' was the opening line. I was in.

Doing the research

The kudos – and the practical benefits – that came with being introduced to people by a union official held in high local regard can hardly be overstated, although there were problems with it too, as we shall see. I was able to sit in on union meetings, access files, meet workers and their families in their homes and go on trips across the Pilbara to union and non-union sites. I joined the union delegates at daybreak, trying to do lots of things at once: take notes, eat a meal, look on top of things and not be too overawed as, on my first day, the leading Mount Newman shop convenor, Rosco, consumed a 'Big Breakfast' that looked like a week's worth to me (I left him to his gym routine later that day).

To get to that roadhouse outside the BHP mining town was a feat in itself. The logistics and the geography of this kind of research are not easy to contend with, and might well be insuperable without a decent level of funding support. The five-hour flight from Sydney to Perth is just the start. Then comes the flight up to the Pilbara itself, another 1,600 kilometres away, followed by hire-car or lifts across the open country between mine sites and between mines and ports.

Being trusted by my initial contacts had led to more work for me to do and to new places. I was asked by the ACTU to run a series of focus groups among non-union workers at Hamersley Iron (now part of the Rio Tinto group), which involved going to four towns 600 road kilometres apart from each other and 400 kilometres away from where I had begun my work in Newman. This was a real breakthrough in my research, taking me from the union sites at Newman and the BHP loading facilities at Port Hedland to the non-union mining towns of Pararburdoo and Tom Price and the port towns of Karratha and Dampier. More than this, I suddenly had dozens of new names and hours of original transcripts. There was more to come, because after this the ACTU ran an organising campaign in Hamersley Iron which I was able to see at close hand. This too had its highs and lows for those involved, and for me. Inspired by union resistance at BHP, some workers put their hands up to reunionise the company in 2001–2002, only to see their hopes thwarted a couple of years later when the union campaign fell apart. Being sympathetic to the cause made it both easy and hard to write about this campaign.

In the non-union towns, it was the homes, the pubs, the accommodation quarters – not the workplaces – that were the sites of the union campaign and of my research. The unions *could not* get on site and I decided that I *would not*. That is, I would not go and interview the local bosses and get the official 'mine tour'. The most I did at the Rio mines was to join a tourist trip to one of the mines. The gigantic nature of the pit and its maintenance and loading facilities were as impressive as everyone had said and photos had hinted. More specifically, to have some idea of the nature of the work and the workplace was not just good, it was essential. It was worth it too for the spin from the tour guide, who talked a lot about ore bodies, derring-do CEOs and technology but appeared not to notice that the company actually employed people until one of my co-travellers asked about wages and unions.

Why not talk to the managers on site and get their support for site visits and the like? I did not feel that I could or should do this. I first went to the Pilbara 18 months after BHP had moved to eradicate union presence. Things were still tense between union members and those who had walked away to sign individual contracts. The term 'wopper' (from the acronym for the workplace agreements these workers signed) was only the politest word then applied. As for the company, it was making its feelings towards high-profile union people pretty plain. Could I write about what I needed through publicly available company material, along with documents from industry and judicial sources? Yes, I thought so. Did anyone need to put the company's story? No, I thought it did a good job of that all on its own, not to mention the aid of the business press, consultants and friendly governments. It seemed to me I would look like just another academic freeloader were I to go off and do those things at that time. I didn't tell any of this to my union friends – as they had become – until after I made the decision. They didn't seem that bothered one way or the other, and I would not recommend this course to anyone else. However, for *me*, then and there on *this project*, it seemed on balance the right way to do it.

At Newman I had been on site without official imprimatur, having been signed in by one of the workers. Here I learnt, of course, a lot more than on the tourist trip. More in fact that I bargained for, as my mentor, known for some reason as Batman, was widely considered to be one of the best talkers in the Pilbara – some claim. He did indeed talk to me without a break for well over two hours. On returning to the union rooms I was asked how I had got on. Before I could reply, Will told the others: 'You'll never believe what Rosco has done... he's only left him in the truck with Batman for two hours.' In true mining-town style they all had a go. But, as I said, I learnt a lot.

I also learnt a lot by socialising. Elsewhere in this book, Chapter 7 talks about how much could be learnt from hanging around with smokers outside workplaces. My research called on me to do plenty of drinking, a lot of it with blokes a lot bigger than me and with a lot more practice at it. Only years after that night at Dessie's did I discover that his lot were considered to be at the serious end of the scale and that I had stumbled in there unknowingly, a lamb to the slaughter. People were impressed I had survived. In the pubs I met just about everyone you could meet and saw some of the social interactions that make up working life. I cannot imagine how I could have done the research without the pub. There were good lines of argument that I probably wouldn't have used myself: 'so you never stand up for yourself then' used as a riposte to the line that 'if I don't like the way the boss treats me I just leave'. There was also the odd impressive head-butt, perhaps surprisingly not in that same conversation. And there were useful discussions with publicans about local economics and politics.

Some of these images fit with the urbanites' stereotypical view of places like the Pilbara: hard, tough, macho, big-drinking. Yet life is always more complicated than that. True, there are more men than women (a ratio of about 120 to 100), but it is mainly the large and growing numbers of contractors and fly-in/fly-out workers, mostly men, who give the Pilbara its 'blokey' edge today. In fact, young families make up the bulk of the population and the median age is younger than the

Australian norm. I soon saw this side of Pilbara life. This would reflect and affect the course of my research, because the question of how life in the towns and in the family related to life at work was of growing interest to me. So I ended up staying in people's homes, eating and talking long into the night about my work and theirs.

The fact is that a lot of this was hard work. When I first flew up to the Pilbara, I was more than excited. I was anxious; I was nervous. This could all go badly wrong, not just professionally but politically. I could look like a complete goose in front of these people. Even when that feeling subsided, I was always edgy. New researchers should be aware that interviewing will almost always be an exhausting process, physically and emotionally. I knew a lot of the necessary background, but I knew next to nothing about details of work processes, local life, shift and roster arrangements. Finding out about all these kinds of details is hard enough in itself. That the people we interview often feel safer in unloading to an outsider about what is really going on in their workplaces and personal lives is, I think, a real privilege, but it also drains the interviewer. Yet here can lie the greatest insights.

The insights I gained were among the best I have ever had in more than 20 years of research. There was still more to it. I was with men and women who were going through hard times in fighting for what they believed in, and they trusted me in those times. Maybe I am a sentimental researcher, but I was a sucker for people who were standing up for things I believed in – not just unionism but unionism of a particular kind. So I formed close friendships and bonds that, to some extent, broke down the division between researcher and 'subjects'. I was aware – and became more so – that I was not the first person to go down this path in this place. In the 1980s other academics who had worked closely with Pilbara unionists had, it seemed to me, been washed out by the experience, either by what they saw or by being caught up in its higher politics (Heath and Bulbeck, 1985; MacWilliam, 1990). I met some former Pilbara workers who had thought about writing up their experiences of the bitter strike defeats only to feel, in the end, that they were too close to it all or too burnt by it to go on and do so.

Even as a researcher I had my moments of pressure. On my way to run the ACTU focus groups I had a call from one of Hamersley's managers (I don't know how he got my mobile number) to ask why I was talking to 'his people'. The same term was used by a group of unhappy BHP managers at a conference to attack me for not talking to 'their people'. At first I thought they meant the managers, but actually they meant the woppers. The fact that workers loyal to the union were not 'their people' was in itself revealing. And then there was the national official of a union unpopular with the locals who wondered aloud what the hell I knew about the Pilbara. I was glad when someone else pointed out that I had spent more time there than had anyone from his office. Not to mention the local official who, after a very long BBQ, told me I should pretty much head back east and study some mines closer to home.

Sites of research

There were many sites to this research. I listened, read, talked and wrote in all sorts of places. Once again there was plain good luck here. According to just where I was, I saw many angles on the research, and I am not sure that any amount of hypothesising or research design could have led to some of these moments (on lucky meetings see Newby, 1977: 120–5).

Some cameos of what happens in these places where I ended up explain this.

I stayed with Jack and his wife Emma: he a leading steward, finally hounded out of his job by a mining company; she a high-profile community critic of the impact of company policy on town life. How else would the researcher hear about the kids sent home from a birthday party because Dad was in the union? How else would I begin to feel, not just think about, what 'community' means here? And what does the so-called expert academic do when listening to the talk about what it will mean in real, personal life to decide whether to fight a dismissal or accept the (big) handout on offer?

Even the car became a research site. My second trip, in September 2001, coincided with the collapse of Ansett Airlines, with which I had flown in and out of the Pilbara. Holding a ticket with Qantas out of Perth, all I had to do was cover those 1,600 kilometres in a day in a hire-car from Port Hedland. Not totally convinced by the claims that I would do it 'easy', I set out at six in the morning and, yes, I did do it easily enough. This was another piece of luck for me (a lot luckier than the company's employees, for sure), because the trip gave me a real perspective on the journeys that, in more than one sense, underpinned much of the Pilbara's past; it emphasised what distance means in a way that air travel cannot; it gave me an unexpected day without phone calls or other interruptions in which to think about what I was doing while all my experiences were fresh. Scribbled notes from that trip formed the basis of much of the rethinking that would go into my writing.

The old 'union rooms' in Paraburdoo to which I had access before and after a union organising blitz in the town in November 2002 were also important to me. That dramatic episode as the unions began to get a toehold in Rio Tinto is another story (Ellem, 2004: ch. 4; 2006: 379–80). The rooms had been barely used since Hamersley Iron was deunionised in 1993 – an archivist's treasure trove, with a rich line on union activity cut short. Runs of files, minutes and broadsheets all came to an abrupt halt, as if the town had been hit by a natural disaster. Most alarming of all, for a union researcher, are the stickers with one union having a go at another – all put up just as the company was planning to take *all* the unions down. Here, too, there were long conversations with the old organisers and Stewart, now handling the Hamersley job, plus workers and their families, the heart and soul of rebuilding a union. Kerriane and Andy's BBQs were at once planning meetings and a lot of fun.

There were plenty of other sites of research: in cars, over those hundreds of kilometres, talking, thinking, trying to remember it all for more formal 'interviews' later on; in a small house back in the east, a few thousand kilometres away, meeting one of the strike-breakers from the Hamersley Iron dispute – having been introduced to a friend of his through a couple of union officials – reading his files, paperwork and clippings, talking about unions and the company then and now; in libraries and offices across the country, trying to make sense of it all when the issues look a bit different to how they do back on the ground; in the Industrial Relations Commission in Sydney, listening to what seemed like the utterly other-worldly playing out of the dispute that killed off the Rio Tinto organising campaign. Sometimes the journey not just over distance but to the heart of the problem was a long one: sitting at a desk in Cardiff University thinking about how to make all this intelligible to an international audience, it finally hit me that the Pilbara, this study, had a wider interest and application because it was, as much as anything, an aspect of globalisation.

Summing things up

I was lucky. I got on well with the people I met. I hate to think what would have happened otherwise. Doors opened, talks started, contacts followed. The role that chance can play in this process is – alarmingly –

important. It can make or break a whole project (Newby, 1977). This research story is like many others in this book. This particular project emerged from a general interest without much prior planning. That it became all-consuming was also unexpected. How I actually did it was equally unanticipated. I do not think I could have done what I did any other way, but the pitfalls were as great as the possibilities. There certainly were problems: because I became so wrapped up in things, I misread some situations, or at least did not suspend judgement when I should have. In light of how things turned out through 2004–2005, some of the things I wrote in the two years or so before that – in tone as well as argument – turned out to be rather optimistic and, well, wrong. In that sense, a peril of the research was exactly the same as its strengths: I was very close to things. Some of my published academic work now reads like part of the Pilbara's history, not an analysis of that history. But, on balance, would I have it any other way? No. Apart from the personal factors, the reason for that is an important one: on reflection, the framework I had for explaining local union success could also explain setbacks and disappointments.

Epilogue

Back in Newman, the day that ended in the drinking session at Dessie's sums up what this type of research is like. The day had begun over 300 kilometres away, in the towns of Paraburdoo and Tom Price, where chance meetings would lead to a swathe of documents landing on my desk later. Through the middle of the day I drove to Newman, taking in the scenery and thinking about what to say at the meeting that afternoon. Then I was off to meet with a local parliamentarian. The women on his administrative staff would later lead me to learn a lot about the Pilbara and provide contacts reaching back to union struggles of 20 years ago. Then we were all off to the function, where I addressed the local union members and their families. My original brief was to speak for ten minutes but other speakers had dropped out, so I was asked to speak, well, for a while. Concerned I would miss out on the fun while talking, Rosco kindly passed me a beer or two as I spoke. Was it destined to be a big night out? Yes. Was it only that? No.

I thought that I had just been plain lucky as an academic outsider to win acceptance here. I do not know how I could have done it in any way other than this. Some research, some places, some research methods suit certain kinds of people, I suppose. Other researchers would make contacts in different ways and therefore write about it in different, maybe better, ways. I am sure, though, that it works best when the research matters most to the people it studies – not as 'subjects of enquiry' but as women and men seeking to make sense of their own lives as workers, citizens and family members.

Acknowledgements

Apart from Des himself, now retired to the coast from the Newman mine, and officials in the public eye, the names of several people herein have been changed. Some of them read this chapter in draft form – for which many thanks. I am grateful to all the people I have met in the Pilbara during my nine visits so far, especially those who provided time, ideas, food and shelter. There are debts, too, to academic colleagues a world away at Cardiff University. Thanks to Ed Heery for the reference to the terrific chapter by Howard Newby, whose account from a generation ago of studying farm workers in Suffolk has uncanny resemblances to my experiences and which I wish I had read before now. From the same conversation, thanks to Steve Davies for coming up with the title for this chapter. Many thanks to Peter Fairbrother for putting me on to the Burawoy reference. I have published a number of articles on this research so far, most recently in 2006, and a book, in 2004, intended for union activists themselves.

Part II
Access for research

5

Combating information suspicion: Guinness, sports and glassblowing

Paul Ryan and Tony Dundon

Introduction

Interviews, no matter how well designed and planned, often fail to elicit meaningful data. Even the most efficient researcher can encounter unforeseen problems. These are especially evident for interviews concerned with management and business-related topics, for a variety of reasons. The most simple is that respondents pull out and cancel at the last minute due to time pressures or unplanned work commitments. A more difficult problem, however, is when a respondent agrees to an interview but is reluctant to divulge the level and detail of information required. This can be as a result of a lack of interest in the research agenda on the part of the interviewee or a reluctance to engage in the research topic. The consequences can be highly problematic, and can even derail an entire research project.

In this chapter we show how an interview had to be turned around from one of almost complete disengagement by interviewees to one characterised by a solid level of engagement. This involved the researchers adjusting to circumstances, providing prompts and exploiting opportunities to develop rapport with respondents. From the outset, it should be recognised that the researcher of a social-science-type research project tends to be against the clock. This is as important for quantitative surveys (questionnaires often need to be kept short) as it is for qualitative interviews (which are often dependent upon the time available to interviewees). The objective is commonly to derive as much information as required with the minimum of disruption and in the shortest period of time. Therefore, the dilemma is a circular 'chicken-

and-egg' scenario. On the one hand, without rapport the interviewee may be disengaged from the process. Yet, on the other hand, developing rapport utilises scarce time available for the gathering of required information.

The remainder of this chapter narrates the story of how a two-person research team moved from a situation of almost complete disengagement to one of close rapport, empathy and understanding between interviewer and interviewee. In the first section we briefly outline the research project from which the interview is drawn. The second section gives a backdrop to the case-study organisation and the respondents. The case study is Waterford Wedgwood Crystal, based in the Republic of Ireland. Employment relations at Waterford Crystal have at times been characterised as conflictual, with a highly charged union-management relationship. The interviewees were the on-site officials of a well-known trade union, the Amalgamated Transport and General Workers Union (AT&GWU). They participated in the interview at the request of management, the latter being the main source of access for the research project. From the outset the union interviewees viewed the project with suspicion, having never had any prior contact with the researchers. The context of a highly conflictual employment relationship at Waterford Crystal is important: there was an awareness of highly sensitive and context-dependent information surrounding an interview process aimed at eliciting deep (rather than broad) data. The third section narrates the interview itself. The final section of the chapter outlines some general guidelines to help develop respondent rapport during an interview-based research project.

The story told in this chapter illustrates how the development of rapport is best viewed as a staged process. Significantly, it describes how these stages have to be subtly moved through at quite a rapid pace while simultaneously ensuring confidence is developed rather than lost. The chapter shows the extent to which interviewee disclosure and data collection can be enhanced after rapport is secured.

The research project and its methodology

The interview story is based on a single case study drawn from a much larger research project that included 15 organisations in total (for details see Dundon et al., 2006). The particular research project was more policy-oriented than theoretical: it was multidisciplinary and involved interviewing multiple role holders at different levels to explore complex social processes at the enterprise level. The research was concerned with the factors influencing change management as a result of European employment regulations (e.g. the European Directive for Employee Information and Consultation). Thus the questions asked and the methodology used were determined by a changing regulatory environment for employee voice that was occurring in Ireland (and the UK) at the time.

The approach is best described as 'social action' research, which 'attempts to come to grips with the meanings of a situation [for] those involved in it' (Silverman, 1970: 224). We were interested in the meanings of employee voice for union officials. A case-study strategy was employed so as to allow role holders to explain and reflect on the detail of information and consultation mechanisms in their own words. Various research instruments were utilised in this regard: semi-structured interviews with different actors, company documentation and in some cases an employee attitude survey. What is reported here is one set of interviews with a single respondent group from one organisation: the union conveners of the AT&GWU based at Waterford Crystal. The approach was qualitative in nature and the interview schedule was designed around several conceptual and analytical themes derived from existing theory and research about the topic of regulating for employee voice. It is important to note that this case-study strategy did not search for broad generalisations across a defined population or sample, but rather sought to understand particular situations as encountered by the respondents themselves. With this approach the researcher is then allowed to place the data in a wider context of explicit and implicit influences surrounding the phenomena under investigation. For this reason, a contextual backdrop to the case study is important.

The case-study context: Waterford Wedgwood Crystal

In finding a case study that is 'suitable', a researcher is often dependent on a combination of accident, fortune and guesswork. This is because there are no clear guidelines for what makes a suitable or robust case. Indeed, it has been argued elsewhere that the meanings and interpretations of complex social relationships can never be fully understood until the research has commenced at the organisational level (Gouldner, 1955). The case study reported here was deemed suitable for the project because the organisation had experienced considerable change during its long and varied history. There were also strong and well-established union-management structures for employee participation and social partnership.

Waterford Wedgwood began its operations as Waterford Crystal in 1783, to manufacture hand-crafted glassware. Waterford Wedgwood plc was established in 1986 with the merger of Waterford Crystal and Wedgwood. With a combined history of over 600 years of heritage, tradition and craftsmanship, today Waterford Wedgwood is among the world's leading luxury goods manufacturers with global brands that include Waterford Crystal, Wedgwood, W C Designs, Rosenthal and All-Clad. At present the company is represented in 80 countries worldwide and has a combined workforce of over 9,000. The company and its workforce have experienced significant change and reorganisation. It faced severe economic recession during the late 1980s, and became known for its lack of technological innovation and combative industrial relations. In response to market pressures Waterford Wedgwood consolidated its position by disposing of unrelated companies. Many of the changes were extremely painful for both workers and the company. Redundancies, wage freezes, wage cuts and changes to work practices were all introduced. These changes culminated in a bitter and protracted 14-week strike in 1990, during which the on-site union convener (the principal interviewee in this research) was sacked by management for making speeches that intimated threats to the company owner, Sir Anthony O'Reilly. After a public apology by the union convenor on a local radio programme, the dismissal was revoked as part of the return-to-work agreement.

The AT&GWU has a tradition as a militant rather than a moderate union. It is perhaps the only union in Ireland that publicly opposes the government's partnership approach to industrial relations, believing vehemently that the concept of partnership is a euphemism for managerial control and the exercise of power over workers. The union is also suspicious of employment regulations that emanate from a supranational body such as the European Commission, believing in free collective bargaining rather than what it would term a form of collusion with state institutions that do no more than support and prop up a capitalist system for employer-dominated interests.

Either in spite or because of its militant values, the union has negotiated several collective-based structures for worker participation at the case-study plant. There is a closed-shop union agreement which ensures 100 per cent union membership as a condition of employment for production workers. Agreements provide for three elected union representatives (conveners) to be released from their daily work tasks to carry out union activities. In addition there are numerous department-level shop stewards who meet with management and conveners on a regular basis. For example, there is a joint negotiating committee (JNC) in which the three conveners meet with company directors on a weekly basis. Senior plant management also consult with union representatives over a wide range of issues at a weekly monitoring steering committee, including full disclosure of commercially sensitive information. At lower levels there are several task groups (TGs) comprising union and management representatives that meet on a regular basis and consider information such as production schedules, shipping quantities, quality issues and production costs. Further participatory structures include sectional consultative committees (SCCs) between shop stewards and supervisors of particular occupational and functional categories, such as glassblowers, cutters or packers. In short, there already exist at the plant extensive collective-based structures for employee information and consultation via the elected representatives of the workforce. These voice channels have been used to facilitate a programme of change and radical restructuring. At times these changes were unpalatable to the union and workforce, with episodes of resistance and non-agreement.

The interview narrative

As with many research projects, obtaining agreement and permission from management is crucial to gain access. It was management that agreed to participate in the research study and insisted – probably in the spirit of cooperation and inclusion – on union involvement. It was certainly an oversight on our part that we took it at face value from management that the union knew who we were and why we would be interviewing them. It was the company management who introduced us to a disgruntled, stony-faced and time-pressed group of three union conveners on a bleak mid-November morning. We were informed we would have about one-and-half hours to interview and discuss the research with the union respondents. Worse still, the interview commenced in what was clearly an alien environment: the HR manager's plush office. The tone thus set was immediate and self-evident: we were 'identified' with management rather than as independent researchers. Two of the three-person union delegation took part, while the third union representative remained silent during the interview.

Stage I: initial suspicions

As soon as the HR manager departed, the researchers were left in little doubt that the interviewees felt that these two clueless academics had been imposed on them at the behest of management. The third union representative, who arrived with the two conveners, remained and was not asked to remove himself while the interview took place, even though he said nothing and it was clear he would not be participating in the interview. This signalled to the researchers that the interview about to commence would neither be of long duration nor provide the narrative, anecdotes and illustrations required to get to grips with complex social processes surrounding union-management consultation. As noted above, there was a growing sense that the researchers were somehow complicit with management in the purpose of the interview. However, there was also a sense that the interviewees were unsure as to what it was the researchers were complicit in. Nevertheless, this was evidently neither the time nor the place to find out. The fact that we allowed management to set up the interview with union officials when negotiating access to the case study meant the respondents had no prior direct interaction with us or the purpose of the research. Thus their suspicion of us should not really have come as a major surprise. We briefly introduced ourselves and the project objectives in the hope of rectifying a glaring oversight and omission on our part. At this point it is worth noting that prior to the case study visit publicly available information had been collected on the AT&GWU (and Waterford Wedgwood). Thus the researchers were to some degree familiar with the union, its broad policy objectives and the company's position concerning things like social partnership and its link to employee voice and union participation.

As the interview began it became evident that one of the researchers is a native of Liverpool, and his scouse accent elicited a mild sense of curiosity amongst the union conveners: 'what brought you from Liverpool to Ireland, what do you do at the university?', and so on. The interviewees commented on the fact that the union's general secretary, based in London, was also a 'scouser'. This signalled an important phase in the first stage of the interview process, as respondents sought to elicit information and some further understanding as to our motives in conducting the research. Notwithstanding this, the overriding sense was one of suspicion. At best, we were a major inconvenience and nuisance who had distracted the union conveners from their more important work. Despite the researchers' attempt to initiate and progress to the more substantive parts of the interview schedule, it was apparent at this point that the respondents were just 'going through the motions' of complying with management's request to partake in the research. Questions and subsequent probes designed to facilitate open-ended responses were met with succinct affirmations or negations. At one level the respondents were respectful of our need to have answers. Yet, at a deeper level, the information given provided neither insight nor the elaborated extrapolations about union-management consultation that we sought.

Stage II: changing direction

The short and succinct answers to our questioning indicated the need for some alternative direction. The way the story unfolds can be illustrated by the metaphor of a typical security guard's role on the door of a nightclub (e.g. a 'bouncer'). A tactic often employed by bouncers when confronted with over-inebriated and aggressive would-be entrants is known as the 'switch'. Rather than face up to the disgruntled customer and argue about access to the club, the 'switch' is a diversionary tactic whereby one bouncer tactfully steps aside and permits another to intervene. This new and more 'reasonable' bouncer explains quite politely the reasons why entry is not possible at this moment in time. While still unhappy, the over-inebriated would-be entrant's attention is diverted away from the initial blocker, the bouncer refusing admission, to someone who seems apologetic and less guilty of the refusal to admit.

At this stage of the interview we were in need of such a switch. The mechanism employed was a request for a drink. The intervention was made by the second interviewer, a non-Liverpudlian Irishman, asking 'in the absence of decent Guinness around here, is there any water?'. The Liverpudlian stepped aside to allow the Irishman to initiate the switch. Significantly, the qualifier of mentioning Guinness in the same sentence as water was not accidental. It generated a further detail to the subsequent conversation around what is and is not 'decent' Guinness. As water was being dispensed from the HR manager's own personal dispenser in his office, the Irish researcher stepped aside to allow the Liverpudlian to invoke a further switch, suggesting that 'such important matters as "decent" Guinness might be best resolved over a coffee, not water'. The coffee option was agreeable. More importantly, this necessitated a trip to the canteen, and as such a much bigger 'switch' than was hoped for ensued.

Stage III: searching for a common ground

Although still in its infancy, the switch offered a temporary reprieve to the respondents' reluctance to furnish the detailed level of information we sought. Such a reprieve signalled another stage on the journey to establish rapport and build a degree of empathy with the interviewees. More importantly, by moving from the HR manager's office to the factory canteen, a more fluid conversation was established in a less intimidating environment. Conscious of the significance of the switch, we realised time was crucial to be able to develop a level of rapport that would be more satisfactory to the research objectives. The transformation from a reluctant to a more supportive atmosphere needed to be rapid and decisive. As the union conveners walked to the coffee dock, the researchers split up. The Liverpudlian chatted with the more senior union convener, who seemed curious about the project and the potential implications of the proposed EU directive on employee voice. The Irishman spoke with the second union official, who was known to be a strong critic of the Irish government's partnership approach. From prior research about the union it was discovered that he is the more militant ideologue: a Marxist. The Irish researcher decided to turn the conversation away from the project and its relevance to union-management power relations, and to talk about something else. This involved an element of risk. The switch described above changed the location and altered the direction of conversation between interviewer and interviewee. However, identifying an alternative and more general, non-threatening topic to build rapport is always risky. The topic can be anything, but the respondent has to be able to engage in a genuine way with its substance. This is a search for a universal subject with a common language. The Irish researcher's knowledge of a game of hurling the day before the interview offered a common ground to open up rapport in new and more engaging ways.

The local sporting team had lost an important game to its neighbours, and it was known that supporters of both teams worked side by side in the plant. The conversation opened with a question: 'So what went wrong yesterday?' The tenor of the question meant that no further elaboration was required. 'Not up to it', replied the Marxist union official. 'It must be tough losing to them', replied the Irish researcher. 'Yes. It's bad in here today. It's been going on all morning. I'm bloody sick of all the slagging', said the union convener. The Irishman, with some empathy: 'Ye had your chances though. The rest of us were for ye. They're an arrogant shower', implying the neighbouring team won only after a hard and proud display by the convener's preferred team. The conversation paved the way for further non-threatening dialogue: 'So where are you from?', asked the convener of the Irish researcher. As the researcher explained his background, where he was born and his father's long-held distaste of the team that had won and caused the militant such discomfort, the first semblance of a bond was beginning to emerge.

Stage IV: establishing empathy

During coffee the conversation stayed off the topic of the research and moved from Gaelic sports to the weather and what life was like in Galway (the city in which the researchers' university is based). The union conveners were still curious about how a Liverpudlian came to work in an Irish university. The conversation eventually turned to how the Liverpudlian had once been a union steward and had previous dealings with officials of several unions in Britain, including the general secretary of the conveners' union, the AT&GWU. The scouse researcher's personal journey from union rep to university lecturer was related. Mutual acquaintances in the labour movement and linkages to others on the political left were exchanged. Existent sympathies with worker concerns and empathy for union organising were swiftly and firmly established.

The nature of the conversation was much more natural and fluid; signalling another important stage in the process of building rapport with reluctant respondents. The substance and details of the conversations were neither intentional nor planned. The subject matter was something that evolved in response to the dynamics of the situation as it unfolded. However, what was conscious was the tactic of a switch, and thus a readiness on the part of the researchers to develop new lines of respondent engagement. Once the less threatening and more common ground for dialogue was found, a degree of empathy between interviewee and interviewer was established. From that moment the interviewers were no longer perceived as being identified with management or on the side of the company. We had shifted from 'outsider' to 'insider' status for the purpose of the interview. At the

Stage VI: post-interview rapport

The most surprising twist in the narrative occurred as the interview came to a close. We initially thought the interview would be very short, with little more than blunt and unelaborated answers, but after the 'switch' (see Stage II above) the interview lasted for about four hours. It was enjoyable, highly informative and peppered with fascinating anecdotes and stories about the company, the union and its workforce. At the beginning of the interview we thought it would be difficult to keep things going for one-and-half hours, a time frame suggested by the HR manager. The concept of a 'tight schedule' was adjusted by the respondents themselves once a level of trust and rapport had been established. After four hours we were extremely pleased with the depth of information collected. However, and unbeknown to us at this time, data collection didn't end as the formal interview closed. As we were winding up the interview and thanking the union respondents for their time, we were offered an unrequested tour of the plant by the two conveners. This is where the most surprising revelation occurred, and the story takes a slight diversion while we were escorted around the factory.

Waterford Crystal is a long-established business that has become an official tourist attraction in Ireland. The union conveners took us across the factory and we joined a mass of (mostly American) holidaymakers who were midway through an official tour of the facility. The company's history and its products were being explained, with photos and replicas of the more famous items and sporting trophies made by Waterford Crystal. Upon arrival the tour guides (company employees) gave a small nod to the union conveners. Our presence was acknowledged but nothing was said: we were in safe and trusted hands and the official guides left us and the union reps to our own devices as we mingled with paying tourists.

The next stage of the tour included an observation deck overlooking a team of about eight workers who were blowing glass and crafting crystal wares. The union conveners, being well known in the company, were allowed to usher us towards the front as the guide was explaining the jobs being performed and products getting made. These workers were evidently highly skilled and worked in hot and sweaty conditions. The job involved a delicate task handling smouldering (melted) glass from a furnace, balanced on the end of a long tube. With intricate hand-and-mouth coordination, the workers would blow an individual item of glass similar in shape and size to a large, round fish bowl. This involved hot melting glass being blown and twisted into shape. When the glass is of a particular shape and size in the blowing process the worker dips it into a coolant, from which is then crafted a piece of crystal ware by other workers in an adjoining team.

In ushering us towards the front we had a privileged position to view the production process, although that was not entirely the motive of our hosts, the union conveners. They facilitated this premium viewing position because they also knew what was coming next in the company's official tour. As the company guide called for a volunteer, the Irishman swiftly and tactically stepped back, leaving for a few seconds the Liverpudlian out in front with the mass of tourists. With a nod and wink from the union convener to the company tour guide, the scouser was seconded to perform the same glassblowing tasks that had just been observed. With the melting glass in flames, loaded on the long tube and now in full view of encouraging American tourists, there was little point in any objection. The best that could be hoped for is the Liverpudlian might be able to display some resemblance of competence alongside the artisan instructing him how to blow the glass. He failed. The skilled craft worker, with what seemed to be minimal effort, demonstrated how to blow the glass while simultaneously spinning the tube to ensure maximum leverage. Within a few seconds he produced a crystal bowl that was perfectly curved and approximate 15 inches in diameter. He dipped it in the coolant and cut it from the tube ready for the next stage. In contrast, the Liverpudlian blew with all the wind he could muster, expelling his lung capacity several times over, and only managed to produce a glass bubble the size of a thumbnail. Instead of skilfully dipping the red-hot flame of glass into the coolant, it fell to the ground with a tiny splat. Nonetheless, the Americans cheered.

As the company guides gathered everyone and moved to another part of the factory to continue with the Waterford Crystal tour, we were taken through an exit to the side. It was explained that we were about to enter a part of the plant that is 'out of sight' from the official tour. Amazingly, here was a scene far removed from the handcraft production techniques we had only minutes before been witnessing and trying to reproduce. There were a number of assembly lines which were spewing out mass-produced crystal pieces that had been designed on computers. The image and brand of hand-made crystal ware were shown to be an illusion: they were exclusive to commissioned pieces, such as major sporting trophies. For the bulk of products, the only human involvement in the process were the hands of packaging workers who removed the finished pieces from the conveyor belt and carefully placed them in boxes for shipping.

The implications of the failed glassblowing attempt and the sight of semi-hidden assembly lines were far-reaching, and beyond the remit of this chapter. Suffice to say that we now believed we had obtained full disclosure, over and above what could have been hoped for or expected. Because the Liverpudlian was willing to 'have a go' at performing a craft without the requisite skill and competence, the respondents were further engaged. At the same time, because the Irish researcher collaborated with the union conveners who helped engineer the scouser's humiliation, a deeper and more trusting 'banter' was to some degree now embedded among researchers and interviewees. Whether this degree of engagement helped facilitate the subsequent observation of mass assembly lines or not, we are unsure. The revelation of mass production may have already been part of the union reps' tour schedule. In any event, the turnaround from complete disengagement at the beginning of the interview to information retrieval was complete. On top of all that, we left with an unexpected gift-wrapped piece of crystal, courtesy of the union conveners, which remains to this day displayed in the researchers' offices.

Conclusion: lessons from our experience

We do not claim that the interview story told here is typical or common. In fact, the initial level of hostility and suspicion among the interviewees is itself an unusual situation. Most respondents in qualitative and interview-based research usually have some prior knowledge and understanding about the topic under investigation, and what is expected of them. Nonetheless, there are important lessons from the experience that show how rapport building, empathy awareness and an appreciation of the changing dynamics of interview research can lead to extensive information discourse. In summary, these lessons include:

- establish your independence and credentials in the research process from the outset
- select an interview venue where interviewees feel comfortable to communicate
- don't rush into the interview schedule
- be sensitive to non-agenda opportunities to expand interaction and develop dialogue between interviewee and researcher

- be prepared – know as much as possible about the interviewee, the organisation and any pertinent issues
- enjoy the discussion – be open to anecdotes and illustrations that add levity to the interview.

6

What lies beneath: the pleasures, pain and possibilities of focus groups

*Barbara Pocock, Jane Clarke, Philippa Williams
and Ken Bridge*

Introduction

We have conducted focus groups in a range of settings around Australia over the past decade. These experiences have been among our most entertaining and challenging experiences as social researchers. Keeping a group of a half-a-dozen ten-year-old boys from a disadvantaged school focused on a discussion about their parent's work, as they alternately run laps of the library and sit patiently on their chairs carefully considering our questions, is both a hair-raising and a rewarding exercise. Focus groups constitute an ethical, reasonably practical way to find out what young people think about key social issues, and provide a means for bringing their perspective to consideration of what affects their lives, to social policy and to what parents, custodians and governments know and do.

We have each come to the qualitative methods of focus groups having spent most of our working and research lives swimming in a valuable sea of quantitative data and analysis: labour force surveys, public health studies, analyses of rates of union density and education participation. These are the essential bread and butter of robust social research. These data remain of immeasurable value to better understandings of social issues. We have each run surveys and also had experience of interviewing people about a range of social issues. However, some of our most creative and enjoyable research experiences – along with the biggest challenges we have faced – have involved the conduct of focus groups.

The focus group, or the focused group interview, has been used to understand the experiences and opinions of groups of people since the 1920s (Wilkinson, 2004). Articulating views and sharing experience within a group allow for the clarification and development of an individual's meaning, and this is, in our view, a first step in the development of a theoretical conceptualisation of meaning around social phenomena. At their best, focus groups encourage the distillation of important issues through the interaction of the group. Participants work together in a synergistic way to determine the issues that they, as a group, consider important.

In this contribution we describe how we have used focus groups, why we like them, where they have come from and the ingredients we see as useful in ensuring a good focus group, based on our practical experience.

The people with whom we have conducted focus groups

Focus groups are a qualitative research method using group processes to help people explore and express their views and experience (Kitzinger, 1995). Using either a series of open-ended questions or a topic guide, a group facilitator guides discussion of a small group of people who share a common experience, such as that of being a child, a worker, a parent, a grandmother, a carer or a union delegate or leader. We have used focus groups in relation to each of these categories of people.

There are numerous texts about choosing appropriate methods for specific research questions, and this chapter is not the place for them. However, it is important to begin the design of any social science project with clarity about the research questions and great care in the choice of appropriate research methods and approach. We have applied the focus-group method in a number of circumstances, generally pursuing large, open-ended questions. The following are some examples of this research.

- *How is work affecting Australians?* Pocock (2003) conducted focus groups among 163 mostly South Australians in 2000 pursing this general question.

- *How is parental work affecting young people and how do they see their own work futures?* Pocock and Clarke (2005) conducted 21 focus groups among young students aged ten to 18 in 2003.

- *How does social support work for new families (i.e. after the arrival of a new baby)?* Williams (2005) conducted focus groups consisting of people with the shared experience of motherhood, fatherhood or grandmotherhood in Sydney in 2002.

- *How are Australians putting together their jobs, homes and communities in a range of new and old suburbs?* Williams and Pocock (2006) conducted focus groups among women and men in a range of urban settings.

- *What are the views of young people (in newly developed relatively well-off suburbs and long-established relatively low-income suburbs) about urban landscapes, work, facilities and planning?* Williams and Bridge conducted focus groups among young people (ten to 16 years) in 2007–2008 (Williams et al., 2008).

In each of these examples we structured participation in focus groups, applying a theoretical sampling framework. The format for this framework has varied. In studies of children, for example, we have included high- and low-income groups. In other cases the framework has included specific representation by age, gender, parental responsibilities, household type, working arrangements or urban/rural location. In our experience this theoretical sampling approach is critical to addressing research questions where issues of place, socio-economic status, gender and household structure are likely to be relevant. What is more, at a practical level such theoretical framing can help structure – at least initially – the process of analysis: for example, while being rural or urban might make little difference to children's perspectives about parental work, it is useful to compare findings between these groups as an entry point to analysis, even if other themes emerge as more important in structuring the final analysis.

Why we like focus groups

Our use of focus groups reflects a constructionist perspective on research. Constructionism maintains that meaning is constructed through the interaction of people with each other and with the world around them, and that this meaning is developed and transmitted within social contexts (Crotty, 1998). Research is not exempt from this process of 'making meaning', and as researchers we inevitably bring our social context to research, whether consciously or not. Indeed – like most researchers – this context shapes the questions that we find interesting and our decisions to spend years of our lives in their pursuit. All researchers bring some elements of a subjective, personal perspective to their work, alongside the directions suggested by the existing literature and theory. Together these affect the choice of questions, the methods applied and the data we choose to examine. We are interested in the social construction of meaning, and we have found that the conversational language and interaction possible in a focus group provide insights into this process and into perceptions of lived experience, which is the material of our analysis.

There are five main reasons that in our experience make focus groups a useful method in the appropriate circumstances.

Firstly, unlike surveys and most quantitative methods, and even some qualitative methods like interviews, chances are that when you run a focus group you will hear unexpected and unanticipated things. Focus groups are almost always interesting. They often include elements of surprise that challenge pre-existing categories or perspectives. They are often funny, sad or vigorous. While one frequently hears repetitive issues and experiences towards the end of focus-group data collection, there are always life stories and experiences among participants that are intriguing, and focus groups – most importantly – permit *depth* of understanding.

Secondly, focus groups are cauldrons of analysis. The collection of the data occurs in the midst of participants' own analysis and response as they interact in a focus group. Analysis of the issue under study often begins in the process of the group, is sometimes intensive in the hour or so immediately after the group (where two researchers conduct it and have time for immediate debriefing) and matures over time with pen and paper or computer-aided analysis. A focus group is, in our experience, often a creative experience where analysis begins immediately because the groups are distinctively *interactive*.

Thirdly, a well-run focus group dilutes the power of the researchers and the weight upon them. It shifts the locus of power from the researcher to the individual and group. It does not in general, in a well-run group, *relocate* the locus of power (which remains with the facilitator) but it *shifts it significantly* to the participants. For example, in a focus group the participants usually talk much more than the facilitator, in contrast to interviews. They also listen and respond to each other, as well as to the facilitator. This gives the facilitator time to pose good follow-up questions where appropriate, to consider whether all viewpoints are getting on to the table and to facilitate the exchange effectively.

This contrasts with the centrality of the researcher in constructing and analysing, for example, a survey where closed questions literally 'close off' responses and guide respondents between a limited range of answers (often with good reason, based on good pre-existing literature, data and evidence about what matters). 'Open' questions in a survey open up possibilities, but of course are usually constrained by both space and time, and perhaps shaped by the questions which precede final 'open' questions inviting comments.

Turning to qualitative methods, one-on-one interviews offer more open possibilities than most surveys. While interviews usually make use of an interview question schedule, there is scope for deeper pursuit of perspectives and open-ended questions. Interviews often permit quite detailed accounts of experience, of individuals' perspectives about their experiences and consideration of their consequences. This gives data both depth and breadth. However, the interview interaction is one on one, as the interviewer asks and the interviewee replies. There is little time for contemplation, as interviewees feel obliged to reply fairly promptly to questions. Interviewees are under examination, as the weight of the interview rests on them alone. This is necessarily a fairly intensive exchange. It can often lead to quite short responses and/or few pauses or opportunities for reflection, as both interviewee and interviewer feel responsible for filling the space – even where quite open-ended questions are used.

We have found focus groups provide much more open opportunities for pursuing discussion of social phenomena. Accounts are immediately 'compared and contrasted'. Participants can give their personal perspectives and also interact with the perspectives of others, and – most importantly in our experience – they have time to consider their views (as others speak) and to enter into conversation and/or build upon different or similar views. As others speak, participants can sit back and think. This relieves the pressure of one-on-one scrutiny and allows participants to consider viewpoints and reflect, then to re-enter the conversation. There is time for an interactive circulation of thought among individuals, who will often revisit a comment or perspective reflecting against what they have heard or previously said. Thus focus groups can result in open, reiterative conversation and exchange.

Consider, for example, the following contributions from high-school students in a country school, discussing housework and relationships –

first the males, and then their female peers in separate sex-specific focus groups:

> You've got to share [housework], otherwise she'll divorce you. You should be able to help for the first few years [of marriage] then it might wear off... (Kevin, 17)

> Most girls today, they're not as into doing housework as 60 years ago. It was expected that housework would be their whole job, but I suppose nowadays they're not as 'Oh yes – I'll do the housework'. It's sort of share, work rate evenly, sort of thing. Maybe not quite evenly. (Kyle, 16)

> Interviewer: So do you think you'll be sharing but not quite evenly, is that your plan?

> Yeah, we hope we do. (Kyle, 16)

Immediately after this focus group, we canvassed the views of young women:

> There needs to be a balance. I think it is disgusting the way it is. (Kate, 16)

> I was thinking the other day... I didn't want to end up like Mum, having to do everything, so... if they are good at home economics or something, they can cook maybe three times a week and I'd do the other bit, and make it balanced. (Judith, 18)

> [You need to share] from the start – because my parents started [not sharing] as they are from the start... I'm not marrying him unless he does the dishes. (Kate, 16)

> It is still going to take a couple more generations for men to start realising they have to do something. That women are now going out to work and they are bringing home money and [men are] not all the time the breadwinner of the family but [women] are contributing equally as the men, so they need to. They're bringing in half the money, the guys are bringing in half the money, so they need to share the work around the house as well. (Judith, 18)

Interviewer: Looking at your brothers, do you think that is going to be easy?

No. My brother is incapable of doing anything for himself. He can make chips – that's the frozen ones. (Kate, 16)

In this transcript participants are listening to each other, reflecting against other comments, and the facilitator is able to pursue issues, following up on Kyle's comment about sharing and Kate's comment about her brothers. Together the two accounts illustrate the contrasting gender tactics of the two groups (Pocock, 2006: 148). Clearly, in this set of focus groups separation of male and female participants was wise. In general, in our experience it has been useful to separate groups where possible by age, gender, geography (rural/urban) and socio-economic status, given that these might reasonably be expected, a priori, to be distinctive lines of analysis.

Of course such group processes can also go wrong – and they have for us: they are open to domination by particular individuals, can lead to 'group think' and can go off-topic and take a lot of time. This means that a skilled facilitator and careful set-up of focus groups and their 'rules' are critical, and we return to these below.

Fourthly, focus groups where social issues are discussed are intensely human experiences. As researchers who are interested in people and what they make of their experiences, we have found that focus groups often include fascinating and sometimes profound moments of human revelation and exchange. This has energised us as researchers. We can each remember particular groups years after their conduct, particular pieces of conversation and particular participants whose stories were especially memorable.

As authors we are fascinated by how and why people do things, what their experiences are (in all their diversity) and what they *make* of their experiences – individually and by exchange in a group. It is fair to say, however, that we have run focus groups about topics that are of personal interest to us, and which – we hope – represent useful contributions to literature and the body of social knowledge. This brings the issue of the disinterested researcher to the fore: given that we are all mothers or fathers, what does the occupation of this subjective position do to our research on children, parents and work? We are not, by and large, too worried about the real and ever-present danger of being personally located in the force field we are trying to understand. This is because we believe it is a convenient fiction to think any social researcher is truly free of social context. All researchers of human phenomena – whether economists, health scientists, anthropologists, historians or philosophers – bring a subject position to their work, the questions they ask, the terrain they investigate, the analysis they undertake and the policy implications they draw. At the very least this relates to gender, but usually much more. The small volume of qualitative research about issues like social support, motherhood, children's experiences of working parents and work-family interaction in part reflects the unconscious biases and methodological and issue preferences of 'care-less' masculinised social science. As researchers we are influenced by our own childhoods, parenting, work, motherhood, fatherhood and gendered experience, just as generations of researchers, like economists, have been influenced by, for example, their gender and lack of responsibility for dependants. And this history has resulted in its own knowledge biases, gaps and costs. How else could the dominant strain of neo-classical economists hold, in effect, that work and gross national product are divorced from social production and reproduction?

In this light, we are strongly in favour of a reflective research practice that works hard at understanding and sifting out our social subjectivities. This is a worthwhile, if usually imperfect, aspiration. We try to do it, and we have certainly each had particular expectations challenged and overturned by what we have heard.

Fifthly, focus groups can be a very efficient means of collecting a lot of data. We are rather more hesitant in arguing this today than a decade ago, given some recent experiences in setting up focus groups in complex systems (for example health and education departments) where long lead times, complex bureaucratic systems and myriad gatekeepers create many obstacles. Nonetheless, when the green light comes on and all the ethics sign-offs are in hand, focus groups can result in a lot of data collection quite quickly, especially compared to interviews. Researchers are always caught in the vice of 'big questions, small resources', and we have each made many pragmatic decisions about methods based on resource constraints.

The ethics of focus groups

All social research raises ethical issues. Focus groups raise particular issues, especially where they are conducted with children. Ground rules are essential. When we conducted our work among children we required written ethical clearance at five levels: the university, each state education system, individual schools, parents and children themselves (recorded verbally). As researchers we were required to demonstrate the absence of criminal records before entering schools, as well as knowledge of reporting systems in relation to child protection.

However, all these systems are thin protection if a researcher chooses to behave unethically. So, for us, the key ethical undertaking exists beyond and in addition to the formal processes; that is, a commitment to *behave* ethically. This has different meanings in different contexts, but includes researching questions that matter; doing research in ways that do not waste time; reporting back to those from whom we draw data; reporting the results of our work publicly and honestly; and connecting our work, wherever we can, to public policy and private behaviours that improve outcomes for people. Ironically, many ethics proposals spend little time on whether the research matters and how it will be linked to impact and public discussion. Fortunately, focus-group research is wonderfully easy to report publicly because it connects to a primitive human curiosity and interest in narratives. Focus groups generate stories; these hold people's attention. They illustrate critical concepts. They are much easier for most lay readers to understand than most quantitative analysis. Not all élite academic refereed publications find them acceptable, but most citizens understand them.

Some ground rules for running focus groups: some lessons

Because focus groups necessitate the sharing of personal information among a group of people, it is necessary to establish ground rules. In our experience these rules reassure participants that their stories will be respected, and not repeated outside the group in any way that identifies them. Ground rules also set up guidelines for respectful conduct within the group that allows each participant to have their say. Such rules usually include a request that views expressed within the session remain confidential within the group. However, we have not been able to guarantee that what young people in a single school say is not repeated outside the focus group, and this is an important failing. We do not know if this happens or its consequences, but we know it is a lot to ask of a child of 12 to respect his/her peer's revelation of a mentally unwell mother or a father who is violent when he is tired. We have had the experience of a child revealing sexual abuse in a focus group (saying 'this is just between us, right?' to the other children afterwards). In this circumstance a mandatory report of the incident was made after the group concluded. It is important to have all such possibilities, and courses of potential action, considered before setting out collecting data.

We have found it useful to do three other things at the beginning of focus groups. First, we explain that the facilitator will be firmly in charge of 'sharing the air-space' so that people are forewarned that they may be 'wound up' in the interests of ensuring that all views are heard. This enables people to relax about speaking: their turn will come and those who habitually hog speaking space will be controlled. Secondly, it is useful to say that some people may not want to make a contribution on an issue. Finally, we explain that focus groups are not about agreeing: they are about canvassing the full range of views and different opinions are actively invited.

Key challenges for focus groups include getting people there in the first place, getting the right people there and finally knowing who you have in the group in terms of their characteristics. We have learned the value of local champions who understand the project, see its merits and have the authority to get the relevant permissions and participants, and will perhaps share your enthusiasm in the final research result. We have found that extensive efforts to set up focus groups are not always rewarded. Sometimes nobody comes, or only one or two. On the other hand, we have run focus groups of up to 16 people, all of whom had travelled long distances in the evening in the country and were not to be turned away.

In our experience by far the greatest cost of focus groups lies in the time required for their organisation. Maintaining a spreadsheet of participants and their key demographics, with data collected in a 'tick the box' survey at the end of the focus group, helps in monitoring the composition of the focus-group population and guides ongoing theoretical sampling.

In running focus groups with children, it has also been vital to be flexible about when, where and how groups are conducted. Schools are sometimes unpredictable places, teachers face many demands and not all children can sit quietly for an hour. In this light, it has been important to find a local champion for focus groups – someone who makes sure parents return consent forms, that a private space is found and that the children are rounded up. Finally, when ten-year-olds need to take a break from questions and run around the library, it is wise to take a break. Food and drink are useful ice-breakers for participants.

We digitally record and transcribe focus groups using an online Australian transcription service. While we have sometimes used computer software for interview transcript analysis, we have shied away from its use for focus groups because it de-identifies, disembodies and decontextualises participants from, for example, their household situation, socio-economic status, household location, rural/urban location and so on. We have not enjoyed reading sets of quotes on specific themes that are disconnected from the whole transcript, and so we have generally manually analysed transcripts from beginning to end.

This can be daunting: for example, 21 focus groups conducted among ten- to 18-year-olds in 2003 resulted in over 700 pages of transcript. Our analysis is generally worked up from a line-by-line reading and coding, identifying issues, various standpoints on these issues, their variation by demographic or other sub-group category, and finally their relation to other literature and to policy and action. This has generally proved an iterative cycle. We have often had two analysts – preferably those who actually conducted the focus groups – to share perspectives, and this has proved invaluable in enriching analysis and checking and comparing perspectives.

Our preference and usual practice is to conduct focus groups with a facilitator and note-taker. This helps to attribute quotes to individuals: the note-taker's role is to sit back from the group and – apart from managing the recording equipment – as unobtrusively as possible take note of who is speaking and key words they use, so that quotes can be attributed to specific individuals. This is resource-intensive, but it does enable the other key thing we have learned to do, which is to debrief together about the focus group soon after its conclusion. We have often been surprised about the subsequent usefulness of this discussion, which we transcribe and use in analysis. Immediate thoughts about the group often note where the 'heat', humour or sadness of exchange lay, help delineate the lines of debate that are critical or dominant, highlight the similarities and differences that are striking (either within the group or in relation to previous groups) and permit reflection on what went well, or wrong. We have learned to make focus groups smaller rather than larger (four to six being ideal), and to allow pauses and silences as people reflect. Larger groups take a long time. We usually begin groups with a round where each participant chooses a pseudonym, and explains relevant demographics and details of their situation – for example, 'I want to be called Sophie and my dad works as a plumber and my mum is a part-time artist and there are five people in my house including my two brothers and we have a dog called Tim.' This kind of introduction breaks the ice, gives the note-taker key information and gets everyone used to talking in an orderly, 'turn-taking' way. It is important to have a room with a closed door if possible and to stick to the nominated finish time. Finally, we have learned through bitter experience that technical failure of all equipment is guaranteed at some point, so we try to have back-up equipment.

The seating of focus-group participants is also very important, as eye contact is one of the main means of communication and control available to the facilitator and can be a real help in keeping the flow of conversation under way and appropriately managed. In our experience, people want to know that someone has things in hand, and that they can trust in effective facilitation.

The limitations of focus groups

It is also important to consider the limitations of focus groups: they are useless instruments for addressing many important social questions. Surveys, document analysis, interviews or other research methods are much more appropriate at many times. Focus groups are most valuable when the question or terrain is relatively unmapped, where the query is very open-ended or where people's own experiences and perspectives matter and are sought. They are not helpful for queries that relate to rates of incidence or population characteristics: for example, they are useless in understanding what causes lung cancer, but they may be very useful to understanding why anti-smoking interventions do or do not work.

In many cases focus groups are a useful complement to survey data and interview material. They can be good precursors to the application of these other methods (to shape questions and map out relevant terrain) or good follow-up tools (to probe survey and interview data to consider issues and explanations that lie beneath the results that emerge from prior collections). We have used them in these contexts both as one of several methods and as a stand-alone method.

Focus groups permit depth: they allow a probing of what lies beneath the surface phenomena of survey results. They permit excavation that is relatively intuitive, following a line of thought or conversation to places that initial research question schedules cannot anticipate. We have often been struck by people's willingness to talk about relatively personal, even intimate, matters in the right kind of environment.

Participants often want to talk about work and, for example, the impact of jobs on their children, illustrating their experience with examples and stories. Many Australians across the socio-economic spectrum are keen to talk openly about social and work issues. While there is sometimes an element of 'performance' in these accounts, it is not common, in our perception. However, it does occur: when Mike, a 17-year-old boy from the North Shore of Sydney, says in a discussion about housework in his future household 'My lady is doing the cleaning. I'll just be on the porch having a beer', he is playing for laughs in a mixed-sex focus group of his peers (Pocock, 2006: 143).

Like all research methods, focus groups are appropriate for some kinds of problems and not others. Much as we have enjoyed running focus groups and witnessing human experience in its great diversity and occasional hilarity and sadness, we know there are many occasions when focus groups are not appropriate, or we cannot afford them or cannot talk people into coming to them. Nonetheless, focus groups can powerfully illuminate the human condition and assist social scientists, especially where they are part of larger mixed-methods studies which allow iterative collection and analysis of data.

Part III
Interviews as a method

behest of the union respondents, we started to return to the substantive topic of the research. The difference, however, is we resumed not in the canteen over coffee or the HR manager's office with its personal water dispenser: we returned to the interview in the confines of the union's own office elsewhere in the plant. Interestingly, on entry to the AT&GWU sanctuary the third union representative, who had been loitering all this time and who we knew was part of the union delegation but said very little, was asked to leave. We never asked who he was or what his role was in the union. Nor was there any need to: we had established a sufficient degree of empathy and trust that the interview could proceed along the lines originally hoped.

Stage V: the dynamic of respondent trust

All changed, changed utterly. A terrible beauty is born. (W.B. Yeats)

The interview recommenced on a much more engaged, interactive plane. Gone were the curt, uninformative answers. In their place were fully fleshed-out narratives, relevant and often amusing anecdotes, elaborations of the union conveners' concerns for the company's future and rich illustrations of their affection for their locality. Their disillusionment with, as they saw it, management inadequacies and details of how 'information and consultation' worked in practice sprung forth in abundance. One particular revelation was the union's acute sensitivity to the market environment faced by the company and its role in calling management to account. The non-militant union convener explained:

> We don't want to be the financial controller of the company [and] management can't be held responsible for economic downturns or war. But if competitors are up then we have the data so management is held responsible.

Almost immediately, the more militant union rep added:

> If people give out that a strike or disagreements will shut the place down, then shut it down. You have to stop somewhere, they can't take it all.

7

Looking through the haze of discontent: smokers as a data source

Robin Price and Keith Townsend

Introduction

In the case of industrial relations research, particularly that which sets out to examine practices within workplaces, the best way to study this real-life context is to work for the organisation. Studies conducted by researchers working within the organisation comprise some of this (broad) field's classic research (cf. Roy, 1954; Burawoy, 1979).

Participant and non-participant ethnographic research provides an opportunity to investigate workplace behaviour beyond the scope of questionnaires and interviews. However, we suggest that the data collected outside a workplace can be just as important as the data collected inside the organisation's walls. In recent years the introduction of anti-smoking legislation in Australia has meant that people who smoke cigarettes are no longer allowed to do so inside buildings. Not only are smokers forced outside to engage in their habit, but they have to smoke prescribed distances from doorways, or in some workplaces outside the property line. This chapter considers the importance of cigarette-smoking employees in ethnographic research. Through data collected across three separate research projects, the chapter argues that smokers, as social outcasts in the workplace, can provide a wealth of important research data.

We suggest that smokers also appear more likely to provide stories that contradict the 'management' or 'organisational' position. Thus, within the haze of smoke, researchers can uncover a level of discontent with the 'corporate line' presented inside the workplace. There are several aspects to the increased propensity of smokers to provide a contradictory or discontented story. It may be that the researcher is better able to establish a rapport with smokers, as there is a removal of the artificial wall a researcher presents as an outsider. It may also be that a research location physically outside the boundaries of the organisation provides workers with the freedom to express their discontent. The authors offer no definitive answers; rather, this chapter is intended to extend our knowledge of workplace research through highlighting the methodological value in using smokers as research subjects.

We present the experience of three separate case studies where interactions with cigarette smokers have provided either important organisational data or alternatively a means of entering what Cunnison (1966) referred to as the 'gossip circle'. The final section of the chapter draws on the evidence to demonstrate how the community of smokers, as social outcasts, are valuable in investigating workplace issues. For researchers and practitioners, these social outcasts may very well prove to be an important barometer of employee attitudes; attitudes that perhaps cannot be measured through traditional staff surveys.

The ethnographic case study

Conducting research as a participant observer within an organisation raises a series of practical and ethical problems for the researcher. The cost of this method in researcher time needed to prepare and undertake the study is of greater import in recent years, as funding constraints in higher education have acted to limit the time taken for research and ethical requirements have tightened (see the chapter by Sappey; Sutcliffe, 1999).

Hence, non-participant observation is more common than 'going native'. Yet this leaves the problem of being an 'outsider', and the research subjects modifying their behaviours accordingly. This is particularly important if the researcher is trying to unearth material at variance with the corporate position, as was the case in the studies discussed in this chapter. Methods need to be found that enable researchers to 'break the ice', establish trust and rapport with research subjects and find those 'unexpected stories' (Behar, 2003: 16).

Many researchers are well aware that entry into workplaces is largely dependent on the goodwill of managers. While an ethnographer attempts to remain objective and independent of influence, maintaining a good relationship with management of the organisation is critical. Unfortunately, this can lead to a perception by employees that the researcher is present as little more than a 'management informer', creating a potentially impenetrable barrier to quality data collection, especially if you are investigating employee resistance. A large part of the problem is the formal setting in which organisational research is conducted. Within organisations, and particularly in confined workspaces, employees are often loath to voice opinions that contradict the management position.

Anthropologists often choose to admit to personal flaws, addictions or idiosyncrasies in order to get research subjects to speak about matters that are otherwise taboo (Sherif, 2001). Knapp (1997) suggests that shared agenda-setting is the most ethical means of providing an exchange of information with research subjects, and also a means by which many issues that the researcher had not thought to ask about are likely to be uncovered. This chapter suggests that smokers are a valuable group of research subjects because they are more forthcoming with information likely to conflict with the management view of the firm. The authors do not believe that smokers are inherently more critical of management, although this is an untested proposition; rather, it is the location of smokers away from the workplace that gives them the freedom to speak openly.

Smoking in the workplace – hiding your butts

The first 'anti-smoking' legislation in Australia, the Tobacco and Other Smoking Products Act, was introduced in Queensland in 1998. This legislation was designed to protect members of the public from the health dangers of smoking and also to reduce the uptake of smoking within the community, especially among children. As a result of this legislation it is generally unlawful for persons to smoke in enclosed spaces in Queensland (s. 26R(1)). Smokers are therefore legally required to smoke outdoors. From 1 January 2005 legislation was tightened to preclude smoking in any sports facilities or within four metres of all building entrances. Many workplaces have developed their own smoking policies which stipulate that smokers are only allowed to do so in designated areas or outside the employer's property line. Consequently, there are often large numbers of employees standing around outside buildings having a cigarette.

For the researcher, standing outside talking to smokers clearly increases one's exposure to smoke. While we recognise the dangers inherent in passive smoking and certainly do not advocate taking up smoking as an aid to research, the following case studies highlight the value of smokers as a means of gaining an additional view of an organisation and its practices.

The three case studies

The data for these case studies were drawn from research conducted across a number of disparate projects in industries as diverse as call centres, food retailing and food processing. In each case the researcher wanted information from research subjects, and in each case this was made difficult by the nature of the work that the subjects were engaged in and the pace at which work was undertaken. In two of the firms, the attitudes of firm-level management towards the presence of researchers also made gaining access to subjects difficult. These cases all highlight the practical value of smokers as research subjects, both for building research relationships and for providing a divergent perspective that is often missed by formal interviews or surveys within the confines of the firm.

Retail foods

This case-study organisation was a large retailer of low-margin, high-volume foodstuffs. In this instance, obtaining research access to the organisation took over six months of negotiation with senior management. The organisation granted permission for interviews with management and staff and a staff survey, and ethical clearance was obtained from the university to cover this research approach. It was then left up to individual store managers to determine the extent to which they were prepared to become involved in the research. Across the stores investigated, store and department managers were prepared to submit to individual interviews, but only one store manager was willing to permit interview access to employees, and then only in the employees' time. In this store it was stipulated that employees were not allowed to stop work to be interviewed, but talking to workers on the job proved problematic and gaining access to off-duty employees was also difficult.

This food retailer used industrial engineers and sophisticated software to ensure that labour was used productively every minute of the day. As a result, the degree of employee performance monitoring was extensive; budgetary targets for staffing levels were in place and religiously adhered to. These workers were so busy that it was hard to find opportunities to speak with them, and when the researcher did so, it was very apparent that the workers were being interrupted. Additionally, in-store 'musak' meant that recording conversations was not a viable option. Initially the researcher talked to employees while working with them. This meant stacking bags of potatoes while talking to the vegetable department employees and squashing cartons flat while talking to nightfill workers. It was not possible to take notes while working, but it was possible to sit down immediately afterwards and write up research notes.

Another difficulty was that staff were often involved in serving customers, or within earshot of customers, and this constrained the type of questions that it was possible to ask, and clearly also the type of response the worker felt able to give. This was particularly the case for checkout operators, who represented nearly 50 per cent of the store's workforce. While the researcher made a point of regularly grocery shopping within the stores being researched and talking to checkout operators while doing so, this was not only expensive but also constrained the range of topics suitable for conversation. This was where the employee survey became valuable (see the chapter by Felstead et al.).

These surveys were undertaken in the tea-rooms of the respective stores. By sitting and chatting to people about the surveys, we were able to discuss issues with the employees that we had not previously covered. This was particularly the case in two stores where the store manager used the tea-room to make coffee, and made a point of chatting with the researcher and the staff sitting there. The store manager's recognition of the researcher helped to break the ice with workers, but it did not overcome the problem of resistance created by the research environment, as workers were often hesitant to speak freely in a tea-room with their colleagues, and often their supervisor, in attendance.

As the researchers were consciously trying to achieve a representative sample of staff across departments and employment classifications, and were therefore tallying types of employees, they became aware that they had not seen any of the meat department employees in the tea-room. When the researchers asked why, they were told that the meat department workers were smokers and took their lunch-breaks outside.

The next step was asking the employees where you were allowed to smoke in the shopping centre. In two of the three stores the management of the shopping centre had designated smoking areas. At the time this research was conducted one of the authors was a smoker, and a native to the smoking outcast group. The original intention was to use this opportunity to survey those workers who smoked and did not use the tea-room, as well as getting a nicotine fix. Instead, the researcher discovered that the employees who were outside smoking and having their lunch were happy to talk quite freely about their experiences within the organisation. Not only that, but their views were often far more critical than those expressed within the walls of the organisation.

Indeed, quite fortuitously, the researcher discovered one particularly valuable smoker. This worker, a service supervisor on his final day of employment with the organisation, was quite prepared to disclose the ways in which the computerised staff scheduling system could be circumvented. This contradicted the previous responses in management interviews that 'the computer rosters staff' so they had 'no control and could not play favourites'. Clearly the software had a series of protocols, but the industrial engineer in charge of the system was not prepared to disclose these. The disgruntled smoker, while standing outside the store, felt free to disclose favouritism in staff scheduling. 'You can chop and change and manipulate it to suit, however you want.' As a researcher, finding such an informant was invaluable and enabled us to present both sides of the staff scheduling story within this organisation. Other smokers provided similarly valuable insights that would not have been captured by either the formal interviews or the survey instrument. Since the researcher did not take a participant consent form outside for a cigarette, but did take a copy of the survey, the informant's consent was provided verbally.

Call centre

At the call centre employees face a high degree of monitoring and performance measurement, high levels of pressure and high turnover. This is not unusual for call centres. The research process at the centre was based around informal discussions with employees about aspects of being organised into teams in an organisation with such individualised work processes. Part of this included attempting to uncover individual and collaborative acts of covert resistance. However, employees initially seemed to hold a degree of reticence in discussing issues of covert resistance with outsiders (Townsend, 2005). Part of this was associated with using this style of methodology in such a research setting.

Call centres are sometimes referred to as 'an assembly line in the head' (Taylor and Bain, 1999) due to the similarities with traditional Fordist regimes in terms of mass production of product (or service in the case of call centres) and short job cycles. The work of call-centre employees is tightly monitored through electronic surveillance, as well as having some scripting of calls and low levels of task discretion (Townsend, 2005). The incoming calls to the centre are placed in a queue, and distributed automatically to customer service representatives (CSRs) through an automated call distribution (ACD) system. This system also provides the rostering and planning officer with a range of information that is used to determine appropriate levels of staffing. Importantly, staff levels are measured to ensure there is always a queue, hence when CSRs are finished with one caller there will always be more calls waiting for them to attend to.

Employees work in an open-plan office space, with each CSR sitting in a partitioned cubicle. While sitting in the workstation the cubicles are slightly above head height for an average-sized adult, limiting the potential visual distraction from surrounding employees. Each cubicle is equipped with a networked computer, a telephone and headset and minimal and ever-decreasing numbers of hard-copy manuals. Although employees have only a semi-permanent partition separating them physically from the adjoining CSR, the overarching requirement to be on the telephone for approximately 85 per cent of their working day limits worker interaction. Each individual CSR is expected to take approximately 90 calls per day. Talk times average between 108 and 126 seconds. In addition, a 90-second post-call wrap period in which follow-up clerical work is completed is measured and included as one of the targets that contribute towards an employee's performance bonus. Within this context, informal conversations remained short and problematic for data collection. Consequently, much of the data were collected from employees while away from workstations.

Commonly, employees would relax in what was known as 'the breakout room' while on breaks. The room was rather small, with a fridge, a television, a table and four chairs plus four lounge chairs. Importantly, this was a non-smoking area; hence all the smokers would quickly grab their lunch from the fridge and congregate outside the building. For the purpose of this research, when the researcher managed to talk to an employee on a weekend without anyone around, he mentioned his reticence to talk openly in the breakout room because of concerns for who may overhear our discussion. The employees' reluctance to discuss issues of resistance did not change immediately when time was spent with the smokers. This was evident in a number of occasions when employees would begin a sentence and then stop, often after glancing in the researcher's direction. However, over time employees appeared to become more comfortable with researcher presence and returned to their everyday conversations.

The time spent with the smokers opened a number of gateways to rich data. Employees spoke about political alliances and disputes within the organisation between particular team leaders and managers or general employees. Such political relationships can be essential contextual information for the ethnographic researcher. As time progressed, employees began to open up and tell of some of their fiddles. The role of 'gossip' in the workplace was highlighted by Michelson and Mouly (2002), indicating that 'gossip' is a potentially rich source of additional information regarding many aspects of the workplace. Importantly, in each of the organisations presented within this chapter, the information collected from the smokers was not to be taken as gospel. Rather, there were two uses for these data. They could be used as signposts or clues to piece together other data collected from within the organisation, or alternatively as information that can be used to progress the collection of data within the workplace. Hence, the 'smoker's word' could be used as a glue to stick together already collected data, or as a wedge to pry open areas for further investigation.

FoodWorks

The FoodWorks plant was a greenfield plant where the managerial team dedicated a great deal of time and resources to the development of a particular managerial culture, aimed to avoid unionisation and promote cooperation and commitment from employees. The investment of time is important when researching topics that may appear as 'deviant' to the organisational hierarchy, and indeed to many workers, so when little resistance was uncovered in initial weeks it was not of concern to the researcher. However, when the employees presented an image of being cooperative, committed people the researcher did begin to wonder what to do.

Commonly, operators were asked about their relationships with managers and team leaders. One operator commented: 'The team leader is good, really friendly, that might be to do with the test we take when we start. Almost everyone here is very friendly.' Months later the same operator had just completed a conversation with a team leader when the researcher entered the workspace. When he approached the operator, without any coaxing the operator put on a decidedly unhappy expression and exclaimed: 'He's a wanker. He's a pain-in-the-arse, fucking wanker.'

The researcher was taken aback; however, this proved to be an opportunity to delve further. Conversation progressed, and the researcher said: 'So, you lot have been telling me for months that this is such a happy place, and "we all get treated so well here", but that's not really the truth. Why have people been telling me that?' The operator's response was forthright, and only partially surprising given what we know about researching deviancy:

> They've all been lying to you, of course. This is a shithole of a place and I'm tired of lying about it. If you want to really know what people think of this place, I'm about to have morning tea, come out with me and spend some time with the 'gutter scum'.

Patience allowed the continuation of the research when it seemed pointless, and a little luck allowed the opportunity to uncover these two significant events that may not seem overly important to the management or employees. However, when searching for dissatisfaction that manifests as resistance and misbehaviour, these two events proved crucial.

As it transpires, the 'gutter scum' is a term of endearment that many of the smokers use to describe themselves. The reason for this is the worksite is non-smoking and the employees must leave the worksite altogether for a cigarette. Throughout the day there is a procession of employees heading out to a street beside the plant, sitting in the gutter smoking cigarettes, drinking caffeine in various forms (coffee, tea and a range of colas) and, most importantly for the research, complaining about management and the organisation. Interestingly, not all members of the 'gutter scum' were as trusting as the operator who had extended the invitation to join them. Nevertheless, entry had been allowed to the inner circle of discontent, and this presented a wealth of data in its own right. Similar to the 'gossip-circle' described by Cunnison (1966: 163), within the protected confines of the like-minded, gutter-scum employees spoke freely about conflicts with team leaders and co-workers, long tea-breaks, hiding instead of working and other activities that were central to this research.

It was after the initial entry to the 'gutter scum' that more data that were central to the research problem came to light. While it was not necessarily the 'gutter scum' who provided these data, it was the recognition and knowledge of dissatisfaction that had previously been hidden that allowed issues to be discussed with other staff members. Importantly, discussions about conflict, misbehaviour and resistance could be addressed with the knowledge that it occurred, and thus without threatening the employee's fear of being the person to initiate such a conversation.

Finding a place for the social outcast

The legitimacy of ethnography as a research method is beyond question; however, the question of the best means to gather data remains. This chapter presents a practical tool for the ethnographic researcher to gather quality data that may not be accessible within the confines of the research site. In discussions during the preparation of this chapter, our views were confirmed by a public service manager, who noted:

> If you want to know anything that goes on in the public service you've got to stand with the smokers. More than that, smoking is really the great leveller. Your youngest, inexperienced clerk will be standing beside your DG [director-general] if they both want a smoke, and that's not going to happen at any other time.

Since the regulation of workplace smoking has led to the segregation of smokers in the workplace, or more correctly outside the workplace, there has been a changing social dynamic in workplaces. Changing community values and legislation have turned smokers into social outcasts. A social outcast is a social outcast, regardless of their employment rank. Furthermore, researchers are able to position themselves within the 'haze of smoke and discontent' to gather a range of data that may not be available through more formal means. In part, this appears to be a direct result of getting outside the physical boundaries of the organisation and out in the gutter, or in the designated smoking area. Research subjects feel much less constrained to offer the company line when they are not within the workplace. Similarly, smokers share a common addiction, widely regarded as socially unacceptable, therefore camaraderie exists among smokers. For a researcher, this camaraderie enables the barriers between the researcher and the research subject to evaporate, even apparently if the researcher is not a smoker but is prepared to congregate with the smokers. We readily acknowledge that these informants may represent a very biased and unreliable source of information, but they provide the opportunity to obtain a story that deviates from the management line.

The authors are not advocating that mingling with a group of smokers is the best way to collect research data. Rather, it is *a method* that can open up further areas of investigation or confirm data already collected. In the three case studies described in this chapter, interactions with cigarette smokers, away from the confines of the organisation, provided a wealth of data that were previously inaccessible. We acknowledge, also, that the use of smokers as a data source raises ethical issues. While each of the organisations discussed in this chapter consented to researcher access and individual staff were aware of the researcher's role within the organisation, written consent was not obtained from respondents. We note that workers who smoke during tea-breaks are doing so in their employer's time, whereas smokers on a lunch-break are on their own time. Deciding what level of ethical clearance is required therefore presents an issue for ethics committees.

Conclusion

This chapter has highlighted the benefits of ethnography as a research method, as well as the practical difficulties. It is argued that it was particularly difficult for researchers to break the ice and establish a level of acceptance within the workplace, such that workers felt able to speak openly about their workplace experiences. The second section of the chapter outlines the anti-smoking legislation that has forced workers who smoke to congregate outside buildings in order to partake in their habit. The third section uses data from three cases studies in which smokers have proved invaluable in enabling researchers to establish rapport with subjects and obtain viewpoints at variance with those of the organisation. The final section reflects on how this was achieved. It suggests that by getting outside the boundaries of the firm, and also by shared social-outcast status, researchers are able to break through the barriers and establish insider status with research subjects. Importantly, though, a particular group of informants, such as smokers, cannot be the sole source of data. Rather, it is one source that can be valuable in particular circumstances.

8

Interviewing men: reading more than the transcripts

Barbara Pini

Introduction

In this chapter I detail my experience of undertaking a doctoral research project investigating women's involvement in leadership in an Australian agri-political group. In particular, I describe one aspect of the research methodology: in-depth qualitative interviews with 15 of the organisation's male elected leaders. I argue that while orthodox interview texts tell us that 'data' are the interview transcripts, the negotiations to conduct the interviews, the silences in an interview and the interactions we have with interview participants outside an interview also constitute data. Before turning to these issues, however, I start with some contextual information on the study and the organisation at the centre of the research.

The context

The agri-political group which was the focus of the study is one of Australia's largest, representing owners of over 6,000 farms. Of these farm owners, at least 3,391 are women in partnership or women as sole operators. At the time of the study, however, no woman held any of the 181 representative elected positions in the organisation. This was across a three-level hierarchical structure: a 26-member board, district-level groups called executives and local area groups called committees. This lack of women in leadership was despite the fact that the organisation adopted a policy in 1994 'to encourage greater participation by women in the affairs of the organisation'. Given the failure of this policy to translate into practice, the purpose of the study was to identify the reasons why women were not involved in leadership and suggest strategies that might be used to address their limited participation.

In its more than 75-year history the agri-political group had not just had an elected leadership of men, but also a managerial staff of largely men. The organisation has a staff of 100 located in 19 district offices in regional towns and a capital city office. Across the 19 district offices there is just a single woman manager. In the capital city office one out of six managerial positions is held by a woman.

Importantly, the agri-political group used as a case study for this research is only one organisational site within this agricultural industry in which men predominate. For example, across the 20 mills where the crop is processed no woman occupies any senior, middle or lower-level management position. Two women have recently been appointed to the eight-member board of the extension and research organisation associated with the industry (for the first time in its 100-year history). However, in the majority of forums – and arguably the visible forums – within this industry, women fail to be appointed as leaders. Further, this is not unusual for agricultural organisations either within Australia or in other international contexts (Pini, 2008).

Methodological overview

The project involved an ethnographic case study of the agri-political group and a broader survey of women constituents of the organisation. The methods used in the ethnography included document analysis, focus groups, interviews and participant observation. As is typical of ethnographic research, I immersed myself in the organisation over the three years of the research. This was facilitated by the fact that the organisation was an industry partner in the research, contributing both cash and in-kind support. The reasons for such support were never made clear, but it was apparent that there was not unanimous support for the project within the organisation. As part of its in-kind support, space in the city office was made available to me where I worked, on average, two to three days a week over the course of the doctorate.

Throughout the entirety of the research project I maintained a research journal. This decision was primarily informed by the fact that the study was undertaken as a feminist research project. While the nature of a feminist methodological approach is multidimensional and includes, for example, a focus on gender relations and an interest in giving value to women's knowledge and voices and political motivation, of concern to this chapter is that it also emphasises the importance of reflexivity (see Pini, 2003). Reflexivity is itself a term that has been somewhat contested in the methodological literature. However, I understand it as meaning critically examining your own position as a researcher as well as the position of those involved in the research, and, importantly, the power relations which may mobilise around these different positions. For example, in this project it meant exploring my own background as a 'country girl', and my emerging identity as an 'academic feminist' working with farm women who were largely antagonistic to feminism but related well to me because of my own background growing up on a farm (see Pini, 2004). Maintaining a research journal is a strategy often recommended in the feminist literature as a means of documenting and critiquing how your social location(s) may impact on a study. While this was my initial motivation in starting the journal, it became much more than that. It operated as what the methodology texts call an 'audit trail' as I began to detail decisions about the research methodology and shifts in my plans and the reasons for such shifts. It also became a source book, as I used its pages for collecting media reports about the study, jotting down contact names and making notes about supervisory meetings. Beyond this, the journal also became a cathartic tool as I dealt with insecurities, frustrations and disappointments along the research journey. On a number of occasions these heightened emotions mobilised around the subject of interviewing and the 15 male elected member participants who were involved in the interviews. It would, of course, be sufficient in itself for these entries to have served a cathartic purpose. However, I was delighted when I came to see them also as data. In the following sections I revisit some of these entries and explain how they demonstrate the need to look beyond transcripts as constituting data.

Background to the interviews

As stated, a range of methods were used to provide data for the ethnography. However, this chapter focuses specifically on the 15 interviews undertaken with elected male members of the agri-political group. The selection of these particular men from the possible 181 elected members was assisted by the general manager of the organisation. As the organisation had committed cash and in-kind support to the study, he acted as a co-supervisor or 'industry supervisor'. In this role he provided assistance in both selecting interview participants and facilitating access to these participants. As well as wanting to elicit the views of elected members from the three levels of leadership, I also wanted to obtain a variety of perspectives on gender relations. With ten years in the organisation, the general manager knew the membership and their views very well, and I therefore used his recommendations to approach participants. Although no one refused, this does not mean that all were equally willing to participate. It is possible that the general manager met some resistance but ultimately convinced members to be involved in the research, given that the project had been approved by the highest tier of leadership.

All the 15 members interviewed were married with children, and all but two were over 50 years old. The majority were, in fact, over 60 and had been elected members of the agri-political group for extended periods of time, ranging from 15 to 27 years. The nature of their duties differed according to the level of their leadership position. The time needed for these duties ranged from two days a week to half a day a week.

After the general manager had contacted the potential interviewees and solicited their involvement in the project, I telephoned each to introduce myself personally. Following this telephone exchange, I wrote to the men thanking them for agreeing to participate in the project, detailing its aims and outlining the more specific outcomes being sought from the interviews. As the interviews did not take place until halfway through the three-year study, I had an opportunity to meet each of the participants face to face before we commenced the data gathering. I used these exchanges, as well as the earlier contact, to develop and build rapport with the men. This typically involved disclosing some aspects of my own upbringing as someone who had grown up on a cane farm, discussing difficulties facing the industry and asking questions about the elected members' farms and families.

Each interview progressed through five stages. The introductory stage centred on my providing information about the interview and research process. The second stage focused on obtaining some background information about the participant and building rapport, as questions were relatively unthreatening. In the third and fourth parts of the interview, I moved to questions about barriers to women's leadership and strategies for change. In the final part of the interview, participants were invited to make further comments or clarify earlier answers.

Listening to interview negotiations

When I contacted participants inviting them to be involved in the research I asked them to nominate what they felt would be the most appropriate time for the interview. I also explained that the interview would take up to an hour. However, when participants came to be interviewed some of the negotiations about time came unstuck. One interviewee, for example, rescheduled the interview twice at the last moment. The day we actually did meet and I began the interview, we were interrupted shortly afterwards by his personal assistant saying that he was needed to attend to urgent business. When I did eventually interview him he was an hour-and-a-half late and left after less than half an hour, having, he said, other 'important business' which demanded his time. In attempting to find a suitable time to meet with this participant, he made numerous references to his busy schedule. He talked about overseas and interstate travel and meetings with particular leaders from government, industry and the finance sector. This was a pattern which was echoed in my negotiations with a number of other male participants. These men engaged in different strategies to demonstrate the demanding nature of their schedule and, indeed, the place of the research I was conducting in this schedule: they regularly looked at their watches, asked how much longer it would take and/or told me that they had other appointments to which they were committed, even though they were informed in writing prior to the interview that it would take one hour. No interviews went over this time, and in fact, given the reticence of some members to answer questions, some were considerably shorter.

My initial reaction to these machinations was one of frustration. With limited time myself and very limited resources for travel, having people cancel or rearrange interviews proved logistically difficult. The verbal and non-verbal cues to hurry the interview along also made me anxious, and I worried about compromising the findings by being rushed. In truth, I also found it somewhat tedious listening to the men's self-referential mode of talk. However, these were very superficial and short-sighted reactions. What I was overlooking in all these interactions were the data and findings inherent in each conversation. Again, I was overly influenced by orthodox methodology texts instructing me that data were what I would obtain once I was in 'the field', and clearly speaking on the telephone while sitting at my desk at the university did not constitute 'being in the field'. However, once I took a more holistic approach to the definition of both the field and data, my sense of frustration shifted to one of excitement. Each encounter to arrange and/or rearrange an interview was not wasting my time (or not entirely); I was collecting data!

In beginning to read the negotiations for interviews as data, I learnt how critical it was to the men of the agri-political group to present themselves as busy, important and well connected. I am not suggesting, of course, that they are not busy, powerful or important. Indeed, interview transcripts are littered with references to their involvement in high-profile national and international committees, interactions with other powerful men outside the industry and media appearances. What is notable about these busy and important men is that they sought to ensure I knew that they were busy and important, and, further, strove to highlight the lowly place my research occupied in their highly eventful lives. Clearly, while these men had hectic lives concerned with high-level business, considering gender equity was not included in this business. This is a powerful statement about how a number of male elected members understood the question of women's participation in the organisation. It was a statement that few made explicitly in interviews, where most were careful to stress their gender equity credentials. It was therefore an important finding in the research.

Listening to silences in interviews

My first interview with one of the 15 elected members also happened to be the first formal piece of data gathering I undertook for the research. By the time this interview took place I had been enrolled in the doctorate for over a year. Like most postgraduate students I had spent long hours reading, planning and preparing, and was quite desperate to start the 'real' research. I therefore remember being full of excited anticipation on the day of this interview. Unfortunately, as it transpired the interview was the most difficult of all that I undertook during the research, and remains today, even after six years and multiple interview-based studies later, one of the most challenging interviews I have ever conducted. At the time I had very limited benchmarks for judging an interview in this way. I therefore simply blamed myself when the participant was overtly hostile, sitting with arms folded across his chest answering questions in monosyllables. When the interview did conclude, long before the official hour was up, I barely made it to the women's toilet before bursting into tears. Part of the issue was that it had been such an antagonistic encounter and I was ignorant and unprepared for it. However, I remember the bigger concern for me at the time was that my PhD was going to be a mess. I was not going to get the type of data I had seen and read in those wonderful papers in those journals I so admired. I extrapolated that my research career was over even before it had begun. After pulling myself together I went to find the general manager. By this time I had moved into problem-solving, deciding that I needed to write the interview off and simply get another participant. Fortunately, while not having a background in research, the general manager proved an expert supervisor on many occasions and did not let me down with his rejoinder to my teary request for the name of another interviewee. I remember him laconically looking up from his desk and commenting 'Well, you wanted a range of views, didn't you?' He also rightly advised talking to my university supervisor. Again I was well served here, as while she was sympathetic to my having had such an unpleasant encounter she was also animated by my description of what occurred, with murmurs of 'How interesting' punctuating her response. I took her advice to 'write it all down' in my journal and thus, again, found later that I had recorded very useful findings that spoke directly to my research questions. That is, there existed a lack of interest, a sense of disapproval and strong resistance to the question of women's participation in the organisation among senior elected men.

The elected member I describe above was not alone in refusing to answer questions posed in interviews. Sometimes this refusal was oblique, in that participants would answer questions with statements such as 'What you need to understand is...' or 'What you don't understand is...', and then subject me to some mini-lecture about the nature of the industry. In these encounters there was seldom any recognition of my own background in the industry and the knowledge such a background would afford, and certainly no recognition of my academic credentials and training. For example, when I asked one elected member why he thought women were not in positions of leadership in the organisation, he cautioned a need to 'take the script back' and suggested I 'ask other questions first', the most important of which seemed to him to be 'Are there actually women involved in the industry?' In this instance, and on other similar occasions, the elected members emphasised their point through a weary shaking of the head or tut-tutting. After one such interview I wrote in my journal of the sense of annoyance at being positioned as child/student/dim-witted by the more enlightened teacher/father/instructor.

However, this response shifted as I came to see what was occurring as being data which added veracity and depth to findings. For example, the men's demonstrations of their knowledge revealed more about the dominance of paternalism in the organisation and the prevalence of paternalistic managerial practices among the elected leadership. These interactions also showed the ways the male elected leadership privileged their own knowledge, gained in almost all cases through engagement in hands-on physical work on the farm. Equally, they had little time for knowledge gained elsewhere. This issue of what knowledge is valued in terms of agricultural leadership emerged as a critical factor in the research, as typically farm women are not involved in on-farm physical work. They are thus, by definition, seen to be disqualified from leadership.

The silence of male elected leaders appeared to reach a crescendo in relation to a survey report I had produced detailing the results from the quantitative phase of the study. The survey had focused on barriers to women's participation and strategies which could facilitate some change. Female respondents to the survey had suggested that a lack of support, the conduct, time and location of meetings and the masculinist culture of the organisation were key factors limiting their participation in the industry. Organisational strategies, education and training strategies, remuneration strategies and support strategies were all considered important to women's increased involvement in the producer group. Seven members said they could not comment on the survey findings report as they had not read it. Five others claimed to be in a similar position, in that they could not recall what was in the report. These responses may be seen as natural and understandable outcomes for what are very busy people. Many of us would relate to being told that someone has simply not had time to read a report they had been given. However, that this lack of comment may have been more manufactured than real was evident from the three interviews where elected members did offer feedback. One of the three talked about the fact that he had concerns with the methodology of the survey, an issue he said he had discussed with others. A second member asked for the tape to be turned off, and proceeded to tell me of the negative reaction the report had elicited from the elected leaders. The third member adopted a more overtly aggressive masculine identity than I had previously encountered, but also revealed that there had indeed been a great deal of discussion about the survey by the elected leadership:

> Interviewer: Can I ask you if you had any comments to make on the survey report I sent you?

Elected member: We had a good laugh about it.

Interviewer: Who's that?

Elected member: Our committee. People thought it was a load of bullshit. Full of bias.

Interviewer: Were there any particular parts?

Elected member: We didn't agree with a lot of it. It's not a boys' club. Our meetings aren't held in pubs. I can see where the perception arises, but if you wait and sit back for them to change you'll never get anywhere. A lot of things in there I see as an excuse.

Interviewer: Can you give me an example?

Elected member: Well, for a start you can't make a meeting dynamic if people don't turn up.

It is difficult for me to read this extract, even years later, without flinching. The elected member's comments were designed to undermine and wound, and I remember them as having this desired effect. My probing question of 'Can you give me an example?' belies the distress that I felt at the time as I listened to him talk about my work as a source of humour and ridicule among a large group of men. Again, he tapped into some very real insecurities I had about the quality of my work (that I now know are common in postgraduate students). However, following a further conversation with my university supervisor about the interaction and her (now much repeated) comments of 'how interesting', I returned to look at these data in a new light. In particular, I was interested in the fact that his comments revealed it is highly unlikely that the survey report would have gone unnoticed or unread by the leadership. The silence around the topic was therefore highlighted, and I began thinking about what this silence exposed. For some, not talking about the report may have been motivated by a desire not to offend, and was perhaps indicative of the culture of gentlemanly paternalism that pervaded the organisation. For others the silence could be read as further unwillingness to engage in the research, and more specifically the issue of women's very real naming of the constraints to their participation. Thus, most importantly, the silence amplified why women continued to be unrepresented in organisational leadership despite the claims by the leaders that they were committed to gender equality.

Listening to informal interactions

As I had a desk in the city office of the agri-political group, I had frequent interaction with many of the elected members over the course of the study. I was also invited to many industry forums and organisational functions (e.g. the Christmas party), during which I conversed with the elected leadership, including some of those who were interviewed. I found some of these occasions, particularly more informal events involving alcohol, very difficult, as sexual innuendos were made and sexual jokes told. While I saw myself attending these types of functions as a 'researcher', it was clear that for some of the elected leaders I was there as a 'woman' and as an available woman. After spending the entire evening at one of the very first such functions I attended attempting to avoid a particular man's harassment and being on the receiving end of a number of gratuitous sexual innuendos, I wrote in my research journal in December 1999:

> Should I not have gone? Should I have been less extroverted? Quieter and more reserved? Tried to be more in the background and watch? But then this would mean not being Barbara, but maybe I have to consciously not be me in these social situations if I'm going to go to them.

This research journal entry is interesting on a number of counts. Besides being mortified at the responsibility I take for the men's behaviour, I see, at this early stage, a limited appreciation of the fact that what I had experienced were 'data' and that these could and should be used to tell a story about the position of women in the organisation. I witness a similar disregard of the need to view informal interactions with research participants as data in my recording of what occurred prior to some of the interviews. I typically met the men being interviewed after a meeting they had attended in the main city office, as this was convenient for them. This meant that other men would see me approach and the two of us walk away to conduct the interview. On these occasions a range of sexual comments and innuendos were made by the male observers. When I approached one member to ask if he was ready for the interview he said, 'I've always got time for a pretty woman.' Another member joked to a participant that he should 'behave himself' with me 'behind closed doors' as we walked away to conduct the interview. Once the interviewee and I walked away from the other males, this overt sexualising of me did not continue. There was, however, an exception.

What two particular participants did throughout their interviews was to call me 'Karen' – one 11 times and one nine – even after repeated corrections had been made before the interviews began, such as in telephone conversations arranging the meeting time, and engaging in small talk before the interview. The 'Karen' to whom they referred is an Australian actress who shares the Pini surname and became nationally famous as a centrefold in the magazine *Australian Playboy*. This association was referred to by one of these participants: when asked a question, he replied, laughing, 'Well Karen, oh... sorry, Barbara. You can see she made a big impression on me.' My post-interview observations note how 'annoyed' and 'frustrated' I was at this apparent mix-up in my identity. Unrecorded, however, is what these comments may mean in terms of data. In hindsight I think I may have been unwilling to see this as data, or indeed the comments made prior to interviews as data, because I worried that it may reflect badly on me – perhaps people would read this as indicative of a lack of professionalism or credibility on my part, and if I was a 'real' researcher this would not have happened.

While I was sexualised on the above occasions, there were also times where, in interactions with elected members involved in the research, I was ignored, dismissed and twice publicly berated. In responding to these instances I relied upon the importance of engaging in reflexively recording what occurred in my journal. As I continue to emphasise, these reflexive accounts were critical in assisting me in reading what occurred as 'data'. For example, on one visit to a district I attended a town meeting on the state of the industry with five other male industry leaders. After the meeting the male local district manager invited all the male guests and other local male leaders back to the office for lunch. I was not invited, and ate lunch alone in a café on the main street. Writing about how I felt in my journal, I began, 'I feel like it is petty even to be writing this down, but I can't believe that they all went off to lunch without me.' Still in the district three days later, I interviewed a woman who explained how difficult it had been trying to set up a local network for industry women. She said, 'I know it sounds petty, but they were supposed to put flyers in the newsletter to advertise the women's forum, but they didn't. They said they got lost or forgot.' What became clear in this instance and so many others is that there were similarities in my experiences of the organisation as a woman and women participants' experiences of the organisation. Thus my informal interactions with the men of the agri-political group were not simply an annoying aside to the 'real' research, but evidence which could add weight to the legitimacy of women's experiences of being sexualised, trivialised and marginalised by the organisational men (see also Cockburn, 1991: 215).

Conclusion

In this chapter I have argued that data analysis must go beyond the interview transcripts. I have suggested that too often as researchers we focus our energies on transcripts when there are also data we may have gathered through negotiating access, through interacting informally with participants or through noting what they do not say in interviews. To be able to take up the opportunities a more holistic conceptualisation of data may bring, I have demonstrated the value of maintaining a research journal. This may seem an onerous undertaking when there are so many other demands on time in order to bring a study to fruition. There is no doubt that it takes energy and commitment. I know that some of the most important entries I made were those when I least felt like writing, and that it took a significant amount of self-discipline to record what had occurred. At the same time I came to enjoy the journal process, and particularly the licence the journal gave me to work through some of the complexities and challenges of the study. As is clear from this chapter (and others), fieldwork is a highly emotional endeavour. It is perhaps even more so for the postgraduate student, who is likely to be less experienced in undertaking research and whose work may be closely intertwined with future career opportunities. Of course, some topics and some research environments will expose a researcher to a higher degree of stress and scrutiny than others. Certainly, addressing gender equity in an organisation where women were not represented in any of the 181 positions of leadership was an ambitious undertaking. Further, the environment of the agri-political group was one where questions relating to gender had seldom surfaced; men's right to leadership was given and taken as a norm. An added complexity was my own status as a young (at the time!) female student asking questions of much older men occupying high-status leadership roles. In dealing with these intersecting forces the maintenance of a research journal was critical for scholarly and pragmatic reasons.

9

Establishing rapport: using quantitative and qualitative methods in tandem

Alan Felstead, Nick Jewson, Alison Fuller,
Konstantinos Kakavelakis and Lorna Unwin

Introduction

Most methodology courses and textbooks treat quantitative and qualitative research techniques in isolation from one another, with lectures and chapters divided accordingly. This division is typically replicated among research scholars, who ply their trade using one or other of these strategies. In contrast, this chapter describes our experience of combining the two approaches. It adds to the growing interest in mixed-methods research, as witnessed by the special issue of *Qualitative Research* in 2006 and the launch in 2007 of the *Journal of Mixed Methods Research*. Debate often focuses on ways in which the evidence generated by quantitative and qualitative techniques complement one another. We wish to develop a more specific, and less often noted, point. In this chapter, we argue that the conduct of quantitative research may provide a valuable vehicle for establishing rapport in the collection of rich qualitative data from respondents. In short, administering a quantitative survey may enable researchers to establish an accepted and legitimate presence within the research site, facilitating further qualitative investigations.

The chapter reports on our experience of studying the establishment and development of a call centre (County Talk) in a local county council in England (Shire County). Our substantive research interest was in how the call centre fitted into the overall structure of the organisation and, in particular, how successfully (or otherwise) it meshed with other stages of the productive system that linked callers with council services. Our analytical approach conceived the call centre as an intermediary point in a process which linked 'back-office' service departments to members of the local community (see Jewson et al., 2007; Felstead et al., 2009).

In this context, we obtained permission to conduct a quantitative survey in the call centre while simultaneously observing how call operatives carried out their jobs. We expected the survey to generate valuable additional evidence and clarify how the call centre functioned within the organisation as a whole. While it did indeed cast light on these issues, we were less prepared for the discovery that the daily process of administering the questionnaire legitimated our presence in the workplace and greatly enhanced opportunities for the collection of qualitative data. Simply handing out and gathering in survey sheets allowed us to 'reside' inside the call centre for two weeks and establish our presence. As a result of being *in situ* as quantitative researchers, we were gradually drawn into the social worlds of call-centre staff, albeit in a peripheral role. We were regaled with their stories, shared their confidences and observed their interactions with members of the public, co-workers and managers. In short, a quantitative data-gathering exercise provided the foundation for the collection of rich qualitative data. This chapter, then, examines some of the benefits of conducting quantitative and qualitative research methods in tandem.

Warming up a cold case

County Talk was set up in 2001. Between 2002 and 2004 call volumes quadrupled, and by 2007 operators were answering an average of over 4,000 calls per week. With 34 full-time-equivalent staff, County Talk dealt with half of all the main types of enquiries the council received. Call volumes grew as access to more and more council services was funnelled through County Talk and the easy-to-remember telephone number was widely advertised.

Our investigations began well. Our 'gatekeeper', in senior management, was helpful and supportive. Initially we made good progress in conducting a series of qualitative interviews with central management, heads of service departments and senior local government politicians. These interviews were full, detailed and frank. Senior respondents understood our project and were willing to answer probing in-depth questions about the origins, purpose and development of County Talk. Nevertheless, we felt that our knowledge of the day-to-day operations of the call centre lacked sufficient detail and that we had not 'got under the skin' of official accounts of what went on within its walls. We were therefore looking forward to conducting interviews with call-centre managers and telephone operatives.

However, we found it difficult to establish rapport in these encounters. Although the interviews were conducted in the County Talk building, they were confined to an office at one end of the call centre. All the interviews were arranged by management, and they ran back-to-back over the course of a few days spread over several weeks. Respondents were required to fit in with this timetable. There was little opportunity to watch, listen to or hear what call operators and managers were doing as they carried out their daily tasks; there was no time to circulate among their workstations on a more casual basis. As a result, we had little opportunity to observe staff at work and little direct experience of the issues that we sought to discuss with interviewees. In particular, interviews with call operators proved to be shorter and less communicative than we had hoped. Although not hostile towards us, these respondents appeared to be unclear about our purpose in conducting research and wary about answering questions about their daily working practices. We felt that we were perceived as the 'suits', parachuted in for a brief and artificial encounter that was not grounded in an appreciation of the realities of interviewees' work.

By now we had used up the access negotiated at the outset of our research with our gatekeeper. Although relations with him were still cordial, we had the distinct impression that further requests for qualitative interviews were likely to be perceived as overstaying our welcome. Moreover, given our experience of the taciturn responses of call operatives, we were not convinced that more of the same would be helpful. Our 'leads' were exhausted; we were stalled. We needed a new source of momentum.

Racking our brains, we remembered the interviews had revealed that, while some data gathering was built into the software used by the call centre, relatively little was known within the organisation about the nature of the calls received by County Talk. Indeed, several management interviewees had lamented the absence of this information. Here, then, was our opportunity to open up a new phase in our research. Accordingly, we proposed to our gatekeeper that we would conduct a quantitative survey of all the calls received by operators over a two-week period. Our offer included the design and production of a questionnaire, daily administration of the survey, inputting the data into a statistical package, analysis of results and presentation of findings in the form of a report. We also suggested that being in the call centre to administer the questionnaire would give us a chance to observe and become better acquainted with the work activities of call operators and managers, subject of course to the proviso that we did not hinder them in any way. We pointed out that the research would entail little or no cost to the organisation, either financially or in terms of service delivery. Furthermore, the involvement of independent academics would give the data-collection exercise greater credibility and enhance the profile of the call centre's operation. Our gatekeeper needed little persuasion, and we quickly received his permission to go ahead with both quantitative and qualitative aspects of our proposed additional research. The advent of the quantitative survey, then, breathed new life into what was becoming a 'cold case'. It also created an opportunity to collect statistical information at the same time as further qualitative material.

Setting up the next phase

The quantitative aspect of the new phase of the research was to be delivered via a paper-based ten-question survey that call-centre operators were asked to complete after each call over a two-week period. Answers took the form of 'tick-box' responses, simplifying and speeding up the process of completing the questionnaire. The first draft was produced solely by the research team, but two further versions were generated in collaboration with County Talk managers, who amended questions in the light of their direct experience of the work of the call centre. This meant that organisation-specific language and terms were incorporated into the wording of the questionnaire, making it easier for operators to understand and complete. At this point the controlling influence of our initial gatekeeper began to wane, while our relations with County Talk managers became more salient. We nurtured these new contacts by taking on board a great many of their suggested changes to the questionnaire. We felt comfortable with this arrangement, since most of the survey questions related to basic factual matters and we assumed that call-centre managers were well informed about how call operators did their work.

The success of the survey, in terms of response rate and coverage, relied on call-centre operators completing questionnaires after each call and dropping them into boxes for collection. Since their cooperation was vital, a number of strategies were employed to allay their potential fears and anxieties. Well in advance, local management, at our request, circulated an e-mail outlining the aims of the survey and introducing the research team. It was also announced that extra 'wrap-up time' – that is, the time between calls – would be built into the system for the duration of the survey. A total of ten seconds was added to the time between calls while the survey was carried out. This concession was greatly appreciated by call operators, since it allowed them time to do the survey as well as providing a welcome distraction from the tedium and intensity of taking calls.

Shortly before the survey began, the research team assembled exhibition boards that provided an overview of the project, explained the aims of the survey and reproduced the questionnaire. It was made clear that, in addition to administering the questionnaire, we would be present in the call centre to observe the day-to-day tasks and practices of call-centre operators. In the week before the survey began, two of the research team briefed all the operators, individually or in small groups. In these sessions we presented the overall aims of the project, described the mechanics of the survey and discussed each of the questions in turn. Call-centre staff also introduced themselves to us, and we quickly got to know their names and roles. These sessions lasted for approximately half an hour.

The questionnaires were produced in pads of 50. After each call, operators took a few seconds to tick the relevant boxes, tear off the completed form and drop it into a conveniently located collection point. We continuously circulated around the building, maintaining a steady supply of blank questionnaires to each workstation and picking up small batches of completed forms. Completed questionnaires were returned to our pod, where they were numbered, dated and time-stamped. Over the two-week period we collected and processed 8,874 returns. The data were inputted into a statistical software package using a laptop. After being processed, the paper returns were tied in bundles and boxed up for carriage.

Unlike our earlier interviews with call operatives, during the administration of the survey we were based in the heart of the call centre, at a circular pod of six workstations located close to the main entry and exit channels. Throughout the survey period, members of the research team were on hand to answer questions or supply information. Towards the end of the two-week period we carried out a series of debriefing sessions with operators; sometimes on a one-to-one basis, sometimes in groups of two.

Getting closer to the action

As soon as we launched the quantitative survey, we found that we had entered into a role within the call centre that was recognised and acknowledged by everyone, down to the most junior call operator. We became part of the scene. It was evident that everybody in the call centre grasped the process of filling in a questionnaire and felt they knew, in principle, what was required of them. Ticking boxes was experienced as a commonplace activity that was understood and with which staff could engage. This may be because questionnaires are widely encountered in everyday life; for example in magazine quizzes, customer satisfaction surveys and even school projects. In contrast, invitations to talk about their jobs at length are encountered more rarely, particularly by those occupying non-managerial roles. Call-centre operatives who had seemed halting, uncomfortable and awkward during in-depth interviews experienced questionnaires as more familiar and comprehensible. Many interviewees had seemed unresponsive, embarrassed or nonplussed by general questions about their work and relationships with supervisors; in contrast, the process of filling in the questionnaire was immediately seized upon by all concerned, leading to lively conversations. Moreover, conducting questionnaire-based surveys was seen as the sort of thing that researchers did. Our role in devising and administering the questionnaire was perceived by respondents as legitimate and transparent. As a result, most call-centre staff willingly volunteered their own perspectives on the quantitative instrument and its likely findings. From the outset, the questionnaire survey established a participative dialogue between the research team and call-centre staff.

During initial briefing sessions it took little time for us to explain the nature of the survey and enlist the cooperation of respondents. Without prompting, staff at all levels quickly became proactive in responding to both the questionnaire and the project more generally. Call operators, in particular, raised queries and sought points of clarification, leading to lively discussions between staff and researchers as well as among staff themselves.

It was in these initial briefing meetings that we first discovered the limits of management's knowledge about how work was actually done in the call centre. Although in devising the survey questions we had relied heavily on their advice, it now became apparent that managers were, to some extent, out of touch with the scope and nuances of the work completed by their staff. We became aware that the wording and structure of the survey instrument reflected how managers thought that calls were handled, not how they were dealt with in practice. We now realised that operators used many 'work-arounds'; that is, informal and unofficial ways of doing things. These were not wholly captured by our questionnaire. Moreover, we discovered that various sub-groups of operatives used different bundles of 'work-arounds', often in ignorance of their colleagues' practices. These included the use of particular internet search engines in preference to the search facility on Shire Council's website, self-created manuals of the 'dos' and 'don'ts' of call handling and personal contact lists of 'friendly' individuals willing to help them deal with particular queries. More generally, call operatives made probing comments indicating that at least some aspects of their tasks were more complex, or involved more negotiation, than managers recognised. They further suggested that some of the questions in the survey would have benefited from refinement. At this point we realised that we should have piloted the questionnaire more widely among workers as well as among managers.

Fortunately, these discoveries did not invalidate the questionnaire and we were able to finesse any discrepancies. Moreover, in the course of initial briefing sessions we gained a great deal of new information, and much better understanding, not only about job tasks of operatives but also the broader functions and implications of the call centre within the overall organisation of the local authority. These insights were recorded in fieldnote diaries kept by the researchers. However, to our surprise it was the closed and formal structure of the questionnaire that prompted most discussion, rather than the open-ended invitation to talk offered by earlier qualitative interviews.

These encounters set the tone for the whole of our two-week stay in the call centre. Completion of the questionnaire triggered conversations not only about the questions but also about broader aspects of work environment, management strategies and organisational structure. Discussion about the questions themselves tended to recede once we got past the launch phase of the operation. The focus of conversations began to move towards what the results might be and what they might mean. This was facilitated by a shift in the character of our rapport with staff at all levels.

Becoming embedded in the action

Members of the research team enjoyed a legitimate and credible reason to roam the shop-floor at will at any time. The method we had adopted for administering the survey entailed a constant process of supplying new questionnaires to workstations and collecting those that had been completed. This continued throughout all working hours and across all shifts. It had to be done carefully and discreetly, so as not to be a nuisance. Nevertheless, it enabled us consistently and constantly to observe the whole of the work process. It provided opportunities for occasional small talk and brief personal interactions. It enabled us to gauge the personalities of individuals and observe relationships between members of staff. We could pick up on the day's gossip, listen to 'war' stories and hear what issues were generating calls. To build further rapport we made cups of tea and brought in biscuits, sweets and cakes. We feared such gestures might have been seen as patronising, but in fact they were well received and interpreted as a 'thank you'. We became part of the ritualised small-scale exchange of gifts that goes on in offices. Favours were returned and reciprocated. We found ourselves included in 'unofficial' practices, such as eating lunch in the call centre on Saturday mornings and watching TV on late-night shifts.

All of this was greatly assisted by the time-scale of the questionnaire. The agreed two-week period of the quantitative survey gave the research team the all-important time to grow connections with staff. We could allow informal low-level contacts and casual observations to build up day by day. We gradually became familiar with folk stories, norms of behaviour and occupational sub-cultures. Off site, in the evening, we were able to spend long hours mulling over within the research team what each of us had seen and heard. We had time to reflect, compare, share, analyse, question and interpret our qualitative observations. We could go back the next day with the intention not only of collecting yet more quantitative survey sheets but also testing, checking, focusing and refining our qualitative observations.

Indeed, the volume and type of qualitative material that became available to us itself posed challenges. We had to find ways of recording a tide of visual observations, snatches of conversation and brief interactions with respondents. The volume and speed with which these impressions came at us meant that we were in danger of losing precious details or making errors in capturing respondents' words. Like all ethnographers, we had to rely on memory and hastily scrawled notes. However, we were aided yet again in recording qualitative data by our role as quantitative researchers administering a survey. We made sure that whenever possible at least two members of the team were on hand, to corroborate each other's observations and recollections. The requirement to dispense and collect questionnaires gave us a legitimate reason to leave and return to our workstations at short intervals throughout the day. We could conduct observations at different times and with different shifts, comparing the ways in which staff behaved alone or in the presence of various others.

It should be added that our relationships with call-centre staff were also enhanced by our visibility. We were seen by everyone when sitting at workstations and walking the shop-floor. Members of the research team were present from 7.30 to 20.30 every day, and sometimes much later in order to catch a night shift. We were on site before nearly everyone else and stayed until after most had left. Our exhibition display boards not only explained the study but also gave some background on the research team. We were to discover that some members of staff had checked out our academic status via the university webpages and had even printed off our publications! Our credentials and our practices as quantitative researchers were thus on display; they provided us with legitimacy in collecting qualitative data.

By the beginning of our second week in the call centre the nature of our rapport with staff changed yet again. We now knew enough to conduct better-informed and more critical conversations. We could ask questions, make comments and seek clarifications in a way that drew us into the work group, rather than underlining our distance from it. We knew who was aware of, or sensitive about, which issues, and could tailor our remarks accordingly. Small talk with at least some staff started to include personal information, on both sides, about children, schools, previous jobs and hobbies. The presence of the research team appeared to have become a source of mild diversion that enlivened the daily routine. Both call-centre managers and operators independently asked whether we would like to listen in to phone calls using auxiliary headsets; an opportunity which, needless to say, we jumped at. It seemed a natural progression of our genuine interest in the challenges faced by call operators.

It was noticeable in the second week that our conversations with operators increasingly centred on the underlying organisational and employment issues that were the focus of the research. These discussions were most pronounced in our debriefing meetings, and produced the kind of dialogue about the work of County Talk that earlier qualitative interviews had largely failed to generate. Ironically, it was reflection by staff on their participation in the quantitative survey that prompted these discussions.

It should be acknowledged that, while active cooperation with the research was widespread, some call operators were more open and welcoming to us than others. By being inside the call centre for such a long time, however, we were able to allay their fears. Furthermore, one of the benefits of our methodology was that we did not have to rely on a few key informants as a channel of entry to the work situation. The questionnaire was our calling card, and enabled us to talk to all call-centre operators. We were therefore able to steer a course between the various factions and informal friendship groups within the workforce. For example, there was a well-entrenched division between staff who had been in post since the start of the call centre and those who had joined during a subsequent recruitment exercise. We were not associated with either of these groups and, as far as possible, cultivated good contacts with both.

Another concern, which recurred throughout our time in the call centre, was our relationship with management. The research had been agreed and endorsed by senior organisational and call-centre management. There was thus a danger that we would be perceived as agents of management. This might have influenced what we were told by workers; indeed, we wondered whether some call operators exaggerated the ease with which they answered calls in order to portray themselves as super-efficient. We therefore took care to distance ourselves from management, both physically and socially. We did not sit on the same workstations as managers. We emphasised our standing as independent academics, and that the research was not funded by the organisation. We promised to make available the results of the survey to all staff, not just managers. We also sought to maintain social separation from management. This latter issue became acute when the research team were invited to a social event solely for call-centre and related managers. We feared that this might compromise our growing rapport with the shop-floor. Accordingly, we found a way of declining the invitation with good grace.

Conclusion

Methodology textbooks and fieldwork monographs often fail to reveal that, in practice, research design is driven not only by scientific principles but also by pragmatic responses to circumstances. For example, a research tool may be employed as a way of kick-starting a stalled project, not solely because of its intrinsic merits. In the study reported here, such a pragmatic decision led to the discovery that the role of quantitative researcher can provide an excellent vehicle for collecting qualitative data. By becoming quantitative researchers we had stumbled into a role that facilitated the collection of rich qualitative data.

The role of quantitative researcher provides a legitimate reason to be present in 'the field'. Moreover, quantitative researchers engage in professional activities that are widely recognised and understood by respondents; in our case, distributing, collecting and analysing questionnaires. Managing a questionnaire provided us with a peripheral role that was not part of the main social activity in which our respondents were engaged, but which was perceived by respondents as having understandable and acceptable meanings and purposes that were legitimately related to their work. Such legitimate peripheral activities may provide the basis for a special kind of participation by researchers in the action going on within a research site. They may enable researchers to become involved in informal social relationships that yield rich and diverse qualitative material. In our study, we found such relationships were more productive than conventional interviews in generating an open and critical dialogue between researchers and respondents. When devising their research designs, therefore, quantitative researchers may wish to bear in mind the implications for simultaneous qualitative data collection. For example, we were able to collect a mass of qualitative data because of the specific, labour-intensive method we had adopted to administer the quantitative survey. Had the questionnaire been delivered electronically we would not have reaped the same benefits.

In trying to capture the nature of the rapport that we forged with our respondents, we hit upon the phrase 'legitimate peripheral participation' to describe our role as researchers. The way in which we employ this term here differs fundamentally from its usage by Lave and Wenger (1991) and Wenger (1998) in their studies of learning processes. We employ 'legitimate peripheral participation' to designate the particular kind of involvement in the research situation that we enjoyed in County Talk. The mechanics of carrying out the survey placed us in a distinctive position. We could not be described as *participant* observers, since we were not doing the same work as the call operatives and managers we were studying. Neither were we *non-participant* observers; we were not just standing watching but, rather, were doing our own work of administering the survey. However, in carrying out our own designated work tasks we were placed in a position where we could conduct intensive and extensive observations of the work of others. We were 'legitimate peripheral participants'. This gave us unique insights into the workings of a call centre in ways which would simply not have been possible had we relied on interviews as our only means of collecting data. It also suggests that quantitative and qualitative methods can work in tandem to produce a much richer set of research results.

Acknowledgements

This research forms part of a larger project which investigates the links between workplace learning, the organisation of work and performance in a range of economic sectors (www.learningaswork.cf.ac.uk). It was funded under the Economic and Social Research Council's Teaching and Learning Research Programme (RES-139-25-0110-A). A full account of the entire project can be found in Felstead et al. (2009).

10

Wrong way, go back! Negotiating access in industry-based research

Paula McDonald, Keith Townsend
and Jennifer Waterhouse

Introduction

Literature addressing methodological issues in organisational research is extensive and multidisciplinary, encompassing debates about methodological choices, data-collection techniques, epistemological approaches and statistical procedures. However, little scholarship has tackled an important aspect of organisational research that precedes decisions about data collection and analysis – access to the organisations themselves, including the people, processes and documents within them. This chapter looks at organisational access through the experiences of three research fellows in the course of their work with their respective industry partners. In doing so, it reveals many of the challenges and changing opportunities associated with access to organisations, which are rarely explicitly addressed, but often assumed, in traditional methods texts and journal publications. Although the level of access granted varied somewhat across the projects at different points in time and according to different organisational contexts, we shared a number of core and consistent experiences in attempting to collect data and implement strategies.

The context

Our responsibilities as research fellows included liaising with human resources and executive committee members in our respective organisations, collecting a range of qualitative and quantitative data, developing and implementing strategies to address identified problems, analysing and publishing our research findings and presenting the findings back to the organisations. We also participated in a range of other typical academic activities during our fellowships, including representation on university and industry committees, service to journals and conferences, postgraduate supervision and the delivery of seminars at conferences and public forums.

Five organisations were involved in the three projects employing us as research fellows. Pseudonyms are used to preserve their anonymity. Project A involved two organisations: Capital, a public body responsible for capital works, and Community, which is a public organisation responsible for community services. The industry partner for Project B was a peak body in the construction industry, though the research was primarily conducted with two of its organisational members, Construct and Assemble, both private construction companies. Project C involved one organisation, Build, which is a public body responsible for the planning, design, construction and project management of infrastructure. The five organisations differed somewhat in size, public/private orientation and core business focus. However, four of them were responsible for major infrastructure development, employed large numbers of engineers, builders and construction workers as well as office-based administrative and project management staff, and were male-dominated. The head office of each of these organisations was located in the same capital city in Australia, but each organisation had offices and sites located across the state (Capital and Build) or across Australia (Construct and Assemble). The remaining organisation, Community, was located in a regional centre and employed predominantly women. Projects A and B investigated work-life balance issues (Capital, Community, Construct and Assemble) and Project C involved managing organisational change (Build).

In all three projects the collaborating organisations made significant cash and in-kind contributions to the research projects. Research protocols were signed off by senior staff in each participating organisation. This was designed to ensure participation by key personnel and provide ongoing organisational commitment to the research project. As will be seen, despite these financial and written undertakings, ongoing access was a major problem for the researchers.

Access as a methodological concern

For the purposes of this chapter we define 'access' not as a single episode but as a process of continually building relationships at multiple points and with multiple actors throughout the course of a study (Walford, 2001). This idea of access being an 'incremental continuum' (ibid.: 34) is relevant for the cases discussed in this chapter, which received indicative senior-level access before the projects commenced via the commitment of funding and formal signing of a contract between the organisation and our university. However, ongoing access to the organisations was a concern throughout many phases of the projects and necessitated multiple agreements with various organisational stakeholders. We also distinguish access from 'resistance', which refers to a participant's reluctance to discuss, open up or be forthcoming (such as during an interview) after access has already been granted (Adler and Adler, 2003).

Significant pressures from industry sectors or society more broadly can affect researcher access to organisations. Troman (1996), referring to studies he conducted in the education sector in Britain, suggests that access to organisations is becoming more difficult due to macro-level changes beyond the organisations themselves. Specifically, he argued that educational policy reform has resulted in an increasing number of researchers in schools, an intensification of teachers' work and greater financial constraints on principals, and that these changes have presented researchers with increasing difficulty in accessing schools to research. Pini and Haslam McKenzie (2007) also concluded that macro-level issues were important in the acquisition of knowledge, discussing their experiences in gaining access to local governments to undertake work on natural resource management. They argued that a range of system-level changes, including increasing financial pressure and an expansion of roles within the sector, rendered access problematic for researchers. At the societal level, Adler and Adler (2003) suggest that an increasing surveillance culture and fear of legal action also influence access to organisations. For example, they describe how their access to a Hawaiian resort hotel, where they were conducting ethnographic research, was systematically diminished following two lawsuits that were brought by employees against the resort.

These studies provide important insights into the range of difficulties faced by researchers when attempting to acquire knowledge via organisational research. Clearly, however, a greater understanding is required of the range of factors affecting access to organisations and what researchers can do to facilitate entry. Indeed, without access, any further knowledge acquisition in organisational settings would cease.

Internal/external pressures

In Project A, Community, access proceeded without difficulty for the first 12 months of the research timeline. A survey on work-life balance (WLB) was administered, interviews were conducted and the results of different phases were reported back to the organisation. Various human resource strategies and interventions were planned on the basis of these 'baseline' findings. Approximately halfway through the second year of the project, as the 'intervention strategies' were getting under way, a cyclone in the local area required a significant refocusing of organisational priorities and the project was delayed indefinitely. Repeated attempts were made to re-establish the goals of the research through contact with key representatives in the organisation. However, the significant loss of momentum that resulted from the natural disaster and the consequent focus on the provision of essential services meant that access to the organisation in the later stages of the research was thwarted.

Managers at Construct and Assemble were all very supportive of the idea of addressing WLB within their organisations and workplaces. The project was built on the premise that employees at all levels of organisations should be entitled to opportunities to be fully engaged in their work while not having to compromise too greatly their non-work interests. However, support for the idea coupled with financial commitment to the research project did not translate readily into access for the researchers or a commitment to initiate the proposed interventions. For example, having begun the larger research project in early 2005, the Construct case was timetabled to begin in August 2006. The Time 1 data were collected on time in September 2005, but then the research project stalled. Managers and designated employees were simply too busy getting through daily tasks to assist the research team; hence by August 2007 the project had not progressed to any substantial degree. Certainly, no more data had been collected, nor had any intervention began despite regular contact between the primary researcher and staff on the case-study site. Commonly, the researcher was told 'we are just so busy, we don't have time to fit this WLB stuff in at the moment'. This response was ironic given that the project was developed on a body of research suggesting that by putting a greater focus on WLB, employees could work more efficiently.

At Assemble the story of delays and inaction was similar. In fact, with some regret from the manager involved, Assemble in essence withdrew from the research project. Commissioned to deliver a major piece of infrastructure, the Assemble site became somewhat of a political football for a short period of time close to an election. After operating for almost 12 months with employees working (based on our Time 1 data) an average of more than 50 hours a week and up to 80 hours a week, the project was ahead of schedule (six months ahead in some areas). The researcher was told that:

> we know that WLB is a problem here – well, nobody actually has a WLB but we are six months ahead of schedule and our leadership team decided that we wanted to stay that way... So we're not going to do it [the intervention], we're just going to keep going as we are.

Within the context of very tight labour markets and high activity within the construction sector, decisions were made within many potential case studies (and actual cases like Assemble) that WLB was not as important an issue as maintaining the status quo. For many people, it seems, the term 'work-life balance' has become somewhat of a cliché.

The aim of Project C within Build (public sector) was to capture staff perceptions of organisational change through the collection of qualitative data at six-monthly intervals from various sites across its jurisdiction. Ideally data were to be collected from the same sites and, as closely as possible, from the same participants at each timeframe so as to gain the best comparative data possible over the seven years of the study. Access for Project C in Build progressed closely to research plans for the first three years of the study, except for one data-collection period that was delayed by three months due to the financial reporting period.

During years four and five Build commenced a major change initiative that sought to address a doubling of its works programme at a time of critical shortages in key skill areas. There was significant ministerial pressure on Build to deliver the infrastructure programme, and it was stated that failure to deliver was not an option. In response to both ministerial pressure and the increased works programme, Build undertook a major restructure and sought to align policy and practice across all its divisions. Some areas of the organisation were significantly affected and researcher access to these areas was blocked, as it was considered that the research would be an added burden to the most affected areas and would not be welcome.

The pressures associated with operational requirements and achieving project timelines were surprisingly similar across the public and private sector organisations in our research. The emergence of 'new' public management principles is likely to have dissolved some traditional differences in emphasis on financial performance and budgetary concerns. Indeed, both Capital and Build have changed substantially over the past 15 years, being subject to external pressures and internal changes to become more efficient and highly competitive within the broader infrastructure environment in Australia. Illustrating views about ministerial (political-level) expectations is the following quote from a senior manager at Capital:

> It's very important that high-profile projects are done on time. When the Minister has made a promise that a facility is going to be open at such and such a date, it would be an embarrassment to him if it is not done on time.

These changes occurring in Australia mirror a range of global labour market trends, such as growing labour insecurity, increased employer dominance in the workplace, the curtailment of third-party influence and government pursuit of labour flexibility.

Despite these operational and industry pressures, access in Capital appeared to be more related to perceptions of risk and research fatigue (described below), while in Build the combination of industry pressures and massive change was most problematic, along with concerns associated with the publication of research findings at a politically sensitive time.

Differential support

Variations in levels of support from key personnel were integrally linked to organisational access in each project. Ethnographic and case-study research typically begins with an individual, known as a gatekeeper, who is a member of or has insider status with a cultural group, and is the initial contact for the researchers and leads them to other participants (Hammersley and Atkinson, 1995). Staff turnover among gatekeepers was a common problem in the level of support afforded to us. For example, the key human resource contact in Capital changed three times during the course of the project. All changes resulted from internal transfer to another position. Following each change, the new contact was briefed by the researchers on the principal objectives of the project and plans for the next stage. While this strategy helped keep the project 'alive', a tangible loss of motivation and a sense that the project was an unwanted task that had been 'inherited' were very apparent with each change of personnel. This resulted in uneven levels of access during the life of the project, especially for variable periods of time following the induction of new organisational contacts. Similarly, in Community the position of director-general changed hands approximately halfway through the project, leaving a hiatus in very senior-level support that was especially critical in this organisation, which was small and geographically removed from the location of the researchers.

Turnover at Assemble meant that within the first six months of the project there were three project managers involved as frontline gatekeepers. All these managers were, in principle, very supportive of the research. However, in practice each manager was focused greatly on the new role as project manager and simply not able, or not willing, to place a high priority on the research agenda. The change of the primary contact gatekeeper at Construct halted the progress of the project for approximately four months. The initial HR/IR manager took maternity leave, and during the period leading up to her departure the research agenda was a low priority. The transition to a new manager was also a lengthy process.

Another central feature of differential support that affected access was the question of who in the organisational hierarchy had ownership of the project. Highest-level support was indicated via financial contributions and sign-off of formal documentation in each enterprise. However, the implementation of the research was usually delegated to lower levels of management, who were not necessarily involved in the inception of the research and/or did not share the same goals as the researchers. Hence, ownership was delivered to a person's desk and often seen as 'just another task' to be completed.

The issue of ownership was important in allowing access for data-collection purposes, but even more critical in getting approval for research strategies or interventions. In Project A, a significant component of the research plan was to implement a number of schemes designed to improve the work-life culture of Capital. These strategies included 'demonstration trials', whereby employees could (with the approval of their direct line manager) try using a flexible work policy, which would then be evaluated following a designated time. Another strategy was to trial recruitment advertisements for part-time positions in skill shortage areas. Both of these interventions were supported provisionally and in principle by the human resource contacts in Capital, and in the original research design by the director-general. However, when the time came for implementation, approval was blocked by the corporate governance board. The members of this board had had no contact with the researchers and presumably felt little personal connection with the project or ownership of its goals. A third intervention was an education strategy to be undertaken during a leadership residential. This was eventually approved as a special session during a one-day training module.

From the outset Project C had the highest level of executive support from within the organisation. The research project had initially been commissioned by the director-general, who had assigned a senior manager to its coordination as well as an administrative support person from the director-general's office who attended regular weekly meetings and organised site visits. The legitimacy given to the research through such high-level and formal support resulted in excellent access during the first three years, when data were collected from 12 sites at Time 1, Time 2, Time 3 and Time 4. Strong relationships developed between the university researchers and their Build colleagues, fostered through activities such as shared office facilities, travelling together, joint conference attendance and joint publications.

However, in the fourth year there was staff turnover in all key project positions within Build: the director-general, the management coordinator of the research and the administrative staff member who had been assigned as a day-to-day contact all left Build. Both the new director-general and the management coordinator came from outside Build. Consequently, the social capital and trust that had been developed through the earlier relationships were lost. New relationships needed to be established with individuals who were not familiar with the project, its aims or the rationale for the processes underpinning it. A new day-to-day contact for the project was never again formally or permanently assigned. Negativity was expressed by the new management coordinator in relation to the data-collection method, as it was considered ineffective, overly invasive and time-consuming. In fact, the new management coordinator blocked access to areas most affected by organisational change, with the researchers being effectively banned from any communication with or access to those areas. This meant that not even individual site access could be negotiated. The effect on the research was that the continuity of data collection from the same sites at each timeframe was lost, and indeed access to these critical sites was never regained. The whole data-collection process and focus of the project were renegotiated, resulting in the research taking a different course to that initially established.

High levels of support for the research came from the upper management within the Assemble and Construct organisations; however, this did not always translate to site-level support the way it did initially in Build. The difference between the three cases appears to be that in Build a staff member from the director-general's office was assigned to broker access across the organisation, which effectively opened doors that may otherwise have been firmly shut. By contrast, within Assemble and Construct site access was substantially problematic, to the point that 'in principle' access was negotiated at seven different worksites. Actual data were collected from five of these sites, but two managers withdrew support prior to data collection (in one case on the day that surveys were to be distributed). Within the five worksites where data were collected, only one site allowed the complete methodological design, with Time 1 testing, an intervention and follow-up measures to determine success. Still, within this single success story, what was designed to be a four- to six-month research project took in excess of 18 months. Simply stated, practitioners within the worksites placed a low priority on the processes of the research project, largely because it was not 'the day to day'. One HR manager, while apologising for the number and length of delays, stated: 'I can't seem to get people moving on this – it's all sort of... out there... while people are wrapped up in what's on their desk for today.'

A final point to note on differential support is that all three of these research projects were designed to effect positive workplace change at various levels. Potential changes included those to organisational policies, organisational culture and the work and non-work lives of employees. This process of introducing change and measuring the outcomes demands high degrees of cooperation on 'the access ladder' (Neuman, 2006). However, the high-level goals of the planned research project meant long negotiations at a strategic and planning level of the organisation were disjointed from the 'gatekeepers', who were at an operational level and perceived substantial risk to their operational requirements.

Perceptions of risk

The vetoing of the interventions in Capital by the corporate governance board was attributed to the level of perceived risk associated with the strategies. These risks were explained in general rather than detailed terms: no explicit reasons were provided by the board directly to the researchers. However, the human resource representatives reported second-hand that recruiting part-time employees was incompatible with the design of jobs in the organisation, which were exclusively structured around full-time workloads. As one employee stated during a research interview, 'Full-time is given here, the culture is full-time so that's not anything unusual.' In the case of the demonstration trials, the board apparently believed that the strategy posed risks to the organisation because allowing such trials would potentially 'open the floodgates' for other employees to request similar arrangements. However, in our work with Capital no more than a handful of employees across the organisation had requested involvement in the demonstration trials. The denial of approval was also clearly at odds with at least one of the principal objectives of the project, which was to facilitate the uptake of flexible policies. The clear disparity between what the organisation had agreed to in project formulation and documentation, and what it was later willing to approve, was also apparent in Project B.

The perception of risk at Construct appeared to be an opportunity for this particular site-management team. In the first meeting to negotiate an access agreement to the case-study site, the project manager stated that he didn't want to 'just do what others have tried'. Rather, he was very interested in being experimental and finding something that was 'truly innovative' and have its 'name up in lights'. Alas, the realities and pragmatism of managing conflicting interests in a workplace meant that the 'truly innovative' was indeed too great a risk – or in practical terms more trouble than it was worth. When developing the interventions that were central to the initial research plan, the management team were confronted with two distinctly different groups of employees. All employees worked long hours, but more than half were earning hourly wages, with the remainder on salaries. Hence a reduction in working hours for waged staff would result in correspondingly lower earnings. In a complicated workplace, what would have a positive impact on one group of employees would have a direct negative impact on another group. The risk of backlash from either group meant a 'minimalist' intervention was by far an easier alternative than one that was 'truly innovative'.

Risks associated with Project C in Build were more of an external political nature than an internal operational one. The nature of Build's business is politically sensitive. An ongoing risk with the research, therefore, was that any report that reflected badly on Build could potentially cause political embarrassment. Despite this risk, Build was initially very willing to share information and make the research public. This intent was a product of the relationship between the initial management team at Build and the researchers involved in the project, as well as the relationship between the first director-general and the then minister. However, with the doubling of the works programme, the appointment of a new minister, a change of director-general and staff changes associated with the project, Build became more risk averse. Although never explicitly stated, risk to reputation was more than likely a factor in the lack of access granted to the researchers to potentially sensitive areas. Research was therefore redirected to head office divisions and the observation of a specific change programme. The growing political sensitivity was highlighted in a comment by a focus-group respondent in the latter stages of the research:

> There's the extra dimension of our Minister and Director General wanting to know what is happening, so tying up a lot of resources in respect to saying do this for me, say this, and for some reason when that process, that once upon a time could have been quite simple, is a bit more complicated.

Concerns about research fatigue

Access to employees of Capital for the purposes of data collection was reasonably unhampered until the final stages of the project. An initial survey was administered with full cooperation from human resource staff to a stratified random sample of half of all employees, some 2,000 individuals. A series of 40 interviews with a range of employees, as well as six focus groups with managers, were also conducted without obstacles or challenges. However, a key issue in administering a second, follow-up survey in Capital was concerns about 'research fatigue' among employees. During the final 12 months of the project, as the researchers tried to identify a suitable date for the survey to go out, concerns were increasingly expressed by human resources staff that this would coincide with a staff opinion survey that had also been planned. It was thought that employees would be unwilling to complete both instruments and that asking them to do so would be overly burdensome. Although attempts were made to compromise on this important phase, such as reducing the number of questions and including them in the staff opinion survey, or changing the timeframe so that several months would elapse between surveys, the final outcome was that the second work-life balance survey was never administered. Similarly, the instigation of employee satisfaction surveys and other research programmes conducted within Build resulted in concerns that staff were being 'over-researched' and would therefore be less likely to participate. This finding concurs with studies done on market research, where consumers repeatedly approached regarding their intention to purchase were less likely to purchase than those consumers approached only once (Morwitz et al., 1993).

Each of the organisations had an active internal research programme, and Build also participates in a number of university-led research programmes due to its size, its professional links with universities through its core business of engineering and its public prominence. As such, gatekeepers were quite eager to ensure external research could either be incorporated into existing research or at least minimise overlap. The most common concern with the gatekeepers was to avoid 'research fatigue'. While there is a developing body of work examining the fatigue of the researcher (see for example Mandel, 2003), there appears to be very little published on workplace and employee-level 'research fatigue'. We have little doubt that research fatigue is a growing phenomenon within society that affects access to organisations and individual employees, and that this will continue to have an impact on academic research in the future. There is, of course, irony and indeed a problem in attempting to develop a research approach that would investigate a workplace's level of research fatigue!

Blockages and new opportunities

There are few opportunities to pursue such longitudinal research as the seven years in Project C. It had been the case from the commencement of the research that sub-projects were undertaken in regard to issues of interest to Build as an adjunct to the major focus of the study. These were undertaken at the request of Build and within the resources of the project, and indicated a willingness by the researchers to investigate not just their own area of interest but also to work with Build on various issues confronting it.

When the continuity of research efforts was frustrated through blocked access, the longitudinal value of the research was lost. Negotiations took place in regard to the type of research and access that would now be useful and acceptable to Build. Twelve separate submissions were made in response to suggestions by BuildCorp, but on each occasion the proposal was rejected, with no clear indication of how it could be adjusted to meet Build's needs. On reflection this appears to be mainly an issue of uncertainty by the management coordinator of what would be acceptable to BuildCorp due to a relatively short association with the organisation. This was therefore an issue of establishing trust, as there had been no history on which to build such a foundation. Not surprisingly, when access to a project was granted it was minor and politically safe. However, over time access was granted to observe the process of a new change initiative and to conduct interviews and focus groups with various participants. While too long a period had elapsed to recapture the longitudinal strength of the initial research, this programme offered an opportunity to research a unique change event that has subsequently resulted in two reports to Build and three academic papers. Project C therefore demonstrates how, through concerted efforts to meet the needs of partner organisations, industry relationships can be re-established to branch research into different and theoretically interesting directions.

How access affected research outcomes

Not surprisingly, given the access difficulties described, the research outcomes for each project were somewhat different to those articulated in the original proposals. In Projects A and B, for example, a key objective was to improve opportunities for employees to achieve work-life balance. In particular, the projects, by implementing a number of specific strategies, aimed to improve access to existing policies and demonstrate the successful use of flexible working in positions where alternative working arrangements are rarely utilised (e.g. among men and employees with supervisory positions). In reality, although some minor technology transfers occurred in the form of changes to human resource policies (such as the introduction of a phased retirement policy and improved access to information via the organisation's intranet), these objectives were not realised and the status quo held firm. Of concern, it is likely that the lack of visible outcomes for employees in Project A (Capital) contributed to increased cynicism among some staff that the organisation merely 'talked up' its commitment to work-life balance without being willing to implement real change. This cynicism was especially problematic for the employees who had volunteered to be part of the demonstration trials, which did not go ahead.

Importantly, our project counterparts in Project A appeared satisfied with the processes and outcomes of the three-year research programme and were not concerned with the divergence between the original research objectives and actual outcomes. This lack of concern was somewhat surprising, but perhaps reflects the lack of shared understandings and goals for the research between the researchers and the key organisational contacts, beyond the initial contractual arrangements. The extended period of time that often elapses between submitting grant applications and the completion of a project (up to five years) is likely to contribute to the diffusion of shared goals as well as to other practical problems discussed previously, such as staff turnover and changes to organisational priorities.

Other goals of the research projects included facilitating researcher training, promoting the development of theory and scholarship in the area of interest and communicating the findings of the research to interested parties, both academic and non-academic. Project A, despite its under-achievement in progressing constructive changes to organisational work-life culture, achieved a reasonable publication output (six journal articles submitted or accepted at the time of writing and five conference papers), mainly due to the relative ease of data collection. These publications made an arguably significant contribution to theory in the area of work-life balance and work-life culture. The findings were also consistently reported back to various stakeholders in Project A organisations on at least six occasions.

The academic outcomes of Project B were not insignificant, but the project could not be held as a flagship for highly successful university-industry partnerships. At least six journal publications and 15 industry reports and presentations to research partners were derived from project data. As a consequence, the knowledge and understanding of the issues generated through the project reached a significant number of people directly affected by the research issue under investigation. Furthermore, the project provided an excellent research training and project management experience for the research fellow. However, problems with access meant that we were unable to compare cases adequately. The publications were therefore single case-study reports and did not have the capacity for generalisation or demonstration of causal effects. For an early-career researcher this was a somewhat frustrating investment of three years, though it highlights the pragmatism required for research within the social sciences. Viewed holistically, the academic and workplace results reached a wide audience and provided an excellent training experience, demonstrating a successful project despite the problematic access issues which arose.

The dynamics and politics of every research project oblige the researcher to consider how to balance the outcomes expected by industry and those required by academic journals. At one time in Build, the researcher was handed a pile of 200 questionnaires – 30 questions in length – and asked if a report would be 'ready for a leadership team meeting next week'. Indeed, the timeframes sometimes expected by industry are not conducive to the standard of analysis required for academic publication. There are likely to be numerous academics with concerns over presenting industry partners with less than rigorous analysis simply to meet partner timelines.

Recommendations for facilitating access

Perhaps, as early-career researchers, we expected too much from the organisations involved and were not prepared for the difficulties we encountered. Our subsequent approaches to industry-based research have been more realistic and perhaps more guarded, but a reflection on our common experiences and the lessons we learned as research fellows provides some potentially useful insights that might be helpful to other researchers.

In preparing for the project, the importance of establishing shared expectations and timelines of the research with key personnel who have legitimate power within the organisation cannot be overestimated. Of course, those with legitimate power and genuine 'buy-in' may not be the same individuals who devised, negotiated or signed off on the project. However, they are likely to be important allies through the course of the project, and identifying them earlier rather than later is, in our experience, critical. As Cheek (2003: 98) notes, 'taking funding from someone in order to conduct research is not a neutral act, but requires that the researcher discuss with the funder all the expectations and assumptions, spoken and unspoken, that both of them may have about the research'.

The problem arises when these key individuals leave their substantive positions, or resign from the organisation entirely. A stalling of momentum is seemingly inevitable during these transition periods, as people become familiar with their new roles and the tasks they inherit from their predecessors. The extent to which the terms and conditions of the research can be renegotiated from that point onwards is dependent partly on the motivation and personality of the new contact, but also on the quality of communication with the researchers. Regular contact is imperative at all stages of the research, but particularly so during transitions in key personnel. In most situations the research project is low down the list of a multitude of tasks needing to be completed, and polite contact in the form of e-mails and phone calls is important for keeping the objectives of the research salient. Offers to conduct seminars or information sessions for various groups of staff are one strategy we found useful to maintain or improve the visibility of the project.

Obviously some events are beyond the researcher's control. The natural disaster and subsequent reprioritising of organisational tasks in Project A are one such example. Increasing pressures from macro-level environments in the construction industry are another. However, Walford (2001) notes that although researchers can do nothing directly to reduce the effects of macro-level changes and pressures, they need to take new and changing constraints into account and, much like sales people in a commercial environment, promote their research more effectively to gain access.

C. Wright Mills suggested 50 years ago that the research process should involve significant record-keeping: the researcher would do well to keep 'ideas, personal notes, excerpts from books, bibliographical items and outlines of projects' in an effort to develop what he referred to as 'intellectual production' (Mills, 1959: 198–9). In an age when accountability for government funding is being increasingly devolved to an individual level, this advice is particularly salient. In many ways a prudent social science researcher should begin a project expecting the worst, indeed planning for the worst, yet all the while hoping and working for the best possible outcome.

11

A sporting chance: workplace ethnographies, ethics protocols and playing by the rules

Jennifer Sappey

Introduction

This is a researcher's story of her student adventures into workplace ethnography. First comes the tale of participant observation of the Queensland commercial fitness industry, which in the early 1990s was one of the last 'award-free' industries in Queensland, Australia. My club membership paid and my access secured, my conservative business suit discarded for spangled leotards and the latest pumps, I went to work. These were the days prior to restrictions on workplace ethnography introduced by the Australian national ethics protocols in 1999. I was free to follow leads as they appeared and report my own observations as just another participant at the gym. Little could I have expected that my observations of the conditions of employment in one particular fitness centre would mushroom into a full-scale industry analysis, as employers took the extraordinary step of discarding self-regulation and seeking a formal industrial award. In May 1994 I sat alone in the public gallery of the Queensland Industrial Relations Commission, conspicuously the only witness to what, at face value, simply did not make sense: private enterprise employers seeking to have government regulate their relationship with their workers. It seemed liked a researcher's manna from heaven.

Second comes a contrasting tale of doctoral research into the changing nature of work for academics in Australian universities. Unlike the freedom of research design and procedures in my fitness industry study, which chased down leads as they appeared, the newly introduced national research ethics protocols with their restrictions on access, design and procedures were compromising the integrity of the research and even threatening to curb the project outright. The challenge was just how to retrieve the research project and still play by the rules, even though the ethics regulations hardly seemed to offer a sporting chance to a workplace ethnographer.

Participant observation in the Queensland fitness industry

Like many who experience the inevitable bulge and spread of middle age, in the 1990s I was lured by the quest for the perfect body offered, in theory at least, by my local fitness centre. I was drawn into a world of workouts where the idealised body of the fitness worker, clad in tight-fitting Lycra to display the six-pack or tiny waistline to best effect, was a walking billboard advertising the employer's products and services. In the fitness centre workplace, the idealised body was a mainstream commodity and the basis of sexual, social and employment success for worker and client alike.

As a student of industrial sociology, what I found curious about this world was that in their quest to attain and display their physical capital, fitness workers such as aerobics and weight-training instructors were prepared to trade off standard employment conditions just to be employed and get access to 'their stage', the space in which they received adoration and a heightened sense of self-worth and celebrity from their admiring clientele. I was intrigued by small incidents which I observed from the gym floor, seemingly out of step with basic conditions of employment enshrined in industrial awards and statute law. For example, poor rostering by the manager might lead to two instructors arriving to teach the same session. One would be turned away by the employer without any call-out pay. As I came to know and socialise with the instructors, it became evident that it was custom and practice for instructors applying for work with a fitness centre to teach up to five classes without payment, in order to secure the employer's favour. They also worked without pay at special fitness centre promotional 'open days' or aerobic displays. These were all casual employees. Sexual harassment of staff seemed rife. I recall one occasion when an employer required a male instructor to don a ballerina's tutu as part of the 'fun', clearly accentuating his genitals for the all-female class. No weekend or evening penalty rates were offered at a time when this was the norm, and most fitness centre employers forbade their casual staff to work for their competitors – a clear breach of freedom of trade. It was my intellectual curiosity to explore and understand the domination of managerial prerogative and its impact on the basic conditions of employment which led me to enrol in a research master's degree in industrial relations.

My enrolment in 1990 was unproblematic. There were no ethics approvals that needed to be secured from my university, merely a proposal on method (participant observation, survey and interview) and expected outcomes to my research supervisor, who 'gave it the nod', and my journey began, free of bureaucratic constraint or surveillance. The initial purpose was to investigate the conditions of employment in the Queensland commercial health and fitness industry, in what appeared to be an industrial setting without the constraints of regulation or the presence of trade unions. It was asynchronous with the wider debate which was raging in Australia at the time, stimulated by employer groups, conservative 'think-tanks' and the neo-liberal political parties, all seeking deregulation of the workplace to lead to what was hailed to be a freeing up of the Australian economy. The broader political timing could not have been better. This 'award-free' industry was unique in that it presented an opportunity to study the brave new world of deregulation. The stage was set for an interesting project which could contribute to a national debate.

The first hurdle was to select appropriate tools which could capture the data in an embryonic industry that was still 'invisible'. The 1990 study took place at a time when the Queensland commercial fitness industry was yet to be clearly defined, the function of 'fitness instructor' was not included in the Australian Standards Classification of Occupations (ASCO) and therefore both were invisible to Australian Bureau of Statistics (ABS) data collection and any professional industry registers of operators. It was this 'invisibility' and the nature of the information sought that shaped the data-collection tools, rather than a process of bureaucratic scrutiny of the method's science by an ethics committee, as was the case in my later research. Given my understanding of the industry structure and the mode of operation of many businesses, I drew from five sources to facilitate cross-validation. I distributed a state-wide mail survey to a non-probability sample of 269 industry employers which I compiled from the 1993 Yellow Pages telephone directories for Queensland and cross-validated with local government records. In order to collect this information I distributed a survey to all

Queensland town clerks requesting listings of fitness centres operating within their jurisdiction. In many ways this method seemed a bit 'rough and ready', but there were simply no other means of identifying an employer sample because of the unregulated nature of the industry, the very phenomenon that I was researching. I also distributed a state-wide mail survey to fitness workers through the embryonic fitness professionals' association to the total population of its 500 members. The questionnaire was designed to cross-validate much of the data collected from the employer questionnaire, with many of the questions replicated. Who was telling the 'truth', if indeed that can ever be known? The data were supplemented by unstructured interviews with the relevant trade union, the employers' association, the president of the embryonic employers' group representing the small number of multi-million-dollar fitness centres, smaller commercial fitness centre owners and managers, fitness instructors, state and local government planning and health inspectors, the Queensland chief industrial inspector and a former head of the Queensland Industrial Relations Commission (QIRC). I thought I had it covered.

'Luck's a fortune', so they say. Although I had seemingly finalised the survey, before posting it to respondents something broke in the national news. It seemed as though I was not the only one becoming aware of the burgeoning industry. The collapse of a large, national franchise of fitness centres had received extensive media coverage and brought the industry to the notice of the Queensland Industrial Inspectorate. However, given the difficulties of locating the industry and its myriad of small gym operators, the inspectorate was prone to target the large, visible employers, many of them having grown out of squash centres in the 1980s.

With this significant change in the larger centres' operating environment, they sought to devise an offensive strategic business move that would strengthen their market position and force many of their smaller competitors out of business. As they felt that they had already been targeted by regulators, they took the highly unusual step of seeking industry-wide industrial regulation, hoping that the additional overheads thereby imposed on smaller 'fly-by-night' operators would squeeze them out of the market. Employers were using the imposition of industrial regulation as a business strategy. There was a clear trail leading from the fundamental conditions of employment in the industry, which I had sought to document and contrast with those of other industries, to the strategic action taken by employers to turn their greenfield site into a regulated environment through the making of the first award, in which the employers were again prescribing the base conditions of employment to the detriment of workers and of smaller enterprises.

Just as the industry operators changed strategy, I too needed to change tack with my research design, to incorporate questions about the award-making process into the surveys which were about to be despatched, and to create a second stage of the research, namely observation and scrutiny of the award-making process itself. Of necessity, it extended my original timeframe for the research project, and required additional financial resources and the development of my skills in award interpretation and industrial commission proceedings. However, I was free to do so, unencumbered by ethical protocols or requirements to seek an extension of the project, which was the case in my later research. If I had been required to do so, the rapid developments towards QIRC proceedings would have meant that the opportunity would have passed by.

On 4 March 1994 the owners of the larger gyms operating in the population centres of south-east Queensland stood in the Queensland Industrial Relations Commission, represented by their employers' association and in partnership with a trade union which my survey had identified had no members in the industry, to agree upon the first industry-specific award. As I sat in the public gallery, conspicuously the only person not associated with the attending employers or union, something didn't seem right.

The triangulation of data collection later confirmed it. In the survey of employers, where I had included a question directly asking if they supported industrial regulation of the industry, 62 per cent said 'no', with 68 per cent specifically supporting self-regulation. Significantly, 93 per cent of both employer and employee respondents did not know that the larger gyms or the trade union were negotiating the first award on their behalf. The only respondents who did know were the four largest gyms, which were spearheading the award negotiations.

Confirmation came from another source. Perseverance is the key to getting any research project finished. It was on my fourth attempt to interview the largest gym operator that I succeeded, each time arriving at the appointed place at the appointed hour, only to find that the businessman had left the premises. Each time I accepted the apology but rejected gifts of fitness merchandise, insisting that all I wanted was another appointment. When I finally gained access to him, I was overwhelmed by the openness of his position. His confidence as a large operator in what was a brash industry led him to boast of the tactic of using industrial regulation to bankrupt competitors and consolidate the market position of the larger operators. A competent shorthand writer, I was able to get him down verbatim, confident that my notes had locked in his confession, unable to renege. I was aware that he could deny his statements, should it come to that at the time of going public, but that he could not withdraw them or refuse to let me use the data, as would be the case in later research. I had not needed his written consent to use his utterances and did not have to offer him the right to withdraw his information at any stage of the research if he so wished, as is now the case. He was a worldly business executive. He had said it. He had said it openly, and in the full knowledge that I was noting his words in front of him. Imprudent perhaps, but imprudence on the part of an interviewee should not be deemed to reach into the realms of unethical behaviour in the recording of those words by the researcher.

In short, the upshot of all this was the making of an award to meet the vested interests of a few in the industry, between the largest employers and a union that had no members in the industry but had secured a preference clause (employers were obliged to give preference in employment to union members). The unusual nature of the occupation meant that the commissioner who made the award was dependent on the collaborating parties to provide information about the nature of the work, its intensity and comparable work in other industries. The outcome was an award that was a poor fit between the award conditions and the realities of the work. For example, the 40-hour week for aerobics instructors was a physical impossibility.

An occupational study of academic work

In 1998 I again ventured into the field of workplace ethnography, this time researching the changing nature of academic work in my own industry of higher education. I chose the established methodology of the extended case method advocated by Professor Michael Burawoy of the University of California, Berkeley. Key to the research methodology was using participant observation, a time-honoured tradition in industrial sociology and the key tool of my earlier ethnography.

My doctoral enrolment in 1998 was unproblematic – until the promulgation of the new *National Statement on Ethical Conduct in Research Involving Humans* by the National Health and Medical Research Council (1999). Until this point, most Australian universities had relied upon the professional judgement of a student's academic supervisor to assess the ethical nature of a research proposal. While there had been regulation of health-related research for 50 years, the broadening of regulation to other forms of social science and humanities research was a relatively recent development since the 1980s, triggered by concern for human rights and an increasingly litigious society. Many universities floundered to come to terms with and operationalise the national statement, which was strongly criticised by social scientists for its application of medical research principles (e.g. the potential harm from collecting tissue samples, psychological testing, clinical trials, etc.) to workplace ethnographic studies. As a student with an ongoing research project, mid-stream, the impact was disastrous.

At this stage I had commenced my fieldwork, with a research design based around participant observation at a single fieldwork site, to be supplemented by interviews with management and workers, and triangulated with content analysis of publicly available policy documents. However, the national statement deemed participant observation, a traditional method in industrial sociology and many other disciplines, to be 'covert', unacceptable and by implication unethical. Unlike my fitness centre experiences, I could no longer record my own experiences and use them as data.

Secondly, the national statement required written approval from the chief executive officer of any organisation under study. Prior to the imposition of the national ethics protocols, when I had commenced my fieldwork my research supervisors advised me on the basis of custom and practice in the discipline that formal permission was not required.

Thirdly, there was the issue of the broadening of the term 'participant'. In that the primary purpose of the protocols was the protection of the welfare and rights of participants, with those rights taking precedence over the expected benefits to human knowledge derived from the research, defining just who was a 'participant' became crucial. The interpretation of one university defined it to be any human, living or dead, who was the focus of the research or alternatively any person upon whom the research findings may impact – a broad interpretation indeed, and significant in its impact on the potential disclosure of corruption and wrongdoing by trade unions, organisations and their managements. The implication of gaining written, informed consent from all participants is that consent must be obtained from every person involved in or sharing the researcher's observations, not just those people who are the focus subjects of the observation. Such a requirement fails to understand the conditions under which industrial sociologists operate.

Fourthly, the nature of working in organisations meant that I had to gain written, informed consent from all within the organisation, starting from the chief executive officer (CEO) and down through all layers of hierarchy and vested interests.

Fifthly, it was deemed that the data I had already collected could not be used, in that they had been gained by covert means (participant observation). The ruling was devastating. Where did this leave me? Where indeed did this leave the entire discipline of industrial sociology? Dare I admit that the tears flowed?

Having negotiated an agreement with my university's ethics committee that I would 'mend my ways' and all future data would be collected in accordance with the new protocols, I was permitted to retain existing data. I then sought permission from the fieldwork site for official access. After some months of delay I was notified that the traditional academic embargo on publication for a five-year period that I had offered to the organisation was merely a gentlemen's agreement and, although accepted by them, had no legal standing. A formal contract would be required, implicitly with the organisation retaining publication rights over the thesis, and, of great concern, perhaps editorial input given that the organisation also required a member of its academic management to be appointed as my external doctoral co-supervisor, and that my research proposal which had been passed by my own institution's ethics committee would need to go through the full screening process of that institution's ethics committee. While access had in theory been granted, I had in effect been kneecapped.

If persistence was the key to success in my first case study, innovation, flexibility and compromise were the keys to this research. There was clearly a need to change tack. I chose a second fieldwork site and approached that organisation's CEO for permission to conduct interviews with staff. After appropriate correspondence and face-to-face meetings with both the CEO and his deputy, permission was granted, with the manager next down the line advised in writing by the CEO of the research which was to be conducted, requesting that I be afforded every assistance. In spite of this, negotiation to interview the manager as gatekeeper to his staff continued for two months via e-mail and telephone. Unable to secure authorisation from him for either a personal interview or access to his staff, I had to abandon the project and simply walk away, given national protocols' clear statement of rights that participation is voluntary and non-participation (particularly where there is clearly a power differential, such as in employment) should not disadvantage an employee. Under these protocols I was unable to report back to the CEO on the failure of the project consequent on his staff's refusal to participate. The result was the besmirching of my own reputation.

Desperate to complete my project, I devised a third strategy – that of conducting an occupational ethnography of Australian academics across a number of university workplaces. Individual academics still retained their traditional right of free speech and perceived themselves to be free agents to grant research interviews. On this basis the doctoral research was able to proceed. The context of the research therefore became the broad occupation within an industry context, rather than a particular workplace. All of the respondents who were approached were full-time academics and academic managers employed in universities on the east coast of Australia. All agreed to be interviewed. The data were captured, but the compromise on participant observation significantly weakened the methodology of the extended case method as I was unable to gain the contextual depth of a single site. The change of direction from a single-site study to an industry-wide occupational case study left the research findings open to challenge, but I finally got there. Some six years after the commencement of the research project, and after considerably more time, financial resources and emotional stress than I had anticipated, the project was successfully completed.

What lessons have I learnt from my early forays into workplace research?

Vested interests and the politics of power

Research in organisations is by its very nature an extremely sensitive political process, as the researcher mediates power relationships and negotiates strategic and tactical compromise. It is a political minefield, in that human action is unpredictable and decision-making within bureaucracies is often irrational. I would suggest that management of the political environment is probably more vital than the correct selection of effective research techniques and tools. At the very least, vested interests and the politics of power will interfere with the researcher's clinical design of techniques and instruments of data collection. At the very worst, political interference will render useless even the broader methodology. As a researcher I will never again assume that consent and a green light from an organisation's CEO will ensure that I can access the data that I need to complete a project. In effect, at no point within a project can I assume that the project is secure, in that the internal politics of an organisation can quickly white-ant any research project, no matter how carefully and scientifically crafted or how passionately pursued.

Unforeseen opportunities and serendipity versus science

Strategic and tactical compromise does not end with navigating one's way through the complexity of bureaucratic hierarchies and vested interests. Organisations are in a constant state of flux in what is for most a dynamic external operating environment. We almost rhetorically teach this to our students, but the realities do not hit home until we venture outside our sheltered university cloisters into the real world and engage with organisations which are aggressively competing for survival and growth. In the current output- and performance-based management ideologies, even public sector organisations which were once fertile ground for research have adopted market-like behaviour and competitive cultures, and researchers are often not welcome unless benefit and a good-news story are guaranteed. Changes in the external operating environment of most organisations (economic, political, social, legal and technological) elicit corresponding offensive and defensive strategic moves by them. Accordingly, our methodologies need to encompass a range of tools and techniques to be able to respond.

Single fieldwork sites are probably a thing of the past, for it is now too precarious for the researcher to assume the completion of a project on the terms under which it began, if indeed at all. Positivists have always criticised workplace ethnographies on the grounds that any one workplace is atypical and tends to produce interesting data but no general principles that can add to theory. Such a view highlights the divide between ethnographic and positivist researchers and the assumptions underpinning both approaches. However, it may be that single-site research will disappear not on methodological grounds, but as the result of better risk management processes in research design. It only takes one article in a major metropolitan daily newspaper to make organisations within the target industry re-evaluate their exposure to public scrutiny and withdraw from a research project. Under the current management fad of risk management, it is probably far better to design multiple-site fieldwork, lest we be evicted from a single fieldwork site consequent on a shift in wind direction on the commercial or political front. The precarious nature of research in such an organisational climate may also call for a rethinking of time, place, financial resources and our own blend of skills, be they qualitative or quantitative. The optimal research design for the researcher may in effect become unviable over the course of the project with the shifts in an organisation's dynamic operating environment. Compromise is inevitable.

The time-honoured method of participant observation

For many workplace ethnographers research ideas come from our immediate work and social environments – we observe, we question and we seek answers. The tool of critical observation through participation and immersion in the phenomenon under study is the foundation stone on which the discipline of industrial sociology has been founded, in that it seeks to understand the complexities of social action and social structures in the reality of the natural workplace setting. In keeping with this focus, it requires a narrative and not a statistical analysis. This has been the tradition with the seminal studies in industrial sociology since the 1930s. Researchers gained employment with an organisation in order to observe, analyse and deconstruct the social relations of the workplace. In most instances the researchers fulfilled their duties as employees, but withheld from management (and perhaps co-workers) their concurrent role of researcher.

However, the time-honoured method of participant observation is now problematic in current research design. The seminal studies of my discipline would not have made it through the scrutiny of their universities' ethics committees, no doubt being labelled 'covert' and by implication 'unethical'. And yet without these studies we would not have the body of theory today which informs analysis of current workplace practices.

Research ethics and the double-bind of the search for 'truth'

The application of a universal ethical code is relatively new to the social sciences, although now common in most Western countries. The

Australian national statement (1999) was revised in 2007, with the National Health and Medical Research Council attempting to soften its negative impact on social science research. However, the interpretation and operationalisation of the statement still lie in the hands of institution-based human research ethics committees (HRECs). Much is still the same for workplace ethnographers.

This raises fundamental ethical questions about the extent to which there is a right to acquire knowledge versus the right to privacy, whether individual, collective, private or commercial. There is clearly potential conflict between the national ethics protocols and industrial sociological research which seeks to deconstruct a workplace and delayer management rhetoric in order to understand the realities and complexities of the social relations of that workplace. There is a fundamental pluralist assumption of the discipline which challenges management's often unitarist view of the workplace as essentially harmonious. While views of the workplace as being conflictual and exploitative need to be tempered with an understanding of the cooperative nature of workplace relations, there is nevertheless a general recognition of acts of both resistance and cooperation in any workplace. An unintended consequence of the protocols' emphasis on the primacy of participants' rights, reinforced by the requirement of written, informed consent (which in the first instance must be that of an organisation's management), may well be a research focus on unitarist consensus which is at best one-sided and at worst seriously misleading. It is unlikely that managerial consent for research of this kind will be granted unless there is guaranteed benefit and management's 'truth' is assured. It may be that management's refusal to grant the researcher access denies the workforce's right to have their 'truth' told, as it is mandatory to have managerial consent before gaining approval from one's university for any organisational research projects.

Even when managerial consent is given, the nature of participants' rights of non-participation or withdrawal from the study at any time, without reason, means that access needs to be negotiated at each level of hierarchy within an organisation, and with each individual participant. This requirement by ethics protocols exposes the researcher to the possibility of even greater interference from vested interests and organisational politics than was once the case. The notion of organisational approval from a CEO, while mandatory, is in effect meaningless in a hierarchical organisational structure. The workplace researcher's position is now quite precarious.

While there can be no disputing the need for research to be conducted in a way that minimises any harm to participants, the difficulties of conducting workplace ethnographic research are significant when confronted by practical impediments which constrain professional procedures and techniques, and in the case of labour-process workplace studies threaten to curb research outright. While research in organisations is by its very nature an extremely sensitive political process, the overlay of unduly restrictive ethics protocols adds an additional complexity to workplace ethnographies which potentially hinders exploration of the hidden processes of power and conflict in workplace relations, and brings into question the integrity of research which only reports managerial 'truth'.

As a postscript to this researcher's story, 14 years after completing my fitness study research I am again venturing into the sweaty world of the fitness centre, about to replicate the original study. Did the employers' strategy work? What long-term impact has the industrial award had on the conditions of employment? Alas, I will no longer be able to jump around a gymnasium as a participant observer and record my own experiences and observations, for that is now deemed to be covert. If research was difficult then, it is even more difficult now.

Part IV
Preparing and responding throughout the project

12

Sitting on a wall in Northumberland crying: semi-structured interviews

Vikki Abusidualghoul, John Goodwin, Nalita James,
Al Rainnie, Katharine Venter and Melissa White

Introduction

Alan Bryman, in the second edition of *Social Research Methods* (2004), has an extensive chapter devoted to 'interviewing in qualitative research' as well as sections on ethnography and focus groups. The chapters provide an excellent introduction to issues such as the difference between semi-structured and unstructured interviews, preparing the interview guide, kinds of question, recording and transcription, etc.

What the chapter does not do is tell you how to deal with the personal trauma of finding out that your tape deck has not worked on one of your very first interviews as a PhD student (sit on a wall outside the factory and cry). Nor does it tell you how to react over 20 years later when a superbly high-tech mini-cassette proves not to have recorded a single word of a two-and-a-half-hour brilliant interview with an old trade unionist (sit in the car outside and cry).

In this chapter we explore the lived realities of qualitative research, particularly the interview itself. We look at issues that arise in trying to gain access (abusive employers, mind-numbing negotiations), the terror of technology (see above), the location of the interview (homes, cupboards, pubs), interviewing in another language (does TQM really translate into Polish as total management control?), transcription (the agency can't understand a word Geordie shop stewards are saying) and electronic and internet-facilitated research.

Before we start, we want to stress that carrying out interviews is probably the most interesting, exciting and addictive part of research (as qualitative researchers we are of course hopelessly biased). The time, openness and frankness with which people feel free to share their experiences are astonishing, and place a huge responsibility on the researcher to treat such confidences, attitudes and beliefs with proper respect. This we hold to be a fundamental and undeniable truth; however, everything else surrounding the interview can test your patience and commitment beyond breaking point.

The chapter draws on the experience of a number of researchers associated with the Centre for Labour Market Studies at Leicester University. We each tell our own stories (our individual accounts are shown in sans serif font), and we have made no attempt to homogenise or standardise our presentation or style. This may make for discomforting reading; it is certainly a little unusual. However, it does follow our contention that interviewing lies somewhere between an art and a craft, and is far more than simply a list of technical skills that can be drawn from the pages of a textbook. This is not to deny the importance of research methods textbooks, but they often downgrade or ignore the importance of the individual and his/her experience and reaction to the research contexts and the person/group being researched. Feminist researchers have sensitised us to some of these issues, but there is more than structural bias at work.

Getting started

As the oldest member of the group, Al is claiming starting rights. Gaining access to undertake the interviews can be far from a straightforward process.

When I started my PhD research I wrote to small clothing firms in north-east England requesting access to talk to managers and women who were shop stewards. My first response was a telephone call (the phone was in the corridor, so everyone could hear). The manager on the other end of the line started to shout at me, demanding to know why I was wasting taxpayers' money on such useless research. Anyway, he argued he had good industrial relations in his workplace based on total ignorance and he didn't want anyone coming in and unsettling his staff. In retrospect this was a fabulous response for a piece of research investigating the small-is-beautiful hypothesis. However, as my first-ever response to a request for access it was decidedly unsettling. But it's not that large firms are any more accommodating. Twenty years later, I was negotiating access for one of my PhD students to a large telecom outfit in Australia. This entailed weeks of meetings, circumlocution, negotiation, confidentiality agreements, consulting with their lawyers and ours and so on. All the while my PhD student could see her precious time ticking away. We got there in the end, but as companies get more litigious and universities more sensitive to what are usually dressed up as 'ethical' concerns, access is going to become more of a problem.

Gaining access is one thing, but the interview venue itself can raise unexpected problems. For example, alcohol and research don't really mix. Long nights discussing the minutiae of your research with friends who are bored senseless is one thing. This is probably OK if you are paying, but alcohol and the fieldwork process are not good partners. One project involved interviewing women who were founders of a cooperative in the clothing industry in southern Scotland and were also former union representatives. I got a lift to the workplace, met my interviewees and was invited to cross the road to the workingmen's club (sic). This was lunchtime, and so on an empty stomach I set up the tape deck and got the first round in. Lager for me, vodka and Irn Bru for my interviewees. Ninety minutes later we left. I staggered out into the Scottish sunshine blinking and burping. The women went back to work. Replaying the tape later, the women maintained a sense of composure and intelligence. I just got maudlin and drunk.

Over the years I have spent a lot of time doing research on union organisation and the labour process in the printing industry. This I believe goes a long way to accounting for the state of my liver. A lot of the research involved interviewing union representatives in many different locations and contexts. Often it would be suggested that we meet in a local pub because it was quieter than work/home. This might have been the case occasionally, but even in quiet pubs sitting with a tape deck on the table between you and an interview schedule on your lap attracts a host of unwanted attention. Often it simply backfires. Having sat down in a quiet nook in a pub in southern England we got started, only for the pub to shake to its foundations every ten minutes as a train went by on the main London to Glasgow route.

As the newest researcher of the group, Vikki continues to outline the unforeseen hazards of when and where interviews take place, particularly when combined with evil technology.

In April 2002 I was conducting research for my master's degree in education at Exeter University into the provision of and interest in in-service teacher training. To do this, I chose to return to Greece, a country where I had lived and worked for seven years, but it was a challenge to get two differing language *frontisteria* to agree to help. (*Frontisteria* are private schools that pupils attend to boost their state school learning outside school time.)

I was most relieved to get quick responses to my 55-point questionnaire on 'the ideal teacher' from three teachers in Lefkada, and I made lots of interesting notes while observing one each of their 50-minute classes. I also got full answers from them to the six questions in my retrospective questionnaire, which related to their perceptions of the observed lessons, and I collated all the data collected thus far to form sets of interview questions relevant to each teacher's responses. The first two interviews went well, in that the teachers were relaxed and spoke freely about their opinions, showing interest in the training issues I raised, and I managed to write all this down in note form to back up the noisy tape recordings that also included babies crying, children running in and out of the room, the phone ringing and some short, whispered, mobile phone conversations.

Now it was time for the third and final interview in Lefkada, which was to be with the school owner/manager who also taught a large number of hours per week. As we'd become good friends while I was working for her, I'd accepted her generous offer of a place to stay and loan of a car during my fortnight there. This proximity, though, made it difficult to settle to do the interview, as we'd got into a chatty evening routine of cooking together, playing with her toddler, sitting down to eat with her husband and gossiping about old times while watching a film. However, this was my last night in Lefkada, so I had no choice but to get the interview done. By the time we'd cooked, eaten, got her son off to bed and husband out to the taverna, it was late in the evening. The house was finally in total silence and the evening was warm, so we sat on the edge of her enormous fireplace and enjoyed the light breeze there as we sipped cool drinks and turned on the tape recorder. I felt quietly confident about my interviewing skills now, and as it was silent in the house and there had been no previous problems with the tape recorder, I took very few notes.

There were many surprises in how she responded to my questions; many stark contrasts with the types of responses her two employees had given. The gist of her response was that because she knew how to get her students through their Cambridge and Michigan suite language exams, her *frontisterio* was successful and her family demanded her free time, she had no need or time for training and so had no interest in doing any. The ways she justified her arguments against training were shocking and yet convincing, and I relished the thought of quoting her in a variety of places in the results chapter and conclusion that were already partly formed in my mind. Amazingly, she had just provided me with the seeds of a strong counterargument that would bark loudly at my whole literature review – this was truly exciting stuff.

Early the next morning, I made my farewells and, with a happy researcher's spring in my step, got on to the coach to Athens. I slept until the halfway point of my journey, the ferry crossing from Rio to Patra, and then opened my notebook to run over the responses to the previous night's interview. I saw that my notes made little sense and were no more than skeletal, so I put on my headphones to listen to the interview on the tape recorder. It took a long time to rewind. When I pressed play, all I could hear was an eerie whooshing sound, like wind rushing along a narrow passageway. As the penny dropped and I realised that the sound of the light breeze going up the chimney had blocked out our voices, my heart sank. With three hours to go until I reached Athens and with a very shaky hand, I started to fill out my skeletal notes from memory, but I knew that without direct quotes from that particular interview, my dissertation would lack a true spark – and unfortunately it did.

Sadly, experience does not always inoculate you against the vicissitudes of events that seem to be (almost) beyond your control. Dealing with sophisticated modern technology doesn't make things any better. Katharine explains.

I remember sitting in the car ten minutes prior to an interview, suddenly discovering as I flicked through my new digital recorder handbook that it would only record for an hour and a half, and I needed to work out (which for me meant reading the handbook) how to set it to long play before starting the interview in a few minutes. Having felt very organised by ensuring I had arrived in plenty of time to find the house, sort myself out and begin in a relaxed manner, I actually started the interview feeling rushed and somewhat less confident with the technology. Doing more to familiarise myself with the technology prior to ever setting out for the interview would have made a lot more sense.

We are often advised in methods textbooks to find a quiet environment in which to interview, and obviously this may be ideal, but how often it is a practical possibility is a different matter. This was vividly brought to light in a recent interview in an interviewee's own home. I had deliberately and carefully timed the interview so that children would be at school and the interviewee had plenty of time and would be the only person in what I had anticipated would be a quiet house. However, as the interview progressed the increasingly loud chirruping of a large number of crickets destined to be the tea of the family's pet lizard somehow seemed to be at just the pitch that the recorder picked up extremely well. This was sufficient not only to provide an irritating piercing noise during transcription but also managed to obscure some of what was being said. On other occasions it simply isn't possible to arrange the interview at a time when others will not be about.

So how does one prepare for an interview where a newly mobile one-year-old is present and determined to chew a small digital recorder wherever it is placed? Perhaps one of the crucial skills of an interviewer is actually to be able to assess circumstances quickly and plan around them, and to recognise that textbook ideals may seldom be a reality.

Being aware of the ideal environment and doing whatever is possible to achieve it are important, but perhaps just as important is to anticipate that the reality may be far from that ideal. This is clearly illustrated by an experience I had as a PhD student in the early 1990s during an interview 30 floors up a skyscraper in central Hong Kong. The interview was going really well when over the tannoy it was announced that Typhoon Signal 10 had just been raised, the office was closing and everyone should leave the building and head home. Prior to the interview I had stood at the railings of the famous Star Ferry pier watching boats already struggling to moor as the water was whipped up into rolling waves, so perhaps the signal number 10 should not have come as a surprise to me. When a signal 10 is raised, offices, shops and transport shut down. In Hong Kong it is like a holiday, and an opportunity for families and friends to get together, but for a PhD student who had never been in Hong Kong during a typhoon it was more alarming. I knew that everything would close down, but I did not know how long it would be before this happened. My interviewee was remarkably (to me) unconcerned by the announcement and showed no sign of wanting to bring the conversation to a close. The interview continued while I wondered distractedly which bus I needed to get, where I would be most likely to be able to get on to it if crowds of people were all trying to catch the same one, how I was going to get food, how long did these things go on for... As my anxiety built I found it increasingly difficult to concentrate on what I was being told in the interview. I was aware that my 'probing' questions were much less probing than they ought to have been, but by then I just wanted to finish the interview and didn't want long responses, as I simply wanted to get back to where I was staying.

More fear

As Katharine's experience demonstrates, as an interviewer you can find yourself in vulnerable and unenviable positions. This can arise not only from environmental threats but also from the identities of both yourself and your interviewees, as John explains.

Over the last 15 years there has been an increase in theoretical and empirical explorations of men's lives. However, while all these accounts provide valuable insight into the construction of masculine identities and give 'standard' accounts of methodology, they offer little insight into the actual, lived, 'real-life' experiences of interviewing and researching men. In contrast, there have been interesting accounts of women researchers interviewing men (see for example Pini, Chapter 8). Lee (1997: 553) suggested that an account of the process of women interviewing men deserved attention, as, when compared to the availability of analyses of women-to-women interviews, 'insights into the character of women-to-man interviewing are disappointingly rare'. Lee proceeds to demonstrate how such vulnerability impacts upon features of interviewing, such as control, rapport and reciprocity. She concludes that women should exercise the level of caution that makes the researcher feel safe when interviewing men, and recommends that they have a second interviewer present. Lee presents fear and vulnerability as if it were only women who experience these issues in an interview situation; yet such a view ignores the fact that male researchers also feel vulnerable, anxious or even frightened in the field.

My semi-structured interviews took place in three parts of Ireland – north Dublin (Baldoyle and Ballymun), Waterford and Donegal. The interviews began with questions structured around what the men were doing at present, be it unemployed, working or participating in training or education. The interview also covered issues such as attitudes to work, experiences of work, home and family, experiences of school, reflections on social class and aspirations for the future. Additional questions were asked based on the answers of the respondents. Some of the men openly discussed their own drug-related experiences, and two reflected on the problems they had with alcohol. Some indicated that they had committed crimes, ranging from social welfare fraud to violent crimes, theft and robbery.

Of all of the interviews, the ones that generated the most concern for me, and that proved to be the most challenging emotionally, were those carried out in Ballymun. Ballymun is often used to represent alienation, violence, crime, social decay and the consequences of working-class displacement. For example, in Roddy Doyle's television film *Family* the main emphasis was on the violence of the father, who was represented as a violent criminal, a wife-beater, a misogynist, an adulterer and an unemployable man capable of incest. Despite the fact that this character had no redeeming features, the film is presented as reality and representative of working-class Dublin life.

From what I already knew about Ballymun, and what I had read and could see in so-called 'fictional' accounts, the prospect of interviewing men in Ballymun was both exciting and terrifying at the same time. As I discussed this with academic colleagues and education and training practitioners in Ireland, my fear became compounded and I really wondered what I was getting myself into. For example, whenever I mentioned that I was going to interview men in Ballymun, my proposed actions were met with both exasperation and bewilderment. There seemed to be a complete lack of understanding as to why I would even want to interview 'those' men from 'that' area. Responses such as 'What do you want to interview them about work for? They are just a bunch of wasters', 'Jesus, you must be mad. Rather you than me', or worse, 'if you're going to do this, stay out of the two pubs, especially The Towers, pretend you're anything but English and make sure you are accompanied by a local wherever you go or whatever you do. That is if you value your kneecaps (ho ho).'

The interviews themselves took place in two locations – a 'portakabin' at a local training centre, and in the flats of the men from Ballymun. No research methods handbook, no matter how popular, academically rigorous or acclaimed, prepares interviewers for the interview process. It has to be experienced. There is no guidance on how to cope with fear and anxiety brought on by what you think you already know about your potential respondents. There is no training to help interviewers with the impending sense of excitement and fear. With the advice of my contacts ringing around my head, and with a training-centre employee sat outside the door, the first few interviews passed without incident. Many of the men were keen to be interviewed – some were almost excited to tell their stories and answer the questions. They conveyed the sense that they were happy to talk as no one else was interested them, save the police. One respondent remarked 'It's great you're writing a book about men, it's grand. That Jackie Collins only ever writes books about women.'

However, not all the interviews were as straightforward and jovial. One respondent arrived at the interview very much the worse for wear. Initially I was unclear whether he was drunk or if he had taken drugs, but he told me that he had taken drugs *and* sniffed glue that morning. His mood swings from the outset of the interview were massive, ranging from very lethargic to very aggressive. It was clear to me that I would not get usable data from him, and I became very concerned for my own safety. The textbooks give very little advice on how to deal with someone 'out of it' on glue and drugs, so I wanted to get him to leave. This made the respondent more irritated, as he really wanted to be interviewed and 'tell his story', and he made it known that he would be very unhappy if I stopped. He would not sit down, and hovered above me in a very menacing way. All I could do was ask the questions while he rambled on about drugs, his family and the various benefit crimes he had committed. It was impossible to concentrate on what he was saying, as all I could think of was getting out of the door. I saw the same respondent two days later in the training centre – he had no idea who I was or any recollection of the interview, and indeed he asked if he could be interviewed!

One person interviewed in this cramped portakabin space was a large man who appeared to have a swastika tattooed on to his forehead; given the proximity, I could not avoid looking at it. However, he noticed my gaze and asked 'What the fuck are you looking at?' It is very difficult to know what to say when you are asked questions in such an aggressive manner, and all I could do was ask him about the tattoo on his forehead – the thing I least wanted to talk about. He then poured out a whole tirade of racist abuse about the increase of immigration into Ireland and so forth.

The final problematic interview I had was in one of the men's flats on the estate. Initially he was keen for me to interview him in The Towers pub, which I had been warned to avoid, but I did agree to visit him in his flat. The flat was perhaps one of the worst venues for an interview. It was incredibly dirty and next to my seat was a full(ish) potty. The flat had a smell that would have made anyone without the most cast-iron of stomachs gag and want to vomit. Smell is a subjective experience, but bad smells are hard to avoid. How does one maintain the stance of a professional researcher when all one can think about is not being sick?

Given the data I had collected and the prominence of location in the responses, I was keen to get a number of pictures of the estate and the surrounding area during my last visit. My contact walked around the estate with me, and I started to get various photographs of key locations mentioned in the interviews. However, shortly after starting this process my contact noticed that the same black BMW car kept passing us. We carried on for a little while, until we confirmed in our minds that someone was observing us and they were not happy about me taking pictures. Whether this was a local, a local criminal, a gang member or the police was unclear, but my levels of anxiety were such that we jogged back to the car and drove off as fast as we could.

Online and comparative research

Technological development in general and the internet in particular have changed the nature of research and research interviews. As Melissa explains, the whens and whys of online interviewing can be unexpected, and the outcomes not always satisfactory.

Comparative research presents a number of challenges for the researcher. Some of the more familiar of these are cultural differences and the uncritical transfer of policies and programmes from one locality to another. One challenge often overlooked is distance. This is especially so for international comparative research, which can often require significant travel and thus access to sufficient funding. For those without research budgets, technology seems to provide an attractive solution. E-mail communication, in particular, can offer the researcher an avenue of access to participants at a distance without great expense. It seems a straightforward process, but it is not without its difficulties. Some methods of data collection, such as questionnaires, lend themselves well to e-mail communication. There seems little difference in encouraging participants to complete and return a questionnaire by e-mail rather than by standard mail. For semi-structured interviews intending to elicit data for a grounded theory approach, however, relying on e-mail for participant interviews can mean a wealth of rich and interesting data may be missed.

My doctoral research, at the University of Toronto, was a comparative study of government-initiated retraining programmes for former fisheries workers in Atlantic Canada and former miners in England, following the collapse of both industries. Interestingly, however, the difficulties I encountered were not in interviewing participants in England, but in Canada. I organised the research in England so that it coincided with two conferences, for which I had funds, and I had family with whom I could stay. Travel within England proved less of a difficulty than in Canada. With a reasonably priced train pass and less distance to cover than in Canada, I was able to meet all but one of the English participants; the one participant I was unable to meet with face to face was a result of that participant's choice, not because of expense or distance. The situation in Canada, however, was quite different. Research participants were located thousands of miles apart, in areas where the programme was implemented, the provinces of Newfoundland and Nova Scotia, and in the national capital, Ottawa, where the programme was developed. Interviewing each in person was just not possible, so I decided to do the interviews by e-mail. I should say that every participant did respond to the questions and provided quite a bit of information that contributed well to the research. In all, though, it was a bit clinical, unlike the in-person interviews where participants talked at length on many topics, not only those related to the programmes but the industry, the communities and the people as well. There is no comparison, I believe, between a three-hour, lively, interactive and dynamic interview versus two or three pages of formal response. Indeed, in experiencing the difference between in-person and e-mail interviews, the term 'rich data' became a reality for me rather than just academic jargon.

There are ways around some of these issues, as Nalita explains.

Qualitative online research can provide an arena such as e-mail in which research participants can be given a voice, and a context in which they can begin to explore how they see themselves. Yet how do research participants construct their identities in such sites? What techniques do they use to present themselves online, and how can researchers be assured about the authenticity of their identities? In such environments there is greater scope for participants to control the presentation of the self, and this can lead to both the production and the disclosure of new online personae, as well as those that can be concealed.

Such issues emerged in my study, which used asynchronous (non-real-time) e-mail interviews to examine academics' understandings of their identities and engagement in their work practice. All the academics in this study were located in higher education institutions across the UK, and due to practical constraints of money, time and travel it was not possible to meet with them face to face. Part of the study involved exploring how e-mail interviewing could be recognised as a legitimate method in the study of academics' lives, and how it could be used to generate narratives of their experience in their voices. I was also interested in the way in which the compression of space and time online meant that geographically dispersed groups and communities were no longer isolated from the contexts and traditions to which they belonged, providing a 'bounded space' within which it was possible to explore how they lived and worked (in the academic community in the UK, e-mail is used on a daily basis in working life for teaching and research; although it is not always perceived as a good thing, this did not make my participants resistant to taking part in the study). I wanted to use e-mail interviewing to gain a better understanding of the meanings that academics generate through conversation, and provided my participants with a more or less open environment in which to compose their narratives, recall and reconstruct their identities and better understand how they came to see themselves in their past and present careers. To facilitate the online interviews I e-mailed to the participants a rubric of how the interviews would be carried out. The rubric adopted a semi-structured interview schedule in which I sent out my research questions one at a time to each participant, rather than sending out a large number of questions at once. This approach formed a platform on which each participant could start to write their online narratives about how they perceived their professional lives. In adopting this approach, I hoped that the e-mail interviews would allow my participants to engage with the questions and sustain reflection on their professional lives.

In conducting the interviews online, I was presented with an ethical dilemma that I had not been aware of in my experiences of face-to-face interviews. I realised that I had to deal with how my participants would engage in the presentation of self in the absence of non-verbal communication such as gesture, tone of voice and facial expressions. As the e-mail interviews progressed I found that while the 'lived body' may be invisible during an online interview, mannered behaviours, pre-interpreted meanings and unstated assumptions were clearly 'visible' during the online conversations, which in turn influenced the nature of their online narratives. In effect, the participants were 'telling' their stories in ways that anchored their identity on the internet. Part of the problem was that conducting the interviews online increased the risk of the participants experimenting with self-presentation. Further, how could I be really sure who the person was behind the name, presenting further dilemmas about how to trust anything that the individual claimed to be? I also began to note that the ability for participants to mask their identity led them to be more active in voicing their opinions, which in turn began to shape the tone and atmosphere of the online interview. The absence of visual cues seemed to make it easier for some participants to start and terminate the e-mail interviews as and when it suited them, despite text-based cues such as 'Haven't heard from you in a while. I wondered if you still wished to continue the interview?' from the researcher. I also noted that some participants adopted the use of emoticons to make up for the absence of conversational cues, or exaggerated punctuation and capitalisation in their written descriptions to emphasise tone and strength of feeling on a particular topic, as illustrated below.

> I wasn't always sure that I knew what you were getting at... some of the questions seemed to overlap and I was concerned about maybe we were sometimes coming at something from different directions and maybe in e-mail communications clarification is not always easy:)!!

The dynamic, playful quality of the medium meant that the participants could express themselves in ways that allowed improvisation and word play to flourish. I also found that their online narratives were sometimes superficial and playful where it was evident that they did not always want to participate in substantive discussion.

What I had not accounted for was that the participants had not only brought place and identity with them but also found themselves simultaneously in a new space in which they could create perhaps new identities. I decided to address this issue by meeting participants offline to triangulate findings and enhance authenticity by examining the connections between their online and offline experiences. I therefore used the offline exchanges to probe further the narratives from the online interviews, and to follow up on issues that remained undeveloped or address those that had been omitted. This approach also enabled me to make more use of the visible body (voice, gesture, tone). Away from the online space, I continued to discuss the research with participants in face-to-face exchanges to 'insert the online world of the Internet into offline contexts, and vice versa' (Hine, 2000: 115). For example, one of my participants mentioned in her e-mail interview that she was concerned about losing her academic identity. When I met up with her at a meeting we were both attending, the participant talked about her experiences again. Later, when the e-mail interview resumed, I probed some more by linking to things that had been raised in the face-to-face conversations. The move between online and offline interaction encouraged the participants to elaborate on their experiences, adding further threads to the e-mail interviews.

Conclusion

Research methods textbooks are slowly beginning to reflect more of the real world of research. They still don't really deal with the questions of fear arising from the interviewee, raised by John, or fear arising from the context, raised by Katharine. Having to deal not only with internet interviews in your own country but face-to-face interviews in your comparator country, as outlined by Melissa, demands flexibility. Having to deal with the possibility that your interviewee is potentially inventing and acting out a completely new persona facilitated by cyberspace, as Nalita found, does not figure highly in the 'how-to' research manuals. As this chapter has repeatedly demonstrated and Vikki outlined in detail, the terror of technology has remained a constant over the working lives of our group.

Finally, there is one factor that can never quite be catered for. The stupidity of the researcher, in this case Al's insistence on combining fieldwork with alcohol, is a factor that will remain a constant over time and never quite get the prominence in textbooks that it perhaps deserves.

13

Researching train-based working

Donald Hislop

Introduction

This chapter presents some reflections upon the practical difficulties that a colleague and I experienced and dealt with in a study of spatially mobile workers' attempts to work while travelling by train, conducted in the UK in the summer of 2006. The primary aim of the chapter is to present some practical insights into the problems and challenges related to planning and executing academic research in this context, and to use these insights to think about some of the skills, such as adaptability, that it is useful for academic researchers to possess. While the research context reported on here is quite specific (moving train carriages), with its own particular characteristics that are different from the contexts in which research is often carried out in (such as offices and homes), some of the issues that had to be dealt with, for example coping with unanticipated circumstances, are arguably generic and relevant to all types of research carried out in any context.

The study reported on here was very enjoyable to carry out, and gave great insights into the difficulties faced by people attempting to work on trains. Further, as outlined below, the study was relatively successful in terms of meeting the research objectives that were set. However, planning for and actually carrying out the research (giving surveys to relevant passengers) involved dealing with a number of challenges, some of which were anticipated in advance and some of which occurred unanticipated while the research was being carried out.

Context

A number of factors have combined in recent years to allow work to be done not only from an increasingly diverse range of locations but also while travelling (Hislop, 2008). Foremost among these is the rapid, ongoing and apparently unending development and evolution of mobile communication and computer technologies. Thus, in the space of approximately ten years, mobile phones have evolved from being simple telephony devices to incorporating a wide range of other business (and personal) functionality, including video, e-mail, internet and computer capabilities. The last ten years have also seen the birth and rapid diffusion (particularly in North America) of the Blackberry mobile e-mail device, which allows people to have automatic access to their up-to-date e-mail in a handheld device that fits easily into the pocket. Thirdly, recent years have witnessed an equally dramatic evolution in computer technologies which have facilitated mobile working, with the development of small handheld computers (often referred to as PDAs – personal digital assistants), and the increasing miniaturisation of laptop computers. Finally, the last few years have seen the development of wireless internet facilities (sometimes referred to as WiFi), with an increasing number of mobile devices having wireless internet functionality built in and an increasing range of locations (such as cafés, hotels, airports, etc.) providing wireless internet facilities.

These technologies have the potential to allow workers to communicate and do computer-based work in a much wider range of locations than has ever historically been possible. Thus in many countries and cities it is now not uncommon to find people working in cafés, restaurants, hotel lobbies, parks, railway stations and airport departure lounges. Further, the use of these technologies is not confined to static locations, with it being increasingly possible for people to work while on the move, such as while commuting or on work-related journeys. Thus people can increasingly be found to be conducting work-related calls on mobile phones while driving, as well as working and communicating on train and plane journeys.

To investigate these issues a research project was designed which focused on one particular domain of activity: train carriages. This context was chosen for two primary reasons. Firstly, my own eye-witness evidence as well as other anecdotal evidence suggested that significant numbers of people are working (or attempting to work) while travelling by train. The second reason was that train-based working appeared to be an interesting context to study, as while utopian rhetoric on mobile computer and communication technologies suggests that armed with relevant technologies people can work 'anytime, anywhere', anecdotal evidence and personal experience suggested that train carriages often prove to be challenging locations to work in. For example, factors such as noise levels, the amount of train movement, the availability of mobile phone signals, constraints of space or even a lack of access to seating all have the potential to disrupt and make difficult people's work efforts.

Thus these personal experiences led me to undertake the research whose methods are reported on here; at the most general level, it was concerned with understanding issues such as the type of tasks that people on work-related journeys attempted to carry out, the extent to which and ways in which they used any mobile computer and communication technologies they had, and how the character of the train context affected their work efforts (for some details of the study's findings see Axtell and Hislop, 2007).

Aims and empirical details of the study

To conduct this research (which was carried out by myself and Carolyn Axtell, from Sheffield University's Institute of Work Psychology) it was felt that the best way to identify participants for a study of business passengers on trains who were working was actually to travel on some trains and identify relevant passengers. Such a methodology required a train operating company to provide access to its trains. Once the permission of one UK train operating company had been received, this research method became feasible. The project that was carried out was small scale and exploratory in nature, as it was self-funded and all research was carried out by Carolyn and myself.

Other studies of train-based working have utilised a range of methods to investigate such questions, including surveys, focus groups, diary studies, ethnographic observation and interviews (Felstead et al., 2005; Lyons et al., 2007). For our study it was decided to use a two-stage methodology. The first part of the research involved handing out surveys to relevant passengers on a number of trains. The second stage involved conducting semi-structured interviews with a sample of the survey respondents. The purpose of using this type of two-stage methodology was to collect both statistical data on broad travel and work patterns and some more in-depth, qualitative data via the interviews. The focus in this chapter is on the challenges and difficulties of the first stage of the study, where the surveys were handed out to relevant passengers.

The surveys were distributed on 12 train journeys spread over three days in June 2006. On each day both parts of two return journeys between a city in Yorkshire and a city in the West Midlands (a journey of approximately 70–80 minutes) were surveyed by one of the researchers. The 12 journeys researched were selected to cover a range of times (from early-morning commuter trains through a number of daytime trains to evening rush-hour trains). This was done in order to get responses from both passengers who were commuting to and from work (but who worked while travelling) and those who made work-related train journeys during the day (for example to attend meetings at different sites).

To ensure that as many relevant respondents as possible completed the survey, the researcher walked up and down through the train during the course of the journey (between one and three stops were made by the trains on the portion of the journey that was researched). Respondents had the option either to complete the survey immediately and return it to the researcher at a later stage of their journey, or post the completed survey back to the researchers at a later date in a prepaid envelope supplied to them.

The research was relatively successful in a number of dimensions, such as identifying a significant number of relevant people to distribute the surveys to (514 were distributed), the high response rate (334 usable responses were received, giving a response rate of 65 per cent), the low refusal rate of relevant passengers declining to complete the survey and the number of people who agreed to be interviewed in the second stage (120). However, there were a number of issues, problems and challenges related to both the planning and the execution of the survey part of the research. The chapter now changes focus to examine these issues.

Issues/challenges related to distributing surveys on trains

The difficulty of predicting the number of surveys needed

The key challenge that had to be dealt with prior to the surveys being distributed was to calculate the number of surveys we would need. We had decided to code the surveys so that we could identify which journey each respondent had travelled on. We therefore had to plan in advance how many surveys would be needed for each of the 12 journeys to be surveyed. The two key questions we had to think about for each journey were firstly how many people would be travelling, and secondly what proportion of passengers were likely to be on work-related journeys. As the journeys to be surveyed were deliberately chosen to cover a range of times, the answers to these questions were likely to vary significantly between the journeys. Even knowing the number of carriages on each train and their seating capacity was of limited help, as we knew that passenger numbers could massively exceed the seating capacity on the busiest journeys, where large numbers of people often had to stand.

Ultimately we had to make educated guesses, with these being shaped by concerns of not having too many surveys printed, and on the other hand not underestimating the numbers needed, which would have meant we ran out of surveys before a journey had been completely surveyed. In the end we decided to have 100 surveys for each journey, even though we thought this would be too many for some journeys, as we felt it was better to have too many than too few surveys.

Overall, this decision proved to be reasonable, as it meant we didn't run out of surveys, but it did contribute to a weight problem we had (see following section), and on one particular route 100 surveys turned out not to be enough. The coding of the surveys to indicate the journey they were distributed on was done by hand, with a very small letter and number being written on the back to indicate the day and journey number (such as M1 for Monday, journey one). On all but one of the journeys we covered, 100 surveys were more than enough (on the quietest journey we only gave out 17), but on the busiest journey I ran out of surveys before having travelled through the whole train. The full extent of how busy this train was didn't become apparent until I had boarded it, thus I hadn't coded the journey details on extra surveys in advance. I began distributing the 100 surveys that I had, and when I ran out I decided to recode some surveys that had been left over from a previous journey, which meant finding a seat and quickly changing the journey coding details. I was able to do this and did manage to complete the surveying of that journey (with 130 surveys in the end being distributed).

The micro-logistics of carrying and distributing a large number of surveys

Due to the context in which we were distributing the surveys, we had to carry with us all the surveys that were to be distributed on a particular day. As we had decided to have 100 surveys for each journey, and only one of us would do the research on a particular day, this meant that on each of the three days of the study the designated researcher for the day began with a bag containing 400 two-page surveys plus 400 envelopes. The weight and space implications of this only dawned on us when we began to prepare for the first day's research. Basically, at the start of each day we had to carry a large, heavy bag full of surveys.

Carrying this bag on the first day's research proved problematic, partly because the weather turned out to be very hot (which made it uncomfortable to carry a large, heavy bag), and also because the amount of congestion on the first train surveyed, an early-morning commuter train, made it impractical for me to carry the bag as I walked through the train. Thus in the process of distributing the surveys on this train I decided to put the bag of surveys down in a storage space between two seats. Unfortunately, when I returned to collect them it took me a few minutes to relocate the bag, as I couldn't remember precisely where I had put it down, which led to a momentary panic that it had either been lost or accidentally picked up by someone else.

Coping with unanticipated events

The distribution of the surveys on the first day of the research was further complicated by an event that we had not anticipated at all. That June Monday happened to be the day after a very large three-day outdoor rock festival (which over 100,000 people attended), and the trains we were surveying stopped at the station closest to the festival site. Thus when the first train I was distributing surveys on arrived at this station, the train was virtually taken over by a large number of tired concert-goers carrying quantities of camping equipment who were making their way home. Not only did they occupy every available free seat, but significant numbers also occupied much of the standing room, making it problematic for anyone to walk through the train. This therefore made it very difficult for me to proceed through the train and distribute the surveys to all business passengers.

However, by carefully stepping over people and their luggage it was possible for me slowly to continue distributing surveys to relevant passengers. But congestion levels were such, on all the trains surveyed on the Monday, that my conversations with passengers, explaining what I was doing and attempting to identify whether they were relevant people to complete the survey, were typically very public, being witnessed by quizzical concert-goers.

Identifying relevant people to ask to complete the survey

In distributing our surveys we were looking for a very particular type of respondent: only those who were in paid employment, who were travelling by train for work-related purposes and who (sometimes) attempted to work while on such journeys. However, differentiating such people from other passengers was recognised as not always being easy. For example, it may be difficult to distinguish passengers on work-related journeys from other passengers on the basis of dress, as focusing our attention on people dressed only in formal business clothes could have biased our survey. Equally, focusing only on people who were actually working when we passed them also had potential limitations, as this may have meant ignoring people who were relevant but who undertook work when we weren't passing them. On the other hand, we didn't want to approach every single passenger due to the time demands this would involve. We thus had to decide on how selective an approach to adopt. In the end we used a relatively broad approach, and agreed to ignore only passengers who seemed to be very obviously not in paid employment or not on a work-related journey (for example the elderly and parents with children).

While this strategy of approaching people to identify their relevance for our research had the advantage of minimising the risk that we would accidentally fail to approach a potentially relevant respondent, its downside became apparent on the busiest trains we surveyed. On such trains it was necessary to approach and talk to a significant number of passengers, which was not only quite time-consuming but also became highly repetitive, with the same question having to be asked repeatedly as we slowly walked through the trains.

Visual data: importance and challenges

As outlined, prior to conducting the research it was anticipated that working on trains was often likely to be challenging, due to noise levels, space constraints, etc. This proved to be the case, and was visually apparent to us during the distribution of the surveys, as many times people were seen attempting to do things like look through a lot of paperwork when they either had to stand or had limited space around them, read a document in a noisy train carriage, discreetly make a private phone call, make use of a number of mobile technological devices when there was limited space, etc.

On some of the journeys when congestion levels were significant, we witnessed a number of notable incidents where people were attempting to work in particularly difficult circumstances. For example, one memorable incident happened on the day that the trains became filled with music festival-goers. This particular incident involved a middle-aged male passenger who was standing in a vestibule area close to one of the carriage toilets, trying to work on a laptop (which was balanced on one of his arms) while surrounded by tired festival-goers on their way home, and who had constantly to stop working and move the laptop to allow passengers to pass him.

Capturing visual data on such incidents has the potential to provide rich and important insights into the challenges and experience of train-based working. However, the *ad hoc* nature of the type of incident that may provide useful visual data, combined with the public nature of train carriages, raises challenges to both capturing them as they occur and gaining the consent of those captured in such images to being photographed.

Discussion

These fieldwork experiences highlight both general issues likely to be relevant to the conduct of any type of empirical fieldwork and some quite specific issues related to researching mobile workers' experiences of working in and travelling through public spaces.

The most general issue that emerged from our study, and one that can be related to the conduct of virtually any type of empirical fieldwork, is the need for the researcher to cope with some level of unavoidable uncertainty, and as a consequence for the researcher to be prepared to be adaptable and flexible in order to deal with changing and potentially unforeseen circumstances. In the case of our study there was an unavoidable level of uncertainty over potential passenger numbers on the trains that we were surveying and the potential congestion levels, if any, we'd have to cope with as a consequence. Ultimately, the end of a rock festival of which we had been totally unaware had one of the biggest impacts on the first day of our research. This required flexibility from us in terms of having to recode extra surveys on one journey due to unexpectedly high passenger numbers, and having to leave some of the surveys in a luggage rack to be returned to later. It also meant having to conduct the research in challenging circumstances, where carriage temperatures were hot, physically moving through the trains due to high passenger numbers proved difficult and there was no scope for any level of privacy in conversations we had with passengers who we were asking to complete the surveys.

This uncertainty was partly to do with the fact that the research we were doing was in a public space, where scope for the researcher to control conditions is virtually non-existent. However, arguably whatever type of research is being conducted, and whatever context it is carried out in, researchers need to be flexible in order to cope with the particular circumstances that present themselves. Thus, for example, conducting one-to-one interviews in a private space, while being a physical context that is more controllable by the researcher, also requires the researcher to be flexible and adaptable in coping with and responding to the often variable and unpredictable ways that different interviewees may respond to the same questions.

However, there are a number of issues raised by these research experiences that relate to the particular difficulties and demands of conducting research on mobile workers in public spaces. Most fundamentally, conducting research in public spaces such as train carriages may be problematic for a researcher who is particularly shy. The research we conducted required us to be reasonably gregarious and extroverted. Firstly, the conversations we had with potential and actual survey respondents had to be conducted in front of witnesses, and in the case of the busiest trains this often involved a number of people watching and listening to what we were asking passengers. Secondly, the nature of the research context meant that we were inevitably approaching people 'cold', as they had had no forewarning that they may be asked to participate in a research project. Thus in approaching people to see if they were interested in participating in our research, we typically had to interrupt them from other activities (such as talking or reading) before we could explain the purpose of our research.

While the focus here has been purely upon the distribution of surveys on trains, the use of other research methods (such as taking photographs, as suggested in the previous section) may also be difficult and challenging. For example, conducting interviews in this context may be difficult and problematic. The benefit of attempting to conduct interviews *in situ* while business passengers are travelling is that doing so may reveal insights that would not be gained by conducting the interview in another context (such as the extent to which tannoy announcements are an interruption). However, space and noise constraints, and a general lack of privacy, make train carriages far from ideal locations in which to carry out research interviews.

Overall, therefore, as the ongoing evolution of mobile computer and communication technologies contributes to changing the nature of people's work experiences, through providing the potential for workers to be mobile and work from a wide range of 'non-traditional' locations, academic researchers, in attempting to 'follow' and understand the experiences of such workers, will have to deal with a new set of research challenges.

14

A story about being engaged in research: buzzing bees, small business and Australian unfair dismissal laws

Rowena Barrett

Introduction

Protection for employees from unfair dismissal (UFD) has been around in Australia under various guises for 30 years or so (Chapman, 2006). Labour standards, and particularly ILO Convention 158 (Convention Concerning Termination of Employment at the Initiative of the Employer 1982), underpin the adoption of a particular form of federal statutory UFD regime which first appeared in the 1993 reforms to the Industrial Relations Act 1998 (Commonwealth). Its existence, however, has not been uncontroversial, and the meaning, operation, scope and remedies have attracted attention over time. In fact, the first reforms to the federal UFD regime were undertaken under the Keating Labor government three months after they were enacted (Chapman, ibid.). Further reforms were made by the incoming Howard Liberal-national coalition government through the Workplace Relations Act 1996 (Commonwealth) (WRA), and arguably these reforms continued down the 'contraction' path (ibid.).

The UFD provisions in the federal legislation are central to this chapter. However, my key concern is with the basis for further contraction, which surfaced in the late 1990s and was championed by various federal ministers for workplace relations, including Peter Reith and Tony Abbott as well as the then Prime Minister John Howard. Jobs, and especially small business jobs – 53,000 of them to be precise, or was that 50,000? – were what the coalition and its supporters said would be the result of further reforms to the UFD regime. With each (failed) attempt to get the WRA amended, the mantra – 'UFD inhibits job growth, especially in small business' – seemed to gain momentum. The bees started to buzz when this mantra penetrated my consciousness late in 2001, entering the space created after returning to work from maternity leave and the award of my PhD on industrial relations in small business.

This chapter is a story about a research project and a series of actions along the way that emerged from the buzzing of those bees in my bonnet. It is not so much about undertaking fieldwork, as perhaps the majority of other chapters in this book are, but instead it is a story about what drove me to undertake a particular piece of work and the array of outcomes that can emerge along the way. Basically, having just completed a PhD on industrial relations in small business, and in doing so reading everything on the topic that I could lay my hands on, I became increasingly aware of this mantra about small business and jobs and was unconvinced that exempting small businesses from UFD would generate the number of jobs proposed. Moreover, in my PhD I had argued that strategies to control the labour process in small businesses could be similar to those used by management in larger ones. In other words, small might be beautiful in some circumstances, but the variety of small business employment relations could only be explained by considering both structural forces and human agency. This meant I was concerned about this assumption that small *was* beautiful. The debate and discussion centred on the creation of jobs, but there was never any mention of the quality of those jobs. For me this was problematic, given the evidence of the poor quality of many small business jobs, especially so when measuring quality in terms of objective factors such as wages, hours, employment security, skills, training and career opportunities.

So my story in this chapter is about the ways in which academics can be motivated to undertake research and use this as a means to voice their concerns and generate different sorts of research outputs. It is a story about becoming engaged in public debate: using your voice but making sure what you're saying is evidence-based. If we want to be academic about this, then my story can be put in terms of wider debates about evidence-based policy and how the research-policy nexus can be bridged. This story is not about ways of collecting data, but research more generally and the non-standard outputs that might result. It's therefore about undertaking research that matters.

Small business is the backbone of the economy...

In Australia the debate around unfair dismissal and jobs came with a figure that initially 53,000 jobs would be created (although this was later amended to 50,000). It was questionable where this figure originally came from, although signs did point in the direction of COSBOA (Council of Small Business Organisations of Australia). However, the Workplace Relations Minister Tony Abbot made the calculation clear when he said in parliament, 'If one in 20 small business employers in Australia took on an extra employee because of a changed legislative framework for unfair dismissal, then an extra 53,000 jobs would result' (House of Representatives Hansard, 13 February 2002: 47).

He of course prefaced his comment with one of my least favourite descriptions of small business, as the 'engine room' – this time of job growth, but it's usually said in the context of the economy more generally. Small businesses are numerous in most developed and developing economies. In Australia the situation is no different, with some 97 per cent of all businesses being small. But it was only really with the work by David Birch (1979) that the importance of small businesses as job generators was highlighted. He claimed that from 1969 to 1976 about two-thirds of employment growth, in a sample of 5.6 million US establishments, came from businesses with less than 20 employees. Further, independent businesses within this sample (those that were not small establishments of larger businesses) accounted for over 50 per cent of the recorded employment growth. Businesses with less than 100 employees were found to generate nearly 80 per cent of the employment increase recorded in this period. In a time of increasing unemployment, governments began to wake up to the potential for small businesses to generate lots of new jobs.

Arguably, 'lots of' doesn't mean much more than that. The Birch study was not without its critiques and critics, and many of the later attempts to establish firmly the relationship between small business and job generation have suffered from empirical and methodological issues (see Kirchhoff and Greene, 1998). Yes, small businesses do create jobs, if only at the point of starting. We can see that in the numbers of small businesses that employ no one except the owner – this is the case for some 80 per cent of all Australian small firms. Moreover, it is well established that many small businesses will not grow and many will fail. David Storey (1982) estimated there was a 0.5–0.75 per cent probability that a new firm will have 100 or more employees within ten years of start-up. That's if they survive ten years, as the failure rate for new small businesses is high and many will not last past their third birthday.

From observer to participant...

All this sort of analysis had been background reading for my PhD, but my concentration was on getting my PhD finished rather than applying this analysis to the debate. However, with the government's renewed attempt in 2001 to exempt small business from the UFD provisions in the WRA, and this time with a revised definition of small business (increasing the number from those employing less than 15 to those employing less than 20), I began to become more interested. The tipping point was two articles in the *Australian Financial Review* (*AFR*) and *The Age* on 3 December 2001. The headline of the *AFR* read 'Labor softens stance on unfair dismissal' (Murphy, 2001), while the article in *The Age* had the headline 'ALP to do deal on unfair dismissal' (Taylor, 2001). The essence of both was – as the headlines indicated – to report that the opposition workplace relations spokesman, Rob McClelland, was considering some conditional support for the coalition's amendments.

So I wrote a letter to the editors of both papers, saying I was curious to see the basis for the ALP's support for the coalition's attempts to exempt small businesses from UFD provisions. I was particularly curious given that in my research I had not found any academic studies showing UFD inhibits employment in small firms; what I had found instead were UK studies, such as those by Dickens et al. (1985) and Westrip (1982), which showed a greater tendency for small-firm employees to be unfairly dismissed. Moreover, I said, I had come across a range of studies (for example Loveman and Sengenberger, 1990; Parker, 2000; Revesz and Lattimore, 1997) showing job quality in small firms to be, on average, lower than that in larger firms. What I drew from this was that employees in small firms appeared to need more, rather than less, protection from the industrial relations system. I finished my letter by saying I thought that 'the ALP should be proactive and focus their attention on developing policy that seeks to ensure small business employers know how to recruit and retain the right people for the business and then, if necessary, how to dismiss employees legally'. This would, I said, decrease the need for small business owners to use UFD provisions.

My letter was published in the *AFR* the very next day (4 December 2001) under the headline 'Unfair dismissal laws for big and small'. Clearly I'd hit a nerve, as not much later in the day I got a phone call from the editor of the *AFR*'s Enterprise section asking me if I was interested in writing two pieces for him around the issue. We had a bit of a discussion about my views on the subject, and he offered me 800 words for a main piece on 'whether there was something in this debate' and a second piece of six to eight paragraphs on the most relevant international study on UFD and small business. That was a Tuesday, and he asked me to get this to him by the Sunday evening.

Journalistic deadlines are quite different to academic ones!

This was the impetus for me to do some 'serious' research on the topic. But I had also stirred up some opposition to my views. On the Wednesday (5 December 2001) a letter from Bob Day of Adelaide appeared in the *AFR* under the headline of 'Employing staff is fraught with danger', which basically said I was bonkers. That was my first reading of it anyway: it actually said it 'beggars belief' that I hadn't found any evidence of UFD legislation inhibiting employment. Bob Day wrote, 'Talk to any small business owner and they will tell you why they refuse to employ people – it's simply too expensive, too complicated and too dangerous. I've lost count of the number of horror stories told to me by owners who have been dragged off to unfair dismissal tribunals.' His argument was 'an impediment to fire is an impediment to hire', and he concluded that 'We have to start making it easier to employ.'

No pressure! On Friday (7 December 2001) that same week two more letters responded to mine. Both were taking me to task for saying there was a lack of published studies showing UFD inhibits employment in small business. One was from Mark Paterson, CEO of the Australian Chamber of Commerce and Industry (ACCI) – 'Unfair dismissal laws are hurting jobs' – pointing to their surveys of small business, including a pre-election survey showing UFD to be an important issue of concern for small business. The other letter was by Jean Raar, an academic at Deakin University ('Proactive approach to hiring is needed'), pointing to a study she and colleagues had undertaken on small businesses in the manufacturing industry which showed UFD was 'a component in a factor pattern that is discouraging small business managers in their staff employment decisions'. Trying to hold my nerve and working to a deadline meant all I could do was think of this as grist to the mill.

Pitching the story...

I used to be a teacher of English in secondary schools and I know that stories need an 'angle' – telling the bare facts is often not enough – and really the same can be said for any academic article, in this case two pieces for the newspaper. I decided that the angle for my articles would be 'What is the problem?' Were the UFD provisions in the WRA the 'problem' for small business owners? Did they make small businesses think twice about employing staff? Or were they a symptom of some other problem? In taking this line I was picking up on the last bit in my letter: 'if small business employers know how to recruit and retain the right people for the business and then, if necessary, how to dismiss employees legally, their need for recourse to unfair dismissal provisions would be reduced'.

So the question became: does UFD inhibit job generation? As indicated earlier, there are a range of answers to that question and they will change depending upon the ontological and methodological approach of the research. As will the answer to whether small business owners are affected in their hiring decisions by the UFD regime.

However, there are some problems when it comes to researching small business, underpinned by a lack of conceptual clarity and hence who makes up the small business sector. As a result, just about any survey can be critiqued, especially for sample size, selection, representativeness and generalisability, and more generally for question wording, assumptions, analysis techniques and the power of the tests, etc. Qualitative research, on the other hand, can attract as many critiques and more.

Moreover, the passion imbuing the letters responding to my own was illustrative of the degree to which, in the small business field, people are labelled as 'those who know' and 'those who don't'. A good example of this came in a letter published in the *AFR* on Monday 10 December 2001. Under the heading of 'An incentive not to employ people', Murray Baker of Roseville, NSW, who had been in business for 14 years, said it was an 'extreme example of hubris' for me to 'pontificate on employment laws' when, as an academic, I would never have employed anyone. His argument was I would not know that 'Business is hard enough without the added burden of petty laws to penalize people taking on the risk of trying to better themselves.' Moreover, it might come as a 'great shock' to me that 'the main focus of business is not to employ people – it is to reward people who are taking the financial risk!' While he could see both sides of the argument, writing 'Naturally, there must be a balance between the interest of the employer and employee', he then went on, 'however, it is difficult to take seriously the view that the role of government is to legislate for the protection of employees and not to acknowledge the risk-takers'. Clearly academics such as me are in the 'those who can't, teach' camp!

The small business field is a funny place. Despite the large number of businesses and the many people employed within them, few academics have made this 'sector' their interest. The loudest voices in this debate therefore come from the small businesses themselves, but only usually when channelled through national or state-based employer associations. The available evidence on the impact of UFD on small business was therefore limited and largely in the form of contract research undertaken for government or groups representing small business interests, or government documents.

Government documents are not a light read. The various parliamentary documents around the issue included a review by the Department of Employment, Workplace Relations and Small Business (1998), which had been prompted by the 1996 Time for Business Taskforce. Then there were the five bills that had been put forward to amend the WRA since 1997. The latest, the Workplace Relations Amendment (Unfair Dismissals) Bill 1998 (Commonwealth), had also been referred by the Senate to the Senate Employment, Workplace Relations, Small Business and Education Legislation Committee for inquiry, so there was another report containing various views on the matter (which was released in February 1999). In addition there were, of course, the various explanatory memoranda attached to the bills and the associated speeches in parliament recorded in Hansard. (The history of the fate of these amendments in parliament is well documented by Pittard, 2002.)

I also searched more widely for international studies of UFD and the effect of employment protection legislation on employment in small business. Unsurprisingly, my search revealed very little other than what I had already mentioned in my letter to the editor. These studies, by and large, focused on why small business employers had developed such a fear of UFD provisions. Essentially they were studies of what happens inside the small business in regards to managing staff. As a result, for academics the critical issue is the informality of small business management and employment practices. So in terms of the UFD debate, the problem is what happens when managing people isn't as commonsense or straightforward as originally thought.

In the article I wanted to address the issue of informality, but also to convey my understanding of the difficulties small business people face. To this end what I did was 'deconstruct' a quote from a small business employer which had been made in the ABS Business Growth and Performance survey and included in an Industry Commission research paper I had found. The quote was as follows.

> We recently employed someone who had been unemployed for 4 years. The hours of work and skill levels did not match exactly what we wanted, but we gave the person a go. The person was completely unsuitable and was dismissed. Now we face unfair dismissal proceedings... never again will I give such a person a go until this legislation is repealed. It is counterproductive to creating employment.

My starting point therefore became, 'what's the problem?' Why did the employment relationship end in such unhappy circumstances? I thought (and still do) that the problem illustrated here was not the UFD provisions in the legislation, rather that encountering those provisions was a result of problems with the employer's recruitment and retention strategies. This didn't just come off the top of my head: it was well established in the little literature that existed that formalised practices were not likely to exist in small businesses, whether as a result of resource poverty, newness, inexperienced management or a lack of managerial skills. I thought this quote clearly showed that it wasn't the legislation inhibiting small business employers from hiring more staff, but them not knowing how to get and keep the 'right' person. Recourse to UFD was an outcome of the larger problem of ineffective recruitment, selection and retention strategies in small (and large) businesses.

How could this be fitted into the wider research on employment relations/human resource management in small business? By writing about studies of recruitment in small business, I could support my argument and point to a reliance on informal, word-of-mouth methods. These studies showed that this increases as firm size decreases, to the point where recruitment in the smallest businesses can be conditional on the availability of a known individual. This is understandable when there are only a few people working closely together and they need to get on. However, the legislation made allowance for this with the three-month 'cooling-off' (probation) period, which was introduced in August 2001. This meant those who didn't 'fit in' could be let go within this period without the UFD provisions applying.

I went on to argue that the use of informal recruitment practices could mean the 'right' person may not be employed because of not having a large enough pool of suitable recruits. Additionally, by using informal methods, employers could leave themselves open to accusations of indirect discrimination. However, all may not be lost if the 'not quite right' or 'almost right' person was employed, as training could be used to fill the gap between the recruit's current skills, knowledge and expertise and what was needed for the job. To reduce costs this could be done in-house or on the job: maybe as simply as having an employee work alongside the new recruit until they'd 'gotten the hang of the job'. However, I also pointed out that research told us that small businesses were less likely than larger ones to invest in formal (off-the-job) training, and this might be problematic for developing non-firm-specific skills or qualifications. A performance management system is how these problems would be identified and rectified – once again, though, evidence suggested performance would be managed informally in small business. Essentially small business people were too busy working *in* their business to spend time working *on* their business.

I finished the article by pointing to the importance of management style. I referred to a UK Department of Trade and Industry (DTI) study of UFD in hotels and catering, transport and engineering sectors by Goodman et al. (1998) and Earnshaw et al. (1998). They found that where a management style emphasising trust, communication and teambuilding prevailed, disciplinary procedures were less likely to be used and UFD cases were less likely to arise. They also found that the immediate response to defending a UFD claim was to implement a dismissal procedure to avoid further claims.

The essence of my article, therefore, was to take the adage 'people are important resources' and say that if small business employers don't think about how these resources are deployed and managed, then problems will occur. I put this under the heading of 'Unfair dismissal and small business: Cure the disease not the symptom'.

In the second article I reviewed the study that I thought best exemplified the cross-over between academia and government, which had been undertaken by academics from Manchester University for the UK DTI. Under the heading of 'A question of evidence', I outlined that the study had sought to examine the major influences on the operation of disciplinary procedures in the context of arguments for and against further change to the UK UFD legislation. I also argued that a number of points from their matched comparisons of predominantly small businesses in the hotels and catering, transport and engineering sectors could be applied to the UFD debate in Australia. Basically the argument was that the non-existence of procedures for dealing with grievances was more important than firm size in whether a firm faced a UFD case. To make my point I suggested we needed to know whether those small business employers who had faced a UFD had a disciplinary procedure in place or not.

However, I also sought to place my argument in the context of the value of evidence-based policy, and concluded that in this whole debate firm size might just be a red herring given that research by the National Institute of Labour Studies in South Australia for a government department had failed to find any statistical significance between firm size and attitudes towards UFD (Wooden and Harding, 1997).

After e-mailing the articles to the editor on the Sunday, I sat back and waited to see whether I would stir up more protest. They were published in the *AFR* on Tuesday 11 December but under slightly different headlines: 'Dismissal law reform is not the answer' (p. 41) and 'Disciplinary procedures can reduce the success of claims' (p. 40).

There was no response! Well, except for a letter from Bob Day (the person who wrote the first letter responding to mine). He wrote to my then vice chancellor calling for my dismissal, as my claim that 'unfair dismissal does not inhibit employment in small business' was 'so absurd that it goes beyond questions of competency' and that 'such public pronouncements bring the University into disrepute'. How do I know this? Well, thankfully, the vice chancellor believed in academic freedom, and sent me a copy of the letter with a brief note saying 'keep up the good work'!

But there was still more evidence to be put forward...

It was fascinating work putting together these articles, but I hadn't exhausted all the material I'd found. What's more, an opinion piece had been published in *The Age* by John Howe and Jill Murray (5 December 2001), who were researchers at the University of Melbourne's Centre for Employment and Labour Relations Law. They opened up a new angle of attack: in arguing their case for a lack of evidence for the government's desire to exclude small business from UFD, they drew on a case that had been heard in the Federal Court the previous month, *Hamzy v Tricon International Restaurants t/as KFC and ors* (16 November 2001) FCA 1589, which dealt with the application of UFD to casual employees.

I knew John from my undergraduate days, so I got in touch and after exchanging pleasantries I asked, given our mutual interests, whether he was interested in jointly authoring an article on the UFD legislation, small business and job growth. Unfortunately he was too busy finishing his own PhD, but he suggested I read the *Hamzy* case in more detail. Essentially the judgment from the Full Court (Wilcox, Marshall and Katz JJ) made it clear that the relationship between unfair dismissal and job creation was questionable.

You know you're a nerd when you get excited by this stuff, and I am and I was! 'Doing' research is like putting together a jigsaw – you must have all the bits and put them in the right place to get the full picture. Here were the bits I had.

- Most small businesses are not covered by the federal workplace relations legislation, and in the explanatory memorandum to the Workplace Relations and Other Legislation Amendment (Small Business and Other Measures) Bill 2001 the federal government estimated some 180,000 (or one in five) small businesses operated in the federal jurisdiction (p. 5). Further, it estimated that in these small businesses only 35 per cent of employees (some 770,000 or one in ten Australian workers) were covered by the federal system (p. 6).

- Most small businesses operate under industrial laws, including UFD, in state jurisdictions. In the explanatory memorandum that was put as 'the number of unfair dismissal applications by employees in small business in the federal jurisdiction has averaged around 7,700 applications in the past 4 years' (p. 10). In other words, less than 2,000 applications per year are from small business. There had been 35,099 UFD applications since the WRA's commencement up to 30 June 2001 (Australian Industrial Relations Commission/Australian Industrial Registry, 2001), and 34 per cent of applications from December 1997 to November 2000 were against employers of 15 or fewer employees (Department of Employment, Workplace Relations and Small Business, 2001). While differences in reporting periods and definitions of 'small business' meant these numbers did not add up, they showed there wasn't an outbreak of federal UFD applications in the small business sector. On the contrary, they suggested a problem in medium-sized and large businesses.

- The WRA (at s. 170CG(3)(a)) already directs the Australian Industrial Relations Commission to take into account firm size when assessing whether dismissal procedures were reasonable (Department of Employment, Workplace Relations and Small Business, 2000).

In summary, this tells us that the countless hours and public dollars spent by the coalition government in trying to exempt small business from the provisions would have saved fewer than 2,000 UFD applications per year. But would it have generated 53,000 small business jobs? This was where the *Hamzy* case came into play, because in determining whether 'the regulation was supported by statutory provision regarding employees in relation to whom the operation of the termination of employment provisions would cause "substantial problems because of their particular conditions of employment"', the Federal Court also tried to examine the relationship between UFD and job generation.

Even when backed by an expert witness (Mark Wooden, professorial fellow, Melbourne Institute for Applied Economic and Social Research, University of Melbourne), the government's claim could not be substantiated. When commenting on ABS figures documenting casual employment growth, particularly among 15–19-year-olds, Professor Wooden stated 'the application of the unfair dismissal provisions of the federal Workplace Relations Act 1996 to the types of casual employees excluded by the regulations would have an adverse effect on job creation in Australia' (p. 69 of affidavit and quoted at p. 59, FCA 1589). Unfortunately no evidence was presented to support this assertion, and under cross-examination he said, 'there certainly hasn't been any direct research on the effect of introducing unfair dismissal laws' (p. 60).

Furthermore, Professor Wooden agreed with the statement that 'the existence or non-existence of unfair dismissal legislation has very little to do with the growth of employment and that it is dictated by economic factors' (p. 66). This left the Federal Court judges to conclude, 'in the absence of any evidence about this matter, it seems to us the suggestion of a relationship between unfair dismissal laws and employment inhibition is unproven' (p. 70).

'There is no evidence' was the theme of an article I wrote and sent to the *Journal of Industrial Relations* (*JIR*) on 8 January 2002. On the advice of the editors and in response to the referees, the revised article became a research note and was returned on 6 March 2002. It was published in 2003 (Barrett, 2003).

Ongoing action...

Another attempt to exempt small business from UFD was made through the Workplace Relations Amendment (Fair Termination) Bill 2002 (Commonwealth). This time the prime minister made it clear the matter was a potential trigger for a double dissolution of parliament (the dissolution of both houses of parliament has only occurred six times in the history of the federal parliament). I wrote another piece for the *AFR* (Barrett, 2002) and met with the opposition minister for workplace relations, Robert McClelland, who gave me a good hearing and then referred to my 'evidence' in parliament (House of Representatives Hansard, 20 February 2002: 377). After the publication of the *JIR* article I was interviewed on *Life Matters* on ABC Radio National (6 March 2003) and kept in touch with various journalists, providing comment on the matter when asked.

The 2002 bill did not trigger a double dissolution, but attempts to exclude small business from UFD continued. In response to the Workplace Relations Amendment (Fair Dismissal Reform) Bill 2004 (Commonwealth), the Senate Employment, Workplace Relations and Education References Committee conducted the Inquiry into Unfair Dismissal Policy in the Small Business Sector in March 2005. I made a submission and gave evidence at the hearings in Melbourne (3 May 2005). Interestingly, during that inquiry a document was tabled by the Democrat senator Andrew Murray which clearly showed that the Australian Industrial Registry (AIR) does not keep accurate records of the numbers of UFD cases lodged by small business employees. In other words, there was no clear evidence that there was a greater or lesser problem for small businesses compared to medium and large ones (see www.aph.gov.au/senate/Committee/EET_CTTE/unfair_dismissal/index.htm).

The prime minister announced on 26 May 2005 that small business would be exempt from UFD as part of the proposed WorkChoices legislation. Shocking, however, is the redefinition of small businesses as those employing less than 100 people. If there was no evidence of the need to exempt small businesses with less than 20 people, where was the evidence for those with less than 100 employees? Moreover, the government was going to underpin this change by extending the use of power in the Australian constitution to regulate corporations. The use of this constitutional power in the past to regulate matters 'outside' the remit of corporations had attracted controversy, as it did this time around. Given my interest, I was invited to participate in a workshop of 'Researchers for Fairness at Work' (20 June 2005). For this workshop a report card on the proposed WorkChoices legislation was produced (for an example see www.econ.usyd.edu.au/wos/Reportchangesreportcard). This led into a larger 'protest' by 151 'work and employment' academics to oppose the reforms, and contributed to a campaign by the Australian Trades Union Council against the reforms.

Unfortunately WorkChoices did become legislation and small businesses were exempted from UFD – but only if they were 'constitutional corporations', given the constitutional basis for the provisions. I stepped out of the debate, but only because I took a job in the UK and my research agenda had to shift somewhat. However, the work I have since conducted around human resource management in small business (see Barrett and Mayson, 2008) has more firmly convinced me that a consequence of exempting firms from unfair dismissal provisions is to encourage firing as the solution to labour management 'problems', rather than investment in better management practices. And this only serves to decrease further the attractiveness of working in a small business.

A conclusion...

In my research note for the *JIR* I made a number of suggestions for research which could be undertaken to examine whether exempting small business from the UFD provisions was necessary. Interestingly (or is that unsurprisingly?), the coalition government never produced any conclusive evidence of its own to show that a small business exemption would create jobs. Having said that, a paper by the Melbourne Institute for Applied Economic and Social Research was influential, having concluded that 77,000 jobs would result from a UFD exemption for small business (Harding, 2002). While the Howard government lost the election in 2007, the current Australian Labor government led by Kevin Rudd is considering its position on UFD and small business, and so there is still research to be done.

In summary, while this chapter is about small business and UFD it is simply being used to tell a story about how researchers and research can be engaged. What I hope I have shown is that 'wanting to make a difference' can drive research – listen to those buzzing bees. Moreover, the outcomes of research may not necessarily be 'traditional' ones, such as a report or a journal article. Publications are currency in academia, but in my view, and perhaps others' also, academics have a responsibility to the wider community to share their knowledge and contribute to the public debate. Thankfully that was also the view of my vice chancellor, who sent me a copy of his response to the person who had asked for my dismissal!

Conclusion

15

Lessons learnt from this madness

Jennifer Sappey, Keith Townsend
and John Burgess

This book has presented 13 chapters of lived research experiences. It is clear on reading these contributions that qualitative research methodologies are not an exact science. This is not chemistry, where hydrogen is hydrogen regardless of where you find it or test it. Perhaps the primary reason for this is the nature of people, and more importantly the subjectivity, biases and personalities of a wide range of people associated with the research process. However, for those of us who are drawn to this field of research, these factors are quite often what makes our work interesting and exciting as well as exhausting and frustrating. As researchers we find ourselves investigating 'new' workplace issues as a means of generating understanding. We also might look at 'old' workplace issues with a new theoretical lens. Increasingly, we are beginning to understand both old and new opportunities and challenges to our research agenda. This final chapter will explore some of the opportunities and challenges that have been developed throughout the preceding chapters. These include the influence of gender on research, technology, the use of images and the increasing requirement to meet national ethics protocols.

It is very easy for those people who are in the 'majority' to forget the experiences of the minority. One example that springs quickly to mind is male researchers interviewing men in the workplace about things that matter to men. Gender has become such a critical aspect of research over the last few decades that one might be forgiven for thinking we have come a long way. Pini's chapter about the complexities faced by a woman interviewing relatively powerful men about the reasons more women are not in these powerful positions is telling. This is a chapter where the issue of gender is at the heart of not only the research question but also the entire research process. Would a male have developed that research project? Would a man have embarked on the project with such passion? Would a male have been confronted with the power plays and attempts at humiliation? These questions, while rhetorical, illustrate some of the explicit and implicit issues that relate to gender in the workplace. A person's gender will influence the research in which they become involved. Gender will influence the theory used to understand a problem. Gender will also influence the interactions between the researcher and the research subject. While Ryan and Dundon did not explore the notion explicitly, one could expect the subjects of Guinness and hurling were topics that allowed the 'blokes' to develop a rapport that might not have been as easily formed for a female researcher. There is a broad societal assumption that men 'do' beer and sports that is easily transposed into the research process, as would equally be the case with many 'female' assumptions. The same observation is present in the very 'blokey' community that Ellem researched in the Pilbara: here notions of male mateship and engagement through copious beer consumption were an important component of the research.

There are a couple of very obvious opportunities for researchers at this point in history. They are in some ways interrelated: technology and images. Technology has long had its drawbacks and will continue to do so. While the advent of digital recorders means that problems with tapes are a thing of the past, flat batteries are likely to remain a researcher's nightmare. The indecipherable accents of research subjects will remain, and perhaps even become a greater issue with the increasing migration of labour. Yet the digital age provides us with some amazing opportunities. Research can be performed anywhere, at any time. We have the capacity through voice and video internet protocols to interview someone on the other side of the world in real time. Historically, the use of images has long shown the world of work. Yet, with some few exceptions (cf. Strangleman, 2004), researchers in industrial relations, industrial sociology, management, human resource management and associated fields have not adopted the use of images to contribute to our story-telling. As we often find it difficult to limit our journal submissions to the required word count, images are a potential source of benefit. It is said a picture is worth a thousand words, but most journals count images as the equivalent of 500 words – clearly a bonus 500 words for the verbose author!

Digital recording equipment, whether in the form of audio recorders or cameras, is increasingly affordable, very portable and extremely useful for the social scientist. Many chapters in this book provide details of experiences that would have been immensely strengthened by the use of images. Ellem's attempts to encapsulate the vastness of the Western Australian outback and the Pilbara region were documented in this book without images, but his 2004 work *Hard Ground: Unions in the Pilbara* provides some fantastic pictures that clearly encapsulate the inhospitable land he describes. Furthermore, this earlier work provides images of the faces of people who were central to the conflict. Photos of the workers on picket lines and in union organising meetings, families at home – all contribute to giving a human face to the abstract images of multinational mining entities' attempts to deunionise.

In addition, Price and Townsend's stories of the smokers and 'gutter scum', Ryan and Dundon's glassblowing failure, Hislop's crowded-train experiences and Sappey's story of the tutu-clad male aerobics instructor would have produced wonderful imagery. Generating these images, however, is not always as easy as snapping a few shots and including the ones that suit. Aside from the practical implications at the time, a more pressing concern for the social scientist is the formalities of meeting ethics committee standards. We suggest that as researchers and journals become more technologically savvy, photo-journalism can provide very evocative and profound images relevant to the issues that the researchers wish to convey. Many books and journals are still wedded to an established pro forma of text only, supported by extensive tables and statistics; but even textbooks are moving on to graphic images and the comic-book format to explain to generation Y the nature of organisational theory (Bauer et al., 2008).

While there has been regulation of health-related research for 50 years, the broadening of regulation to other forms of social science and humanities research, including workplace studies, is a relatively recent development. One can trace the increasing desire of universities, and indeed governments, to regulate through ethics protocols to the 1980s, triggered by concern for human rights and an increasingly litigious society. It is symptomatic of the inevitable ethical tensions which social researchers confront as the changing politics of community values precipitates changes to ethical frameworks for the conduct of research. This is a natural evolution of community values and social change. However, operating within the new regulatory ethics frameworks presents major challenges for social science researchers in general, and workplace researchers in particular. Indeed, the authors of this chapter see this as one of the greatest challenges to workplace research.

This is evident in the experiences of the authors in this collection. Although diverse in methodology, design and content, the cases in this book have raised two important questions which are worthy of reflection. The first is the fundamental ethical question about the extent to which there is a right to acquire knowledge and pursue 'truth' versus the right to privacy, whether individual, collective, private or commercial. Research in organisations is by its very nature an extremely sensitive political process, as the researcher mediates power relationships and negotiates tactical compromise (Beynon, 1988; Bryman, 1988). However, the pursuit of knowledge and 'truth' is becoming increasingly complex as vested interests exert their rights of control over information and its promulgation. This is particularly significant for university academics and student researchers, given that the withdrawal of public funding from universities over the last decade has placed the burden of funding on the researcher, who must secure sponsorship and project resources through partnerships, often with business organisations. As the chapter by McDonald et al. suggests, having a financial contribution to the research project and explicit approval to provide research subjects and collect data is simply not enough for some projects. Furthermore, the provision of sponsorship and indeed access is unlikely when there is a fundamental pluralist assumption in much workplace research that challenges management's often unitarist view of the workplace as essentially harmonious. We cannot and should not only research 'good-news stories' that might mean workplace access is more readily available.

While views of the workplace as being conflictual and exploitative (Braverman, 1974) need to be tempered with an understanding of the cooperative nature of workplace relations (Burawoy, 1979), there is nevertheless a general recognition of acts of both resistance and cooperation in any workplace. The cases in this book attest to that fact. An unintended consequence of ethics protocols' emphasis on the primacy of participants' rights, reinforced by the requirement for written, informed consent (which in the case of workplace and organisational studies must be that of an organisation's management), may well be a research focus on unitarist consensus which is at best one-sided and at worst seriously misleading (Belanger et al., 1994: 7). This must bring into question the integrity of research which only affirms management's 'truth', albeit having come about through the researcher guaranteeing benefit to the organisation in order to gain access in the first instance, or through the regulation of information which management provides.

Cases in this book illustrate that both are at play. From these cases it is clear that conflict exists between ethics regimes and workplace studies which seek to deconstruct a workplace and delayer management rhetoric in order to understand the realities and complexities of the social relations of that workplace. Unless researchers are able to explore the range of pluralist views in any workplace, an unintended consequence of a consensual view is that workers may themselves be denied the right for their 'truth' to be told.

Second is the question of the difficulty of conducting research, be it qualitative or quantitative, when confronted by practical impediments which constrain professional procedures and techniques and may even threaten to curb research outright. As we have seen from many contributions in this book, researchers must be innovative and responsive, based on intuition gained from experience. Impediments and barriers will present themselves in every research project. When the researcher is confronted by such an obstacle, it is often only through experience that one can determine whether it is an impenetrable barrier or one to climb over, go around or smash through. Rarely is a research project completed in strict accordance with its original design. And yet ethics protocols require researchers to anticipate all interactions with participants, outcomes and consequences prior to commencement of the study. Certainly, variations of ethics approvals are possible, but, as this book has demonstrated, many research projects present opportunities that do not lend themselves to returning to the university, applying for a variation and waiting for permission to proceed. This poses the challenge of developing research designs which are flexible and incorporate contingency plans, for rarely, if ever, will things go strictly according to plan. Within the constraining framework of restrictive ethics protocols, the researcher must build into research design the potential to respond effectively to impediments and opportunities which present themselves.

However, flexibility and responsiveness will not always overcome. Take, for example, the time-honoured method in industrial sociology of participant observation, often as a worker at a particular workplace (Mayo, 1933; Roy, 1952; Kapferer, 1972; Beynon, 1973; Kriegler, 1980; Gamst, 1980; Thompson and Bannon, 1985; Burawoy et al., 1991; Calvery, 2000). Participant observation effectively juxtaposes what management and workers say against what they actually do. But under many ethics protocols participant observation is severely constrained, and what is now deemed to be covert participant observation (e.g. working in an organisation and recording observations without the consent of management while withholding information about the primary researchers' identity or institutional affiliation) is banned other than in the most exceptional of circumstances. Justification for this is the protection of the welfare and rights of research participants.

It is significant that under the restricted use of participant observation, seminal workplace studies, from the early factory studies through to the 1990s' labour process studies, could not have been conducted. For example, Roy's (1952) seminal work on 'goldbricking' in a steel-processing plant's machine shop is unlikely to have made it through the current ethics regime:

> I here report and analyse observations of restrictions made during eleven months of work as a radial-drill operator in the machine shop... For ten months I kept a daily record of my feelings, thoughts, experiences and observations. I noted down the data from memory at the end of each workday, only occasionally making surreptitious notes on the job... I did not reveal my research interest to either management or workers. I remained 'one of the boys on the line', sharing the practices and confidences of my fellows and joining them in the ceaseless war with management, rather indifferently at first, but later wholeheartedly. (Ibid.: 427)

Similarly, under current ethics protocols Kriegler's (1980) significant study of work and factory life at BHP's Whyalla shipyard in South Australia is unlikely to have received ethics approval. As a labourer he found that:

> working as a manual worker, albeit for only a brief period, gave me the opportunity to experience some of the routine, discipline, danger, feelings of satisfaction and achievement, frustration and disappointment that working men encounter in their daily lives. There is considerable merit in the view that understanding human beings and explaining their actions requires that one put oneself in their position, thereby closely identifying with them, and that only then, through a process of introspection and learning, will one find oneself in a position to understand behaviour. (Ibid.: vii)

We are not suggesting that we return to the days of deliberate deception, such as was the case in the 1920s and 1930s in the seminal work of Elton Mayo, the 'father' of industrial sociology. Mayo's workplace studies led to the foundation of the human relations approach to managing the workforce, which acted as a springboard from which contemporary human resource management has evolved over the last 75 years into an all-encompassing philosophy and strategic business tool for the management of labour in a competitive marketplace. As significant as Mayo's studies were, how many of us have scrutinised the research design employed in his seminal research? It is not generally known that in his 1923 study into labour turnover in a Philadelphia textile mill, when Mayo (1933) was finding difficulties in getting qualitative data from workers on the factory floor, he established a small dispensary in the plant with a qualified nurse in his employment who collected data through the many confidences that were told to her by the factory workers visiting her for medical assistance, unaware of her research role. The problem of gaining access to and data from participants has always existed. However, such deception is unacceptable in twenty-first-century research paradigms. Had such a methodology gone before an institutional ethics committee today, it would surely have been unequivocally rejected, and rightly so.

There are other such seminal cases where current ethics protocols would fail to understand the conditions under which the social scientists operated. Given the risk aversion of many ethics committees, we doubt that race-sensitive research such as Kapferer's (1972) study of the social relationships between African workers in an Indian-owned clothing factory in Zambia and Rimmer's (1972) study of race and industrial conflict in a group of Midlands foundries in the UK would have been approved.

Similarly, under the current requirement of written, informed consent being obtained from any person who is involved in or witnesses an incident, or indeed who may be affected in any way by promulgation of that incident, Beynon's (1973) seminal workplace ethnography based on observations of and interviews with workers at the Ford Motor Company could not have been conducted. If applied to Beynon's account of a dead Ford worker's corpse lying unattended on the factory floor for ten minutes while management insisted on co-workers continuing to work on the line, who would be deemed to be the participants from whom written consent needed to be obtained: the supervisor, the deceased, the deceased's family, the co-workers, the Ford Motor Company? It is unlikely that any organisation would give written consent for the publication of facts which would adversely reflect upon it. Not surprisingly, Ford vehemently denied this incident at the time.

Herein lies the challenge for the researcher. In a liberal democratic society, public policy and private practice should be informed by high-quality social research which is independent and free of capture by the participants and phenomena which it seeks to observe and explain. Unfortunately, this is at odds with ethics protocols' primary focus on the protection of the welfare and rights of participants in research, with those rights taking precedence over the expected benefits to human knowledge derived from the research. This is the double-bind which confronts researchers of all persuasions. The argument can be made that ethics regimes are now so risk averse that data collection and findings are potentially compromised. No one could argue that research should be conducted without any protection of participants and their interests, but the burden on workplace researchers in satisfying regulatory bodies of the justification for their research and the adequacy of their methodology is now great indeed. Faced by such a dichotomy, the solution lies in the transparency, integrity and flexibility of our research design.

Despite these challenges, those of us researching the world of work play an important role in the generation of knowledge and in interpreting and understanding the changing and consistent nature of workplaces and industry. We are drawn to the work because it interests us, intrigues us and satisfies some intellectual curiosities. We all investigate slightly different areas of the broad topic, and all have slightly different approaches driven by our personalities, ideologies and interests. The authors of this book all hope that the book, while not a recipe for research, provides interesting and worthwhile accounts for both novice and experienced researchers.

References

Adler, P. and Adler, P. (2003) 'The reluctant respondent', in J. Holstein and J. Gubrium (eds) *Inside Interviewing. New Lenses, New Concerns*. Thousand Oaks, CA: Sage.

Allen, J. and Henry, N. (1996) 'Fragments of industry and employment: contract service work and the shift towards precarious employment', in R. Crompton, D. Gallie and K. Purcell (eds) *Changing Forms of Employment: Organisations, Skills and Gender*. London: Routledge.

Ashforth, B. and Kreiner, G. (1999) '"How can you do it?" Dirty work and the challenge of constructing a positive identity', *Academy of Management Review*, 24(3): 413–34.

Australian Industrial Relations Commission/Australian Industrial Registry (2001) *Annual Report of the President of the Australian Industrial Relations Commission and Annual Report of the Australian Industrial Registry, 1 July 2000 to 30 June 2001*. Canberra: Commonwealth of Australia.

Axtell, C. and Hislop, D. (2007) '"All aboard!": trains as mobile offices', paper presented at British Psychological Society Division of Occupational Psychology Conference, Bristol, January.

Barrett, R. (2002) 'Coalition knows its job creation claim is spurious', *Australian Financial Review*, 19 March, p. 47.

Barrett, R. (2003) 'Small business and unfair dismissal', *Journal of Industrial Relations*, 45(1): 87–93

Barrett, R. and Mayson, S. (eds) (2008) *The International Handbook of Entrepreneurship and HRM*. Cheltenham: Edward Elgar.

Bauer, T., Ford, D., Rado, K. and Short, J. (2008) 'Testing the motivational effectiveness of graphic novels: a new idea for student learning', Irish Academy of Management, Dublin City University, September.

Behar, R. (2003) 'Ethnography and the book that was lost', *Ethnography*, 4: 15–39.

Belanger, J., Edwards, P. and Haiven, L. (1994) *Workplace Industrial Relations and the Global Challenge*, Cornell International Industrial and Labour Relations Report No. 25. Ithaca, NY: ILR Press.

Beynon, H. (1973) *Working for Ford*. London: Penguin.

Beynon, H. (1988) 'Regulating research: politics and decision-making in industrial organisations', in A. Bryman (ed.) *Doing Research in Organisations*. London: Routledge.

Birch, D. (1979) *The Job Generation Process: MIT Project on Neighbourhood and Regional Change*. Cambridge, MA: MIT Press.

Bourdieu, P., Accardo, A. and Parkhurst Ferguson, P. (1999) *The Weight of the World*. Cambridge: Polity Press.

Bowe, J., Bowe, M. and Streeter, S. (eds) (2000) *Gig: Americans Talk About Their Jobs*. New York: Three Rivers Press.

Braverman, H. (1974) *Labour and Monopoly Capital: The Degradation of Work in the Twentieth Century*. London: Monthly Review Press.

Broadbent, K. (2003) *Women's Employment in Japan: The Experience of Part-time Workers*. London: Routledge Curzon.

Broadbent, K. (2008) 'Gender-specific organising in Japan: new frontiers for union renewal or splitting the union movement?', paper presented at British Universities Industrial Relations Association Annual Conference, Bristol, June.

Bryman, A. (ed.) (1988) *Doing Research in Organisations*. London: Routledge.

Bryman, A. (2004) *Social Research Methods*, 2nd edn. Oxford: Oxford University Press.

Burawoy, M. (1979) *Manufacturing Consent: Changes in the Labor Process under Monopoly Capitalism*. Chicago, IL: University of Chicago Press.

Burawoy, M. (2000) 'Introduction: reaching for the global', in M. Burawoy, J.A. Blum, S. George, Z. Gille, T. Gowan, L. Haney, M. Klawiter, H.L. Lopez, S. O'Riain and M. Thayer (eds) *Global Ethnography: Forces, Connections, and Imaginations in a Postmodern World*. Berkeley and Los Angeles, CA: University of California Press.

Burawoy, M., Burton, A., Ferguson, A., Fox, K., Gamson, J., Gartrell, N., Hurst, L., Kurzman, C., Salzinger, L., Schiffman, J. and Ui, S. (1991) *Ethnography Unbound: Power and Resistance in the Modern Metropolis*. Berkeley, CA: University of California Press.

Calvery, D. (2000) 'Getting on the door and staying there: a covert participant observational study of bouncers', in G. Lee-Treweek and S. Linkogle (eds) *Danger in the Field: Risk and Ethics in Social Research*. London: Routledge.

Cavendish, R. (1982) *Women on the Line*. London: Routledge & Kegan Paul.

Chapman, A. (2006) 'Unfair dismissal laws and work choices: from safety net standard to legal privilege', *Economic and Labour Relations Review*, 16(2): 237.

Cheek, J. (2003) 'An untold story? Doing funded qualitative research', in N. Denzin and Y. Lincoln (eds) *Strategies of Qualitative Enquiry*. London: Sage.

Cockburn, C. (1991) *In the Way of Women: Men's Resistance to Sex Equality in Organizations*. New York: ILR Press.

Cresswell, J. and Piano Clark, V. (2007) *Designing and Conducting Mixed Methods Research*. Thousand Oaks, CA: Sage.

Crotty, M. (1998) *The Foundations of Social Research: Meaning and Perspective in the Research Process*. Sydney: Allen & Unwin.

Cunnison, S. (1966) *Wages and Work Allocation: A Study of Social Relations in a Garment Workshop*. London: Tavistock Publications.

Denzin, N. and Lincoln, Y. (2005) 'Introduction: the discipline and practice of qualitative research', in N. Denzin and Y. Lincoln (eds) *The Sage Handbook of Qualitative Research*, 3rd edn. Thousand Oaks, CA: Sage.

Department of Employment, Workplace Relations and Small Business (1998) *Twelve Month Review of the Federal Unfair Dismissal Provisions*, December. Canberra: Commonwealth of Australia.

Department of Employment, Workplace Relations and Small Business (2000) *Annual Review of Small Business 2000 – What the Federal Government Is Doing for Small Business*; available at: *www.dewrsb.gov.au/smallbusiness/publications/annualreview/fedgovt ...lwrr.html* (accessed: 20 April 2001).

Dickens, L., Jones, M., Weekes, B. and Hart, M. (1985) *Dismissed: A Study of Unfair Dismissals and the Industrial Tribunal System*. Oxford: Blackwell.

Dundon, T., Curran, D., Maloney, M. and Ryan, P. (2006) 'Conceptualising the dynamics of employee voice: evidence from the Republic of Ireland', *Industrial Relations Journal*, 37(5): 492–512.

Earnshaw, J., Goodman, J., Harrison, R. and Marchington, M. (1998) *Industrial Tribunals, Workplace Disciplinary Procedures and Employment Practice*, Employment Relations Research Series No. 2. London: Department of Trade and Industry.

Ellem, B. (2004) *Hard Ground: Unions in the Pilbara*. Port Headland: Pilbara Mineworkers Union.

Ellem, B. (2006) 'Scaling labour: Australian unions and global mining', *Work, Employment and Society*, 20(2): 369–87.

Emerson, R., Fretz, R. and Shaw, L. (2001) 'Participant observation and fieldnotes', in P. Atkinson, A. Coffey, S. Delamont, J. Lofland and L. Lofland (eds) *Handbook of Ethnography*. London: Sage.

Ezzy, D. (2002) *Qualitative Analysis: Practice and Innovation*. London: Routledge.

Felstead, A., Jewson, N. and Walters, S. (2005) *Changing Places of Work*. Basingstoke: Palgrave Macmillan.

Felstead, A., Fuller, A., Jewson, N. and Unwin, L. (2009) *Improving Working as Learning*. London: Routledge.

Flick, U. (2005) *An Introduction to Qualitative Research*, 2nd edn. London: Sage.

Fraser, R. (1969) *Work*, Vols 1 and 2. Harmondsworth: Penguin.

Gamst, F. (1980) *The Hoghead: An Industrial Ethnology of the Locomotive Engineer*. New York: Holt, Rinehart & Winston.

Goodman, J., Earnshaw, J., Marchington, M. and Harrison, R. (1998) 'Unfair dismissal cases, disciplinary procedures, recruitment methods and management style: case study evidence from three industrial sectors', *Employee Relations*, 20(6): 536–50.

Gouldner, A. (1955) *Wildcat Strike*. London: Routledge & Kegan Paul.

Hammersley, M. and Atkinson, P. (1995) *Ethnography: Principles in Practice*, 2nd edn. New York: Routledge.

Haraszti, M. (1978) *A Worker in a Worker's State*. Harmondsworth: Pelican.

Harding, D. (2002) *The Effect of Unfair Dismissal Laws on Small and Medium Sized Businesses*. Melbourne: Institute for Applied Economic and Social Research, University of Melbourne.

Hearn McKinnon, B. (2007) *Behind Work Choices: How One Company Changed Australia's Industrial Relations*. Heidelberg: Heidelberg Press.

Heath, C. and Bulbeck, C. (1985) *Shadow of the Hill*. Fremantle: Fremantle Arts Centre Press.

Hine, C. (2000) *Virtual Ethnography*. London: Sage.

Hislop, D. (2008) *Mobility and Technology in the Workplace*. London: Routledge.

Howe, J. and Murray, J. (2001) 'Abbott, in fact, is attacking the fair go', *The Age*, 5 December, p. 15.

Japan Institute of Labor (2006) 'Labor situation in Japan and analysis: general overview 2006/2007'; available at: *www.jil.go.jp/english/laborinfo/library/documents/Labor2006_2007.pdf* (accessed: 12 December 2007).

Jewson, N., Felstead, A., Fuller, A., Kakavelakis, K. and Unwin, L. (2007) 'Transforming knowledge and skills: reconfiguring the productive system of a local authority', Learning as Work Research Paper No. 10. Cardiff: Cardiff School of Social Sciences, Cardiff University.

Kamata, S. (1982) *Japan in the Passing Lane*. New York: Pantheon.

Kapferer, B. (1972) *Strategy and Transaction in an African Factory: African Workers and Indian Management in a Zambian Town*. Manchester: United Press.

Kawanishi, H. (1986) 'The reality of enterprise unionism', in G. McCormack and Y. Sugimoto (eds) *Democracy in Contemporary Japan*. Sydney: Hale & Iremonger, pp. 138–56.

Kersley, B., Alpin, C., Forth, J., Bryson, A., Bewley, H., Dix, G. and Oxenbridge, S. (2005) *Inside the Workplace: Findings from the 2004 Workplace Employment Relations Survey*. London, Routledge.

Kessler-Harris, A. (1975) 'Where are the organized women workers?', *Feminist Studies*, 3(1/2): 92–110.

Kirchhoff, B. and Greene, P. (1998) 'Understanding the theoretical and empirical content of critiques of US job creation research', *Small Business Economics*, 10(2): 153–69.

Kitzinger, J. (1995) 'Qualitative research: introducing focus groups', *British Medical Journal*, 311: 299–302.

Knapp, N. (1997) 'Interviewing Joshua: on the importance of leaving the room for serendipity', *Qualitative Inquiry*, 3: 326–42.

Kriegler, R. (1980) *Working for the Company: Work and Control in the Whyalla Shipyard*. Melbourne: Oxford University Press.

Lave, J. and Wenger, E. (1991) *Situated Learning: Legitimate Peripheral Participation*. Cambridge: Cambridge University Press.

Lee, D. (1997) 'Interviewing men: vulnerabilities and dilemmas', *Women's Studies International Forum*, 20(4): 553–64.

Loveman, G. and Sengenberger, W. (1990) 'Introduction: economic and social reorganisation in the small and medium-sized enterprise sector', in W. Sengenberger, G. Loveman and M. Piore (eds) *The Re-Emergence of Small Enterprises*. Geneva: International Institute for Labour Studies.

Lyons, G., Jain, J. and Holley, D. (2007) 'The use of travel time by rail passengers in Great Britain', *Transportation Research A: Policy & Practice*, 41: 107–20.

MacWilliam, S. (1990) 'Marginalizing opposition to the Accord', *Arena*, 92: 146–50.

Mandel, J. (2003) 'Negotiating expectations in the field: gatekeepers, research fatigue and cultural biases', *Singapore Journal of Tropical Geography*, 24(2): 198–210.

Massey, D. (1994) *Space, Place and Gender*. Cambridge: Polity Press.

Mayo, E. (1933) *The Human Problems of an Industrial Civilization*. New York: Macmillan.

Mayo, E. (1949) *The Social Problems of an Industrial Civilisation*. London: Routledge & Kegan Paul.

Michelson, G. and Mouly, S. (2002) '"You didn't hear it from us but…" Towards an understanding of rumour and gossip in organisations', *Australian Journal of Management*, 27: 57–65.

Mills, C. Wright (1959) *The Sociological Imagination*. New York: Oxford University Press.

Morehead, A., Steele, M., Alexander, M., Stephen, K. and Duffin, L. (1997) *Changes at Work: The 1995 Australian Workplace Industrial Relations Survey*. Melbourne: Addison Wesley Longman.

Morwitz, V., Johnson, E. and Schmittlein, D. (1993) 'Does measuring intent change behavior?', *Journal of Consumer Research*, 20(1): 46–61.

Murphy, K. (2001) 'Labor softens stance on unfair dismissal', *Australian Financial Review*, 3 December, p. 3.

Neuman, W. (2006) *Social Research Methods: Qualitative and Quantitative Approaches*, 6th edn. London: Allyn Bacon Education.

Newby, H. (1977) 'In the field: reflections on the study of Suffolk farm workers', in C. Bell and H. Newby (eds) *Doing Sociological Research*. London: Allen & Unwin, pp. 108–29.

Nichols, T. and Beynon, H. (1977) *Living with Capitalism: Class Relations in the Modern Factory*. London: Routledge & Kegan Paul.

O'Reilly, K. (2005) *Ethnographic Methods*. London: Routledge.

Parker, R. (2000) 'Small is not necessarily beautiful: an evaluation of policy support for small and medium-sized enterprises in Australia', *Australian Journal of Political Science*, 35(2): 239–53.

Pini, B. (2003) 'Feminist methodology and rural research: reflections on a study of an Australian agricultural organisation', *Sociologia Ruralis*, 43(4): 418–33.

Pini, B. (2008) *Managerial Masculinities and Agricultural Organizations Worldwide*. Aldershot: Ashgate.

Pini, B. and Haslam McKenzie, F. (2007) 'Access and local government research: methodological reflections', *Local Environment*, 12(1): 31–42.

Pittard, M. (2002) 'Unfair dismissal laws: the problem of application to small businesses', *Australian Journal of Labour Law*, 15: 1–16.

Pocock, B. (2003) *The Work/Life Collision; What Work Is Doing to Australians and What to Do About It*. Sydney: Federation Press.

Pocock, B. (2006) *The Labour Market Ate My Babies: Work, Children and a Sustainable Future*. Sydney: Federation Press.

Pocock, B. and Clarke, J. (2005) 'Time, money and job spillover: how parents' jobs affect young people', *Journal of Industrial Relations*, 47(1): 62–76.

Pollert, A. (1981) *Girls, Wives, Factory Lives*. London: Macmillan.

Rengō-Osaka (2001) *Kigyōnai Jugyōin tō ni Kansuru Jittai Chōsa Hō koku (Report of Survey of Employees)*. Osaka: Rengō.

Revesz, J. and Lattimore, R. (1997) *Small Business Employment*, Staff Research Paper. Canberra: Industry Commission.

Rhodes, C. and Brown, A. (2005) 'Narratives, organisations and research', *International Journal of Management Reviews*, 7(3): 167–88.

Rimmer, M. (1972) *Race and Industrial Conflict: A Study in a Group of Midland Foundries*. London: Heinemann.

Roy, D. (1952) 'Quota restriction and goldbricking in a machine shop', *American Journal of Sociology*, 57: 427–42.

Roy, D. (1954) 'Efficiency and "the fix": informal intergroup relations in a piecework machine shop', *American Journal of Sociology*, 60: 255–66.

Ryan, S. (2007) 'Dirty deeds done dirt cheap? Employment relations and the organisation of work in the NSW commercial cleaning industry', PhD thesis, Work and Organisational Studies, University of Sydney.

Schwartzman, H. (1993) *Ethnography in Organisations*. London: Sage.

Sherif, B. (2001) 'The ambiguity of boundaries in the fieldwork experience: establishing rapport and negotiating insider/outsider status', *Qualitative Inquiry*, 7: 436–47.

Silverman, D. (1970) *The Theory of Organisations*. London: Heinemann.

Smith, H. and Thompson, H. (1987) 'Industrial relations and the law: case study of Robe River', *Australian Quarterly*, 59(3/4): 297–305.

Smith, V. (2001) 'Ethnographies of work and the work of ethnographers', in P. Atkinson, A. Coffey, S. Delamont, J. Lofland and L. Lofland (eds) *Handbook of Ethnography*. London: Sage.

Storey, D. (1982) *Entrepreneurship and the Small Firm*. London: Croom Helm.

Strangleman, T. (2004) 'Ways of (not) seeing work: the visual as a blind spot in WES?', *Work, Employment and Society*, 18(1): 179–92.

Sutcliffe, P. (1999) 'Interviewing, observation and ethnography: techniques and selection criteria', in D. Kelly (ed.) *Researching Industrial Relations*. Sydney: Federation Press, pp. 136–50.

Swain, P. (1995) *Strategic Choices: A Study of the Interaction of Industrial Relations and Corporate Strategy in the Pilbara Iron Ore Industry*. Perth: Curtin University of Technology.

Taylor, F. (1911) *The Principles of Scientific Management*. Toronto: General Publishing.

Taylor, P. (2001) 'ALP to do deal on unfair dismissal', *The Age*, 3 December, p. 4.

Taylor, P. and Bain, P. (1999) 'An assembly line in the head: work and employee relations in the call centre', *Industrial Relations Journal*, 30(2): 101–17.

Terkel, S. (1972) *Working*. New York: Avon.

Thompson, H. and Smith, H. (1987) 'Conflict at Robe River', *Arena*, 79: 76–91.

Thompson, P. and Bannon, E. (1985) *Working the System: The Shop Floor and New Technology*. London: Pluto Press.

Townsend, K. (2005) 'Electronic surveillance and cohesive teams: room for resistance in an Australian call centre?', *New Technology, Work and Employment*, 20(1): 47–59.

Troman, G. (1996) 'No entry signs: educational change and some problems encountered in negotiating entry to educational settings', *British Educational Research Journal*, 22(1): 71–8.

Walford, G. (2001) *Doing Qualitative Educational Research. A Personal Guide to the Research Process*. London: Continuum.

Wenger, E. (1998) *Communities of Practice: Learning, Meaning and Identity*. Cambridge: Cambridge University Press.

Westrip, A. (1982) 'Effects of employment legislation on small firms', in D. Watkins, J. Stanworth and A. Westrip (eds) *Stimulating Small Firms*. Aldershot: Gower.

Wilkinson, S. (2004) 'Using focus groups', in D. Silverman (ed.) *Qualitative Research*, 2nd edn. London: Sage.

Williams, P. (2005) 'What is social support: a grounded theory of social interaction in the context of the new family', PhD thesis, Department of Public Health, University of Adelaide.

Williams, P. and Pocock, B. (2006) 'Fitting it all together: work, home and community in two Australian master-planned communities', research report, September, Centre for Work + Life, University of South Australia, Adelaide.

Williams, P., Bridge, K. and Pocock, B. (2008) 'Kids' lives in adult space and time: how work and community accommodate teenagers in suburban Australia', paper presented at Tenth Australian Institute of Family Studies Conference, Families Through Life, Melbourne, July.

Winton, T. (2001) *Dirt Music*. Sydney: Picador/Pan Macmillan.

Wooden, M. and Harding, D. (eds) (1997) 'Trends in staff selection and recruitment', report prepared for Employment and Purchasing Division, Department of Employment, Education, Training and Youth Affairs, Australia.

Index